To

From

Date

MY
QUIET TIME
devotional

CHRISTIAN ART
PUBLISHERS

My Quiet Time Devotional

Published by Christian Art Publishers
PO Box 1599, Vereeniging, 1930

© 2019
First edition 2019

Devotions taken from *The Traveler's Devotional Bible*

Designed by Christian Art Publishers
Cover designed by Christian Art Publishers

Images used under license from Shutterstock.com

Printed in China

ISBN 978-1-4321-2912-5 (Softcover)
ISBN 978-1-4321-3096-1 (LuxLeather)

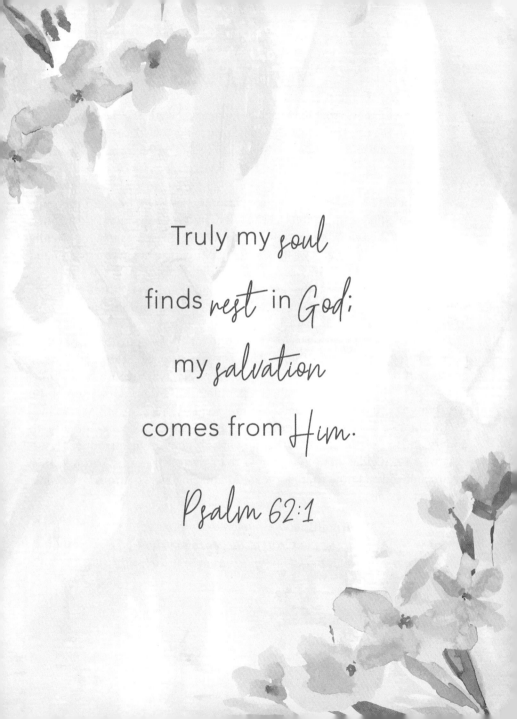

Truly my *soul*
finds *rest* in *God;*
my *salvation*
comes from *Him.*

Psalm 62:1

STARTING WITH THE BIG PICTURE

*All those listed above include fourteen generations from
Abraham to David, fourteen from David to the Babylonian exile,
and fourteen from the Babylonian exile to the Messiah.*
MATTHEW 1:17

Matthew sees perfect – divine – harmony and symmetry in the long, detailed genealogy of Jesus the Messiah. While we might be inclined to glaze over the relentless parade of utterly foreign names like Jehoiachin, Shealtiel, and Zerubbabel, if we look a bit deeper, we can begin to comprehend just how important this list is.

Matthew shows from the genealogy that there were three perfectly symmetrical stages of fourteen generations each leading up to the arrival of Jesus Christ.

From Abraham to King David, the people of God were tribal; from King David to the destruction of Jerusalem, the monarchical state and Temple priesthood developed; from the Babylonian exile, when those institutions collapsed, to the time of Messiah, the people of God waited for a son of the great King David who would restore Israel to glory.

Matthew's overview provides a comprehensive and coherent way to understand the significance of the long list of names that introduces Jesus. In it we find regular people with less than perfect records. Through this, we are amazed to know that God can do amazing works through the most imperfect vessels.

*You're just you – flawed and imperfect.
As with the people in Jesus' genealogy, however,
God can use imperfect people to do great things for Him.*

SOMETIMES, IN THE DARK OF NIGHT …

After the wise men were gone, an angel of the Lord appeared to Joseph in a dream. "Get up! Flee to Egypt with the child and his mother," the angel said. "Stay there until I tell you to return, because Herod is going to search for the child to kill him".

MATTHEW 2:13

The tense drama of Matthew 2 unrolls on a darkened stage as the leading actors play elaborate cat-and-mouse games, each seeking to outwit the other. But one side in the contest is clearly favored by divine interventions.

An air of protective secrecy surrounds the young child and His parents. Throughout the narrative, Jesus' adoptive father Joseph was instructed via the most secure communication channels: a private dream, words spoken in his own head that cannot be onverheard and betrayed to those who would harm the child. The wise men, too, were directed "in a dream."

In fact, almost the whole story takes place under the curtain of night: a bright star led the foreigners to the child; angels appeared again and again giving direction to the participants in their sleep; the holy family traveled to safety by night.

When the "all clear" sign was given in Egypt in a dream, Joseph brought the family home. But at the border, a final detour to Galilee was counseled to Joseph, once more in a dream.

The point is not that our dreams are always God talking – that would be a dangerous route to take! Instead, the point is that we must always be talking and listening to God. He will give guidance when we pay attention.

*How can you make talking and listening
to God a daily priority?*

HE'S COMING

The prophet Isaiah was speaking about John when he said,
"He is a voice shouting in the wilderness,
'Prepare the way for the LORD's coming!
Clear the road for him!'".
MATTHEW 3:3

John was an odd character, no doubt about it. Looking at him, no one could deny the fact that he was hearkening back to the prophets of old – Elijah, Elisha, Isaiah, Jeremiah. In fact, he took his words directly from the prophet Isaiah.

The voice of God had been silent for some 400 years, since the Old Testament had closed with the hopeful words of Malachi, "Look, I am sending you the prophet Elijah before the great and dreadful day of the LORD arrives" (Mal. 4:5). Jesus Himself would later identify John as this one prophesied by Malachi: "I tell you, Elijah has already come" (Matt. 17:12). Of course, we're also clued in to John's identity by the story recorded by Luke. When Gabriel prophesied John's birth to his father Zechariah, the angel said, "He will be a man with the spirit and power of Elijah. He will prepare the people for the coming of the Lord" (Luke 1:17).

John was a man ordained by God and given a mission to fulfill. And he did it with grace, knowing that his job was simply to point people to the Messiah. Our calling is no different. We need not wear coarse camel hair clothes or have a diet of locusts and wild honey as John did, but we ought to have a passion for pointing others to the Savior.

Where is your wilderness?
Whom are you pointing to the Savior?

COME AND FOLLOW ME

Jesus called out to them, "Come, follow me,
and I will show you how to fish for people!".
MATTHEW 4:19

J esus' invitation to two brothers, Simon Peter and Andrew, marks the beginning of a formal training process. For three years they hardly ever left His side, and He never stopped teaching them how to be what He wanted them to be and how to do what He wanted them to do.

It was intense, sometimes terrifying, always exhilarating, from the moment they dropped their fishing nets and began to walk with Jesus until the day three years later when they found themselves heading up the fledgling movement after the Master's departure.

Many do not enter into full discipleship with Jesus because they are afraid of failure; afraid of not being able to do what they sense is far beyond their natural abilities. However, Jesus knows not only our interests and abilities but also our potential. When we are enabled by Him, we can do far more than we normally would attempt.

When Jesus calls us to follow Him, He promises it will be worthwhile. He also lets us know that He personally will equip and train us to do what He calls us to do. After all, He did use the phrase "show you how to fish" when He issued this particular call to two fishermen! And He promises us today, "I will show you how." Who could ask for more than that?

*Jesus wants to use your interests and abilities
for His Kingdom – after all, He made you the way
you are for a reason! Are you ready to follow?*

COSTLY LOVE

*"If you love only those who love you, what reward is there for that?
Even corrupt tax collectors do that much. If you are kind only to your friends,
how are you different from anyone else? Even pagans do that.
But you are to be perfect, even as your Father in heaven is perfect".*
MATTHEW 5:46-48

Remember the "love notes" you used to send by way of friends back in elementary school? They usually took the form of "Do you like me? I like you."

Our first ventures into the risky world of love often involved exploratory efforts. We thought we might like someone, but we couldn't risk exposing ourselves to rejection, so we attempted a romantic reconnaissance. We wanted to ensure a proper response before we took a chance.

Unfortunately, real love doesn't work that way. Jesus pointed out the reason when He described love as the decision to take the first step – to love the unlovely, to reach beyond the comfort zone of family and friends. Once we decide how we would like to be treated, we are to treat others that way – regardless of how they treat us. Loving in return is easy, compared to loving first. God's kind of love, however, acts without guaranteed response.

What could possibly make us love that way and take those risks? The knowledge that we already have been loved that way! The life of Jesus can be read as the greatest example of how to love others, but it should be read first as God's demonstration of His love for us. At its best, our love for God will always be responding love, but loving others as Christ has loved us is our opportunity to actually imitate God, to "be perfect" even as He is perfect.

*God loved us not because we were lovable,
but because He is love.*

A PRAYER FOR GUIDANCE

I look to Thee in every need, and never look in vain;
I feel Thy strong and tender love, and all is well again.
The thought of Thee is mightier far than sin and pain and sorrow are.
Discouraged in the work of life, disheartened by its load,
shamed by its failures or its fears, I sink beside the road.
But let me only think of Thee and then new heart springs up in me.
Thy calmness bends serene above, my restlessness to still;
around me flows Thy quickening life, to nerve my faltering will.
Thy presence fills my solitude, Thy providence turns all to good.
Enfolded deep in Thy dear love, held in Thy law, I stand;
Thy hand in all things I behold, and all things in Thy hand.
Thou leadest me by unsought ways,
and turn my mourning into praise. Amen.

Samuel Longfellow

Day 7

MY PRAYER FOR
GOD'S GUIDANCE

_____

_____

_____

_____

_____

_____

_____

_____

_____

_____

God never guides us at some time in the future,
but always here and now. Realize that the Lord
is here now, and the freedom
you receive is immediate.

Oswald Chambers

WHY WORRY?

"And why worry about your clothing? Look at the lilies of the field and how they grow. They don't work or make their clothing ... And if God cares so wonderfully for wildflowers that are here today and thrown into the fire tomorrow, He will certainly care for you. Why do you have so little faith?".

MATTHEW 6:28, 30

*F*ood, drink, clothes – these comprise some of the basics of life. Why shouldn't we worry about them? No one wants to be hungry, thirsty, or unprotected.

The answer begins by understanding the difference between concern and *worry*. Concern means being aware of specific needs and then taking steps to meet those needs – concern leads to responsible action. It would be irresponsible and sinful, for example, for a father to be unconcerned about the basic needs of his family, for a mother to not care that her children are clean and clothed.

Worry, on the other hand, is extreme concern – concern gone to seed – an obsession with those needs. Filled with anxiety and fearing the worst, worriers nervously wonder about the future. They tend to spend more time filling their minds with ideas of the worst that could happen than working to make their dreams for the best that could happen come true. Concern mobilizes you to action; worry immobilizes you and makes you unable to function.

The answer to the worry question is understanding that God is the ultimate source of everything good and that He loves us, knows our needs, and shares our concerns.

When tempted to worry about life's basic necessities, rely on this promise from Jesus: God will take care of you. As you live and work, trust Him to meet your needs.

Would you say you have healthy concern – or
unhealthy worry – about the needs of yourself and
your family? How will you find the right balance?

WHO TOLD YOU TO DO THAT?

"Not everyone who calls out to me, 'Lord! Lord!' will enter the Kingdom of Heaven. Only those who actually do the will of my Father in heaven will enter".
MATTHEW 7:21

Many people's "religion" originates from within themselves. That may sound inherently contradictory since religion by definition has to do with forces and powers exterior to ourselves and to the material world in which we live. But the truth of the matter is that we human beings tend to create our own religions. We give to God what we think is reasonable service and presume that He had jolly well better be happy with it. This can be just as true for those who call themselves followers of Jesus as it is of others who belong to other faiths. Many call Him "Lord" but basically do as they please, creating religious structures, rites, practices, and traditions. The more elaborate those sets of rules and restrictions are, the more religious they think themselves to be.

Jesus warns, however, that the gate into the Kingdom is narrow (Matt. 7:13). Many will be confounded at the judgment when He tells them that their works, even those done in His name, were *not* in fact authorized or called for by the Father. It's a sobering prospect.

It is better – and safer – to build upon the solid rock of Jesus' instruction than to build on the shifting sand of our own ignorance. In short, do what *Jesus* says, not what *you* think you need to do. And the only way to know that is to be in communication with Him, through prayer and through the Word.

There's no way around it. To stay close to Jesus,
you need to stay in communication with Him.
How are you doing?

LOOKING AT THINGS A NEW WAY

*"And I tell you this, that many Gentiles will come from all over
the world – from east and west – and sit down with Abraham,
Isaac, and Jacob at the feast in the Kingdom of Heaven".*
MATTHEW 8:11

hat? *Gentiles* sitting down with the Hebrew patriarchs at the feast in the Kingdom of Heaven? How can that be?" To us at twenty-some centuries removed from Jesus' historical context, the notion of Gentiles populating the Kingdom does not seem far-fetched. After all, most of us qualify as Gentiles. To us, these are words of invitation. Jesus wanted *us* in the Kingdom! To Jesus' contemporaries, however, these words were outrageous. Jews and Gentiles did not cross paths – ever! And certainly not *for*ever!

But that was the plan all along. Jesus came not just to His people, but to all people. And we see this in His actions. As Jesus descended from the mountain after preaching, the first person to throw himself at His feet was a loathsome leper (Matt. 8:1). Such people were to be sent far away, into exile so that they could not spread their disease. Instead of recoiling from him, Jesus reached out to heal him. The next person to approach Jesus was a foreigner – not only a Roman, but an officer in the Roman army of occupation. To the astonishment of onlookers, Jesus gladly served *him* as well.

The followers of Jesus looked at one another wonderingly. *What is this Kingdom going to be like?* They may have even wondered to themselves, *Do I really want to be part of it?* To do so would mean letting go of long-held prejudices and looking at things a new way – God's way.

*What prejudices might you need to let go of
in order to look at life God's way?*

WHO IS GOING TO DO THIS JOB?

"So pray to the Lord who is in charge of the harvest;
ask him to send more workers into his fields".
MATTHEW 9:38

Jesus seemed to be ever concerned with completing the task, with getting the job done. Toward that end, He constantly was seeking others to involve in His mission. Unlike many bright stars in the social firmament, He showed no inclination to garner attention and hoard it, but rather delegated His ministries generously.

We are all familiar with individuals who work solo, not trusting others to share the workload and not willing to patiently coach lesser talents into performing brilliantly. But Jesus was exactly the opposite; though flawless Himself, He patiently repeated lessons to His imperfect protégés and continuously called more and more disciples into action. Seeing the great need all around Him – the people were "like sheep without a shepherd" (Matt. 9:36). Jesus recruited as many workers as He could to meet the need, then told His closest followers to pray to the Lord to send out *more* workers.

Ironically, after telling them to ask the Lord to send workers into the harvest fields, only a few verses later (in chapter 10), He *sends* them out two by two to do the job.

First He made them aware of a need, then He urged them to pray that God would do something about it ... then He sent *them*.

In what ways are you committed to helping Jesus
get the job done in your corner of the world?

WHY WOULD ANYONE DO THIS?

"And all nations will hate you because you are my followers.
But everyone who endures to the end will be saved".
MATTHEW 10:22

Serving Jesus is no picnic. He never masks the difficulties that His followers will encounter. We have a great reward that may serve as our motivation to follow the Lord (eternal life in heaven!), but Jesus spent more time warning of how terribly difficult it is going to be on earth than He did in portraying the benefits of heaven. Odd method for recruitment ...

Strangely, many contemporary evangelists have it exactly the opposite: They describe in glorious terms what a wonderful life God has planned for you and urge wavering potential converts to cash in.

But in Jesus' day, many would-be disciples who approached Him were rebuffed with curt responses like, "Are you sure? Do you *really* think you're up for this?" and Jesus would lay out the manifold troubles and tribulations that they were likely to encounter if they embarked on this journey. To His closest committed disciples He addressed detailed descriptions of just how they should conduct themselves in ministry and just how badly most people would respond to their message.

Jesus assures us that neither earthly benefits nor popular acclaim will be forthcoming in large supply; in fact, He says, "All nations will hate you." Those who really understand what following Jesus means don't do it for an easy life; they do it because it's the *best* life.

So, why do you follow Jesus?

THE LORD'S PRAYER

Our Father in heaven,
may Your name be kept holy.
May Your Kingdom come soon.
May Your will be done on earth,
as it is in heaven.
Give us today the food we need,
and forgive us our sins,
as we have forgiven those who sin against us.
And don't let us yield to temptation,
but rescue us from the evil one.

Matthew 6:9-13

Day 14

A PRAYER FROM MY HEART

_____

_____

_____

_____

_____

_____

_____

_____

_____

_____

In prayer it is better to have a heart without words,
than words without a heart.

John Bunyan

COME TO ME

*"Come to me, all of you who are weary and carry heavy burdens,
and I will give you rest. Take my yoke upon you. Let me teach you,
because I am humble and gentle at heart, and you will find rest for your souls.
For my yoke is easy to bear, and the burden I give you is light".*

MATTHEW 11:28-30

*A*d agencies know how to sell product. They find a hole and promise to fill it; they find a need and promise to meet it; they find a problem and promise to solve it. Then with airbrushed pictures, polished actors, and glib celebrities, they make their pitch for their products, each guaranteed to satisfy.

After you have been fed a steady diet of Madison Avenue, it's easy to build an immunity to its messages. And after dealing with a procession of products that fail to meet expectations, it's easy to take a cynical look at any new claim.

So when we hear, "Come to me ... and I will give you rest," we may turn it off in our minds. Certainly we are weary from carrying heavy responsibilities and working to please God, ourselves, and others. But this claim, like so many others, seems too good to be true.

Until we realize who is speaking. It is Jesus – God in the flesh – one of us, yet the Savior. Jesus tells the truth; He always comes through and lives up to His billing. After all, He's been there. He's been tired. He's carried burdens. He knows what you're going through.

You're probably tired of life's hectic pace, the busyness of your schedule, and the demands being placed on you at work, at home, at church, in your community. You don't know if you can keep up the pace. Add to that the cares you experience about your spouse, your kids, your family, and the needs you see around you.

Jesus says, "Come to me. Let's talk. Let's strike a balance. Let me help. I will give you peace."

*Are you in need of a lighter burden,
a time of rest? Come to Jesus.*

THE OBJECT OF OUR DEVOTION

"I tell you, there is one here who is even greater than the Temple!".
MATTHEW 12:6

We religious people love our institutions. Whether it's a beautiful sanctuary or a nice neat set of laws and restrictions or a flawless program of worship, we love the religious structures that we fabricate for ourselves.

The religious leaders of Jesus' day were probably no different from us on such matters, only their foibles jump out at us because Jesus confronted them over and over on their excessive "religiosity."

The truth is, Jesus was usually responding to their initial attacks. His disciples would break off a few heads of ripened grain to snack on while walking through a field on the Sabbath, and the religious gatekeepers would blow a shrill whistle and call, "Foul!"

Jesus would say simply to someone with a shriveled arm, "Stretch it out," and when the leaders saw that a healing had taken place on religious "downtime," they angrily plotted to do away with Jesus. In their game of life, the rules mattered more than the players.

Jesus tried to get them, and us, to understand that He Himself is to be worshiped, not all of our artificial trappings. But for some strange reason, too many seem to prefer the edifices they construct to the person they should honor.

To whom or what are you truly devoted –
to the living person Jesus or to a building,
a denomination, a set of rules?

WORTH MORE THAN EVERYTHING ELSE

*"The Kingdom of Heaven is like a treasure that a man discovered
hidden in a field. In his excitement, he hid it again and sold
everything he owned to get enough money to buy the field".*
MATTHEW 13:44

What could be worth so much that we would sell everything we have to acquire it? Most of us couldn't think of anything we currently desire that is *that* valuable – which gives us a clue: The Kingdom of Heaven is beyond our wildest dreams.

It is not the fulfillment of some lifelong ambition or finally getting what we've wished for all along. It is more like discovering something completely unexpected, Jesus tells us, which we immediately recognize as surpassing the value of everything we've accumulated thus far in life.

But many of us don't invest much in assuring entrance to the Kingdom, perhaps because in the back of our minds we pretty much figure that if we give up all that is valuable to us, we're losing out on this life. So we hedge our bets, "diversify our portfolio," as it were, rather than putting all our eggs in one basket.

The man Jesus described in the story was so excited by his discovery that he didn't hesitate to sell everything he had in order to get the hidden treasure he had found. Perhaps we don't yet perceive just how valuable the Kingdom is, which is why we fool around with lesser things.

What do you believe about the Kingdom of Heaven – really?
How valuable is it to you?

EVERYBODY GETS TO PARTICIPATE

*Then he told the people to sit down on the grass. Jesus took the five loaves
and two fish, looked up toward heaven, and blessed them. Then, breaking the loaves
into pieces, he gave the bread to the disciples, who distributed it to the people.*

MATTHEW 14:19

*C*an you imagine what it must have been like that day, to be one of the twelve disciples? Going from the frustration of being told to do an impossible task to the elation of participating in the unbelievable-but-true miraculous accomplishment of that assignment ... What must they have thought and felt as they watched Jesus hold up the small bread and fish toward heaven and bless them, then break off pieces and hand the pieces to them as He nodded toward the enormous crowd, indicating that the disciples, in turn, should do exactly the same.

As they kept handing out bread and fish, and more bread and fish, to dozens, then hundreds, of hungry people, a giddy, unanticipated joy must have rushed over them. They probably shouted to one another, "Hey, Thomas! Do you need some extra bread? I've got more than I know what to do with! Ha!" "No thanks, I'm fine. I keep giving it away, and there's still more in my hands!" And they grinned at each other and laughed merrily, and went on serving.

It was a day they would never forget. Jesus did an incredible miracle for thousands of men, women, and children, but He shared the glory, letting them be part of it – handing the food to them and letting *them* give it to the people. That seems to be His modus operandi: getting us involved in the good He is doing.

*What does Jesus want you
to "hand out" today, and to whom?*

"DID YOU SEE THAT?!"

*The crowd was amazed! Those who hadn't been able to speak
were talking, the crippled were made well, the lame were walking,
and the blind could see again! And they praised the God of Israel.*
MATTHEW 15:31

Let's face it: Jesus' enormous popularity and renown was based primarily on scenes like this one. Okay, some were impressed by His teaching; still today even people who don't consider themselves followers of Jesus frequently admit admiration for His "great teaching."

What brought thousands of people to Jesus was the possibility of days like this one: where a whole circus of the sick, diseased, demon-plagued, and variously crippled would all be released from their afflictions and suddenly start walking around as normal people – sane and sound! It must have been a stunning spectacle to watch. And for those most affected by His ministry – the afflicted themselves – it was, of course, astonishing and wonderful to be free at last from whatever had plagued them.

Why did Jesus do this? To fulfill the ancient prophecy of what the Messiah would do and to bring glory to God. Jesus doesn't always heal everyone. Sometimes God has other purposes for permitting our continued suffering. But it is recounted that there were days in His earthly ministry when huge crowds brought their innumerable afflicted friends and relatives and laid them at Jesus' feet and, it says, He "healed them all" (Matt. 15:30). All of them ... just imagine. The miracles proved who He was; it was up to the people to accept what He taught.

*What do you believe about Jesus? Is He more than
just a great teacher or miracle worker to you?*

A REQUEST FOR GOD'S LOVING CARE

Watch Thou, dear Lord,
with those who wake, or watch, or weep tonight,
and give Thine angels charge over those who sleep.
Tend Thy sick ones, Lord Christ.
Rest Thy weary ones.
Bless Thy dying ones.
Soothe Thy suffering ones.
Pity Thine afflicted ones.
Shield Thy joyous ones.
And all, for Thy love's sake.
Amen.

St. Augustine

Day 21

MY PRAYER FOR GOD'S CARE

_____

_____

_____

_____

_____

_____

_____

_____

_____

_____

_____

_____

Be not miserable about what may happen tomorrow.
The same everlasting Father who cares for you today,
will care for you tomorrow.

St. Francis de Sales

WHO DO YOU SAY I AM?

Then he asked them, "But who do you say I am?".
MATTHEW 16:15

When all is said and done, it doesn't much matter what everyone else says about Jesus. What determines your lot, in this life and in eternity, is what you yourself believe about Him. What Jesus first asked His disciples at Caesarea Philippi, "Who do people say that the Son of Man is?" (Matt. 16:13), may have been good didactics, warming them up to the subject so to speak, but He will not ask that question when you see Him face-to-face. All that will matter then is whether you have confessed Him to be your Lord in *this* life.

No doubt about it, Jesus was controversial. The disciples expressed some of the views that circled through the gossip columns of ancient Israel. But then Jesus looked His followers squarely in the eyes and said, "Okay, what about you?" You see, that's the bottom line.

You may have heard lots of opinions about Jesus from all kinds of people in all areas of your life. But the burning question Jesus asks you is, "Who do *you* say I am?"

As Jesus warned moments later, if we try to guard and keep our life, we'll lose it, but if we give up our life for His sake, we'll find real life. His true followers cast aside self-protecting devices, heave their crosses upon their shoulders, and fall in behind Him as He marches forward to where He, and we, must go.

So who is Jesus to you? How are you following?

WHO IS HE? AND WHO SAYS SO?

But even as he spoke, a bright cloud came over them, and a voice from the cloud said,
"This is my dearly loved Son, who brings me great joy. Listen to him".

MATTHEW 17:5

Who is Jesus? We may speculate, we may investigate, we may extrapolate from the data to form a reasonable hypothesis ... but ultimately it is God who bears witness to His Son, just as the Son bears witness to the Father.

The Bible says that Jesus, as Son of the divine Father, is uniquely qualified to reveal the nature and character of God having existed eternally with Him in intimate communion before He took on flesh to live as a human being. Some may doubt those extravagant-sounding claims – in fact, from Jesus' day until ours most human beings *do* dispute the uniqueness of Jesus' privileged knowledge of the Father.

So God the Father provides a certain amount of testimony that corroborates Jesus' claims. That evidence is splayed all over the Gospels in the form of miracles, divine wisdom manifested, authoritative teaching, and supernatural understanding of Himself, His destiny, and the hearts of those around Him.

Some specially privileged individuals – in this case, His three closest friends – got to see and hear direct divine revelation of Jesus' glory. Most of us never have such extraordinary mystical experiences, but nearly all who follow Jesus do receive *some* sort of verification that satisfies our longing for certainty. Not always with an audible voice, but in different ways, the Father assures our hearts that Jesus *is* who He claims He is.

Ask the Lord to burn the reality of Jesus' presence and person upon your heart, so that you might believe and serve Him, without wavering or doubting.

WHO IS THE GREATEST?

Then he said, "I tell you the truth, unless you turn from your sins and become like little children, you will never get into the Kingdom of Heaven".

MATTHEW 18:3

Most adults are busy climbing upward somewhere on the ladder of success. We expect that as we are faithful and productive with whatever duties have been given to us, promotion to greater responsibilities (hopefully coupled with greater rewards!) will be granted. It seems natural to us (at least in the Western world) that this is the way we advance higher and higher in career positioning, prestige, and material benefit.

While Jesus certainly has nothing against us moving upward and onward in our jobs and careers, He would have us keep a certain perspective on ourselves and our priorities. When the disciples were jockeying for position in the Kingdom, wondering which of them would be "greatest," Jesus answered, "The greatest? Listen, you won't even *get into* the Kingdom unless you abandon this ceaseless one-upmanship and rivalry and learn to be humble, like this child. My Father cares deeply about little ones like these, whom you apparently don't even notice in your competition to get ahead of one another. Wise up and realize that searching for and restoring straying lambs – or straying brothers and sisters – should be your priority. That's how you will become 'the greatest'."

So keep your perspective about your purpose on this earth. Consider your true priorities. Think about where you're storing your "treasure." Then consider what Jesus said about being "like little children."

What have you been aiming for as your "next promotion"? Does this correspond to, or conflict with, God's intentions for your life?

THE DANGER OF TOO MANY THINGS

Then Jesus said to his disciples, "I tell you the truth, it is very hard
for a rich person to enter the Kingdom of Heaven".
MATTHEW 19:23

This may be one of Jesus' best known sayings. Often cited by those who do not consider themselves to be rich, it would likely be repeated and widely circulated as a sort of consolation for their present lack. As Tevye said in *Fiddler on the Roof*, "God must really love poor people – He made so many of them!"

Why are riches such an impediment to spirituality? It is not evil to be rich, as is clear from God's blessing of ancient figures like Abraham, Job, or Solomon with material riches. That He continues to do so today can be seen in works like Billy Graham's autobiography *Just As I Am*, which repeatedly mentions how well-to-do supporters of Graham's ministry (and thus the Kingdom in general) gladly dug deep down into their pockets to make many important ministries possible.

As shown in the story of the young man who turned away from Jesus at the end of their encounter (Matt. 19:22), and as Jesus mentioned elsewhere, it is the extra *cares* that trip people up. A wealthy life is not a carefree life; in fact, the more things (or investments or "stuff") people have, the more they have to worry about and pay attention to. It's that simple – or that complicated.

It's hard for wealthy people to get into the Kingdom simply because they have much that distracts them and takes their focus off of what is most important.

Are you rich in things of this world?
If you consider yourself to be so, do you own
those things or do they own you?

THE FIRST WILL BE LAST, AND THE LAST WILL BE FIRST

"Those people worked only one hour, and yet you've paid them just
as much as you paid us who worked all day in the scorching heat".

MATTHEW 20:12

I t just didn't seem right. Not to us, not to the disciples who were listening
to Jesus the first time the parable of the vineyard workers was told (Matt.
20:1-16), and certainly not to the principal characters in the story, those hired
at the beginning of the day who received exactly the same compensation as
those hired only at the last hour of the working day. Boy, were they ticked!

And they let the owner of the vineyard know it, too. After bearing the
heat, sore and tired from bending over grapevines all day, and then to see
some latecomers treated equally for less contribution ... well, it just wasn't
right or fair.

The owner, whom Jesus obviously meant to represent His heavenly
Father, was not vexed by the complaint but gently corrected their mistaken
concept of fairness. He kept His word with all those whom He hired. If He
wished to be generous with the very last person to enter into His service,
why should that make any difference to them? They had received what they
had agreed upon.

Jesus' point in telling the story, of course, is to forewarn His closest
disciples that just because they'd "given up everything" (Matt. 19:27) to
follow Him and were His earliest followers, they should not be surprised – or
miffed – when others who would come into the Kingdom later and perhaps
with seemingly less sacrifice receive the same benefit.

*Do you see yourself as deserving special deference because
of your length of service in the Christian community?
What do you feel about the latecomers?*

A PRAYER FOR A STEADFAST FAITH

O Lord, give us a mind that is humble, quiet,
peaceable, patient and charitable,
and a taste of Thy Holy Spirit
in all our thoughts, words, and deeds.
O Lord, give us a lively faith, a firm hope,
a fervent charity, a love of Thee.
Take from us all lukewarmness in meditation
and all dullness in prayer.
Give us fervor and delight in thinking of Thee,
Thy grace, and Thy tender compassion toward us.
Give us, good Lord, the grace to work for
the things we pray for.
Amen.

St. Thomas More

Day 28

MY PRAYER FOR A STEADFAST FAITH

_____

_____

_____

_____

_____

_____

_____

_____

_____

_____

_____

Every tomorrow has two handles. We can take hold of it
with the handle of anxiety or the handle of faith.

Henry Ward Beecher

WHAT DO YOU THINK?

"When the owner of the vineyard returns," Jesus asked,
"what do you think he will do to those farmers?".
MATTHEW 21:40

To conclude His shocking parable of the wicked farmers (Matt. 21:33-46), Jesus suddenly threw the ball into His opponents' court. They were forced by the logic of the story to react, which they did with vigor, denouncing and pronouncing a death sentence upon the wicked farmers and saying the vineyard should be entrusted to more worthy tenants. But their response backfired on them as they realized that *they* were the usurping tenants on borrowed terrain, ungratefully and ungraciously refusing to honor the terms of their agreement with the owner, God, and plunging headlong in a plot to kill His Son.

Throughout this climactic series of encounters near the end of Jesus' earthly ministry, He repeatedly asked His antagonists, "What do *you* think?" It would be one thing for Jesus, having been rejected over and over by the unrepentant religious establishment at Jerusalem, to pronounce judgment on them. It was a decision He had a perfect right to render, as His parables illustrate. But it was all the more effective for Him to let them reason out the consequences of their rejection and actually articulate it themselves.

Jesus gives us clear and reasonable grounds upon which He will one day act as judge. He spells out both what He expects and what He offers, and then asks us to consider, "What do you think?"

You cannot pretend that you don't understand
what Jesus expects and what He offers.
The ball is in your court. Where will you go from here?

THE MOST IMPORTANT COMMANDMENT

"The entire law and all the demands of the prophets
are based on these two commandments".

MATTHEW 22:40

Jesus makes it so simple and clear: Love God, and love your neighbor as yourself. The context of the question that led to His answer was one of hostility and animosity: The religious leaders wanted to get rid of Him, to stop Him from teaching the people. But why? He wasn't proposing an overthrow of Jewish religious doctrine.

Not only was Jesus' teaching harmonious with the body of Jewish Law derived from Moses, He said that all the other commandments and prophetic demands were based upon this foundation. If they were the rivers that refreshed the people of God, this was the source, the headwaters, the spring from which the nurturing streams flowed. If it hadn't been obvious before, this answer to the question, "Which is the most important commandment in the law of Moses?" (Matt. 22:36) should have settled the matter.

In one sense it did, since no one dared ask Him any more questions. Yet for those who considered religion to be their personal franchise, He was still a dangerous threat. He made a relationship with God available to anyone.

Perhaps that is what irritated the authorities. They would much rather that people felt helpless and dependent on them for religious direction. Unlike the subtleties and obscure regulations of the religious teachers, Jesus' teaching may be summed up in a single breath, in the simple straightforward command: Love God and love your neighbor. Anyone can understand that.

*Are you keeping this simplest and most important of
all the commandments? Or do you get sidetracked
on minor issues and legalistic paraphernalia?*

WHAT YOU SAY AND WHAT YOU DO

"What sorrow awaits you teachers of religious law and you Pharisees.
Hypocrites! For you are so careful to clean the outside of the cup and the dish,
but inside you are filthy – full of greed and self-indulgence!".

MATTHEW 23:25

Whew! Did He blast them, or what? "Lowly Jesus, meek and mild," intones the nursery song, but that is not the persona we meet toward the end of Matthew. This chapter of the Bible is hard to swallow for those who prefer to guard for themselves an illusion of a "safe" Jesus with no backbone. But we had better recognize that the Jesus who walked the earth was no such person. In C. S. Lewis's *The Lion, the Witch and the Wardrobe*, when asked about the lion (and Christ figure) Aslan, "Is he *safe*?" Tumnus answered, "I should say NOT! He's not a tame lion, you know."

After whirling around dispensing one adversary after another who came at Him from different corners of the Temple courtyard, Jesus was the unanimously acclaimed victor in every theological "match." Next He stepped into an aggressive posture and denounced His defeated opponents for their hypocrisy. Interestingly enough, He did not dispute their teachings, but approved of them, and warned the people that they should indeed *do* what their religious authorities told them to do – but that they should be very careful not to copy their blind guides' behavior, for what the religious leaders said did not match what they did.

Jesus warns all of us today that exterior pretenses of holiness are all the more fraudulent when they are belied by interior filth and deceitfulness.

The Lord sees all the way through you.
What "filth" might there be that needs to be cleaned up?

THE VERY LAST THING
BEFORE HE COMES

"And the Good News about the Kingdom will be preached throughout the whole world, so that all nations will hear it; and then the end will come".
MATTHEW 24:14

What we are concerned with and what Jesus is concerned with are not identical. This is as true when it comes to the end times as it is with many other themes and subjects about which Jesus' disciples asked Him. They, and we, want to know some clear signposts so we can get ready. Jesus, on the other hand, puts the end in the same perspective as everything else He discussed: It's all about the *Kingdom*.

So right in the middle of His definitive discourse on the end times, He returned to His beloved central theme: "The Good News about the Kingdom will be preached throughout the world, so that all nations will hear it." By this time, just two days from the completion of His earthly ministry, Jesus was speaking openly of the universality of the gospel. There had been hints all along that the Kingdom was inclusive, that some Gentiles would get in, but now He declared without ambiguity that in the end all ethnic groups – some from every tribe and tongue and nation – will have heard and been given the opportunity to accept the Good News.

So we keep on sharing the Good News. Missionaries go to the far corners of the earth, deep into the darkest jungles, far across the tundra, into the mountains. They seek those who have not heard. They translate Scripture into unwritten languages. And with every new group who hears, the end comes closer. "Amen! Come, Lord Jesus" (Rev. 22:20).

What direct relationship is there between openly declaring the approaching Kingdom to those around you and Christ's triumphant return?

AM I READY FOR HIM TO COME BACK?

"So you, too, must keep watch! For you do not know the day or hour of my return".
MATTHEW 25:13

*A*s the old saying goes, "When the cat's away, the mice will play." In the workaday world, there seems to be a natural affinity between productivity, efficiency, diligence ... and the presence of the supervisor. "When is the boss coming back?" is a standard question for which every employee wants reliable information, so that he or she may resume a more vigorous pace – just before that luminary appears.

On numerous occasions Jesus referred to this human tendency to relax and take responsibilities lightly when there is no one present to elicit more diligent behavior. He warned against treating His own temporary absence as King in such a foolish way – foolish because "you do not know the day or hour of my return." It could be at any time, and it almost certainly will be at a moment when we *don't* expect Him.

Several of the parables Jesus told to illustrate the conditions of His return emphasized this matter of being found faithful and ready when the Lord (the Bridegroom, the King, the Master) suddenly surprises everyone by showing up.

"You had better live every hour of your life getting ready for that moment," He solemnly warned. "Those whom I find working for me will be rewarded very generously. And those who thought maybe I wasn't coming back any time soon, and goofed off ... well, you *don't* want to be one of them."

What if He really were to appear today? Are you ready?
If not, what needs to be done before you can face Him?

A PRAYER OF THANKSGIVING

It is good to give thanks to the LORD, to sing praises
to the Most High. It is good to proclaim
Your unfailing love in the morning, Your faithfulness
in the evening, You thrill me, LORD,
with all You have done for me!
I sing for joy because
of what You have done.

Psalm 92:1-2, 4

Day 35

MY PRAYER OF THANKSGIVING

_____

_____

_____

_____

_____

_____

_____

_____

_____

_____

God is in control, and therefore in everything
I can give thanks – not because of the situation
but because of the One who
directs and rules over it.

Kay Arthur

PREPARING FOR THE WORST

On the way, Jesus told them, "Tonight all of you will desert me. For the Scriptures say, 'God will strike the Shepherd, and the sheep of the flock will be scattered'".
MATTHEW 26:31

Jesus knew exactly what was coming at Him that night. In fact, He had known it all along and had tried to prepare His followers for the experience by telling them, repeatedly, that He was going to be betrayed into the hands of His enemies, that He would suffer intensely, and He would die. Here He told them that this dreadful event was upon them and that they would abandon Him in the hour of His greatest need.

Of course, they didn't believe it and took turns assuring Jesus that "*I* won't forsake you, I'll be there for you," and so forth. But Jesus' preparation for the imminent crisis was not based on illusive optimism but on Scripture. He *knew* what had to take place, and He steeled His spirit for it by facing it head on.

He understood His coming death in the right theological perspective ("*God* will strike the Shepherd," or as He said in John 10:18, "No one can take my life from me. I sacrifice it voluntarily"). Yet He spent intense moments in agonizing prayer dealing with how He felt about that which He wished to avoid. What He admonished sleepy Peter about was true of Himself as well, and He knew it: "The spirit is willing, but the body is weak" (Matt. 26:41). So, knowing His friends would all desert Him, Jesus got ready by submitting to His Father.

When He'd won that battle, He stood up and said resolutely, "Let's be going" (Matt. 26:46).

You can turn whatever difficulty you're facing today into a great victory simply by saying, "I want Your will to be done, not mine," and meaning it.

TOOK HIS PLACE; TOOK MY PLACE

*So Pilate released Barabbas to them. He ordered Jesus flogged with a
lead-tipped whip, then turned him over to the Roman soldiers to be crucified.*

MATTHEW 27:26

Barabbas was a hardened criminal who had robbed, killed, and stirred up insurrections; Barabbas was the very first person to be redeemed by Jesus. In his case, the word *redeemed* is not metaphorical, as we use it with reference to all the rest of us down through the ages whose sins have been paid for by Jesus' death. That day Barabbas was literally redeemed – set free – when Jesus stepped into his place in the executioner's line and replaced him.

Every physical pain that Jesus experienced that day – the whippings, the beatings, the mocking torment by brutal soldiers, the onerous trek to the killing place carrying the heavy, splintery wooden cross, spikes nailed into His hands and feet, and then the long, slow suffocation of crucifixion it all should have been Barabbas's lot.

What we read about in the Gospels' depiction of the crucifixion is how torture as a deterrent to rebellion was carried out upon thousands of condemned prisoners in public squares throughout the empire. Barabbas had been sentenced to what Jesus actually experienced.

Whether he watched from a prudent distance we don't know. But every one of us since that day who looks at this scene should say in our hearts, "That is what I deserve. Jesus replaced not just Barabbas – He took *my* place. That is what it cost to redeem me."

*Ask the Lord to help you not to distance yourself
from His sufferings, but instead to realize that He
deliberately took the punishment your sins deserved.*

FINAL WORDS

"Teach these new disciples to obey all the commands I have given you.
And be sure of this: I am with you always, even to the end of the age".
MATTHEW 28:20

M atthew ends his Gospel with Jesus giving His disciples a final command and a final promise. The first is natural and fairly obvious for a teacher and coming King: As you go into all the world making disciples of all the nations, teach them to obey everything I have commanded you. Of course. But the second is much more heartening. "I am with you always." Always!

The command must have been daunting. He had warned them over and over that the process of proclaiming His Kingdom would be fraught with rejection, even with persecution. Worse yet, they had seen that hostility come to its ugly culmination in the torture and death of Jesus Himself only a few days before; they knew He was not exaggerating. What happened to Him could very likely happen to them.

But He promised that as they went in obedience to His commission, making disciples of the nations, *He would be with them*. That must have been enough, for we see in the book of Acts that they did exactly that. Having Jesus with them had become their highest value. After experiencing three days of His absence when He was dead, and now the unparalleled joy they felt as He was again among them, they needed no further motivation. Just His promise that He would be with them was enough for them to launch the perilous but exciting mission of taking the Kingdom message to every corner of the world.

Is the prospect of having Jesus with you enough to
obey Him wholeheartedly and to fearlessly make Him
known to those who don't yet know Him?
What else could you possibly need as motivation?

Day 39

NONSTOP BUSYNESS

*But Jesus replied, "We must go on to other towns as well,
and I will preach to them, too. That is why I came".*
MARK 1:38

Mark's Gospel is an adventure story from the get-go. One of Mark's favorite words that appears throughout his book may be translated by such urgent English terms as "immediately, instantly, suddenly, at once." In chapter one he uses the word eleven times!

By the ninth verse, the adult Jesus is already striding into action; only a few lines later, back from forty days of being tested by the devil, He is already preaching. He's always on the go, moving on to serve in "other towns as well."

When He called disciples to follow Him, they dropped their work tools and hastened to catch up. He cast out evil spirits, healed hundreds of sick people, and dazzled the fast-growing crowds by the sheer energy of His output and the dynamism of His preaching.

In contrast to the long and detailed teaching discourses of Matthew's Gospel, Mark streamlines the verbal aspects of Jesus' ministry and focuses on the activity.

The person who practically jumps out at us from Mark's portrait of the Messiah is no pale ascetic or abstract moral philosopher; He's more like an action hero. With a sense of purpose in every move and God's guidance with every stride, Jesus was a man on a mission. He knew what He had come to do, and there was no slowing Him down.

*What is your overriding purpose in life,
even as you move through the busyness of each day?*

GET UP AND WALK

*And the man jumped up, grabbed his mat, and walked out through
the stunned onlookers. They were all amazed and praised God,
exclaiming, "We've never seen anything like this before!".*
MARK 2:12

Look at the action-packed, visceral language in this verse! "Jumped up ... grabbed his mat ... walked out ... stunned onlookers ... praised God."

Wherever Jesus went He stirred up excited reactions. Whether He was healing helpless people or in the company of notorious sinners, Jesus always evoked animated responses.

His popularity soon attracted the attention of the religious elite who were critical of the excitement that His ministry provoked. Jesus generally either ignored them or showed that their astringent interpretations of religious law were both wrong and harmful. Then He went on His way, attending to those who most needed His intervention. "Healthy people don't need a doctor," He explained, "sick people do" (Mark 2:17).

Jesus made it His personal business to raise to achievement and purpose people who had become, for whatever reasons, immobilized. Imbued with an insatiable propensity for action, Jesus marched through the Gospel narratives telling people who are comfortably seated (like Levi) or inexorably stretched out (like the paralyzed man), "Get up! Pick up your stuff, and come on! There's work to be done!"

*Where are you in your spiritual life today?
Lethargic? Immobilized? Distant?
What will it take for Jesus to get you to get going?*

A PRAYER FOR DIRECTION
ON LIFE'S JOURNEY

Steer the ship of my life, good Lord, to Thy quiet harbor,
where I can be safe from the storms of sin and conflict.
Show me the course I should take. Renew in me
the gift of discernment, so that I can always see
the right direction in which I should go.
And give me the strength and the courage to choose
the right course, even when the sea is rough
and the waves are high, knowing that through
enduring hardship and danger in Thy name
we shall find comfort and peace.
Amen.

St. Basil of Caesarea

Day 42

MY PRAYER FOR GOD'S
DIRECTION AND LEADING

_____

_____

_____

_____

_____

_____

_____

_____

_____

_____

_____

What Jesus would do, and how He would do it,
may always stand as the best guide.

Charles Spurgeon

CLOSE TO JESUS

"Anyone who does God's will is my brother and sister and mother".
MARK 3:35

The various followers of Jesus seem to have formed several concentric rings around Him. "Vast numbers of people" came from distant regions to see Him (Mark 3:8). A "crowd" pressed in on Him (Mark 3:9). "Many" needy people received healing (Mark 3:10). From the many people who followed, Jesus called out certain ones to go with Him, and from among them He selected a group of twelve apostles "to accompany" Him (Mark 3:14).

The religious establishment, in contrast, soon recognized that Jesus had no interest in joining their aristocracy. Piqued by His apparent indifference to their status, they accused Him of belonging to a more insidious society – that of Satan. "That must be where He gets His powers!" they charged.

Even Jesus' own family members, alarmed by the huge crowds roiling around Jesus – and that He actually seemed to welcome them – came to take Him home. But when they sent word in to Him, He set the record straight about who His closest associates were: "My mother? My brothers? These," He said, indicating fondly with a sweep of His arm the devoted followers eagerly pressing in all around Him, "these are my mother and my brothers and my sisters." Why? Because these are the ones who are seeking to do God's will. These are the ones who get to be closest to Jesus.

In which circle of Jesus' followers are you right now?
How close do you want to be?

Day 44

DIGGING DEEPER

In fact, in his public ministry he never taught without using parables;
but afterward, when he was alone with his disciples,
he explained everything to them.

MARK 4:34

Jesus habitually used colorful, entertaining stories to attract and regale a wide swath of people, and "to teach the people as much as they could understand" (Mark 4:33). His stories, drawn from the everyday lives of everyday people, made clear to His hearers that He was no abstract, removed holy man – He knew what life was like. He knew about planting seeds and the constant reality that much of the seed is lost in less-than-accepting soil. The result? The people listened to Him gladly.

To His disciples Jesus disclosed that He taught with parables to actually disguise the deeper meaning of His teaching – a level of understanding He reserved for His closest followers: "When he was alone with his disciples, he explained everything to them" (Mark 4:34). He compared the Word of God to a seed that was planted gladly and began to show promise, but later was quenched and never became fruitful.

Jesus urged His hearers to listen carefully and dig deeper, to make every effort to understand the full meaning of the Word of God, to not just be entertained by it, but to be like good soil and produce a huge harvest.

What kind of soil are you today?

WELL, WHAT DO YOU EXPECT?

But Jesus overheard them and said to Jairus,
"Don't be afraid. Just have faith".
MARK 5:36

What Jesus did and said often did not correspond to what people expected. Given who He is, that should seem natural. Yet over and over in the Gospel narratives we find that people were either surprised by Jesus' actions or words, or else He was surprised by their reactions to Him. When such dissonance occurs, who do you think should adjust to whom?

Jesus freed a wild man from the demons that had tortured him, but the change in the man was so shattering to behold ("sitting there fully clothed and perfectly sane") that the citizenry of the town the man had menaced actually begged Jesus to leave (Mark 5:1-20).

A suffering woman reached out from within the anonymity of a crowd, believing even clandestine contact with Jesus' clothes could heal her. As Jesus felt healing power drain out of Him into her, He turned, surprised, and required that she reveal herself and in so doing receive His spiritual touch as well (Mark 5:24-34).

When Jesus arrived at the home where a child had just died, He implied that there was still hope. Hearing His words, the raucous crowd instantly shifted from weeping and wailing to hoots of derisive laughter. But what He did next – raising her to life again – astonished everyone (Mark 5:35-43).

So what do you expect from Jesus?

In a world where most voices are skeptical, or resigned,
Jesus says, "Don't listen to them. And don't be afraid. Just trust Me."

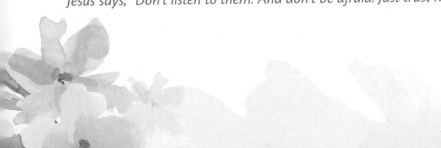

WITHOUT AMBIVALENCE

*Herod respected John; and knowing that he was a good
and holy man, he protected him. Herod was greatly disturbed
whenever he talked with John, but even so, he liked to listen to him.*

MARK 6:20

*R*ighteousness has a compelling attraction to it. Even those who are least inclined to right living, find themselves fascinated by lives that are apparently free from sin and evildoing and by messages that boldly declare moral truth. Hard-bitten politicians, cynical journalists, and even seasoned criminals have found themselves softening and backing off when confronted with a personality like the pope, Mother Teresa, or Billy Graham. But to listen is not the same as to commit; fascination is not dedication.

Herod Antipas, one of the real scoundrels of the first-century political milieu, felt this kind of ambivalence toward his prisoner John the Baptist. He couldn't resist calling the preacher in for frequent consultations where John's words resounded with the clear ring of truth. But Herod found himself disturbed by John's talk, like a later governor Felix would experience when his prisoner, the apostle Paul, would discuss "righteousness and self-control and the coming day of judgment" (Acts 24:25).

Sooner or later Herod would have to resolve the ambivalence. To his everlasting chagrin, his evil wife decided for him. Appalled by his own cowardice, Herod nevertheless ordered that John be silenced.

Those who are fascinated by believers who love and live for the Lord but reject what they see are making a grave and eternal mistake.

*Ask the Lord to help you always give Him
full attention without ambivalence,
no matter what situation you face today.*

HEART SCAN

*"For from within, out of a person's heart,
come evil thoughts, sexual immorality, theft, murder ... ".*
MARK 7:21

*A*nd the list of perverse attitudes and actions goes on. Jesus revealed that the heart is the source from which all evil actions come pouring forth. We are accustomed to blaming evil on sources outside of ourselves – bad choices in friends, socioeconomic disadvantages, poor parents, even the devil. But Jesus says it all starts right inside ourselves.

Criticized by the religious rulers and teachers of His day for not keeping ceremonial hand-washing laws, Jesus wearily recognized the issue to be the same that had plagued the people of God since Isaiah's day – religious leaders who emphasized external rules rather than internal purity.

The latter is difficult to assess: How can you know when your heart is clean and pure and focused on pleasing God? It requires living with a steady consciousness of the propensity to evil in your heart so that you keep constant vigil over it, repeatedly returning to the presence of God after momentary (or longer) lapses of attention. You must, as King Solomon wrote, "Guard your heart" (Prov. 4:23).

It's much easier to keep a list of man-made rules and to check them off each day: "Well, I've done what I'm supposed to. So, I'm okay." But Jesus says, "No, that's just it. You're not and never can be on your own. You need Me."

What does the Lord see in your heart today?

A PRAYER FOR ALL SEASONS

God, Thou made the sun and moon
to distinguish seasons and day and night.
And we cannot have the fruits of the earth
but in their seasons.
But Thou hath made no decree
to distinguish the seasons of Thy mercies.
In paradise the fruits were ripe the first minute,
and in heaven it is always autumn.
Thy mercies are ever in their maturity.
Thou never sayest we should hath come yesterday.
Thou never sayest we should come back tomorrow, but today,
if we will hear Thy voice, Thou wilt heareth us.
Thou brought light out of darkness, not out of lesser light.
Thou canst bring Thy summer out of winter,
though Thou hath no spring.
All occasions invite Thy mercies
and all times are Thy seasons.
Amen.

John Donne

Day 49

A PRAYER FOR THE
SEASONS OF MY LIFE

_____

_____

_____

_____

_____

_____

_____

_____

_____

There are far, far better things ahead
than any we leave behind.

C. S. Lewis

DO YOU GET IT?

"'You have eyes – can't you see? You have ears – can't you hear?'
Don't you remember anything at all?".
MARK 8:18

Working with fallen, limited human beings must have been excruciatingly difficult for the Son of God. Even in the voluntarily reduced state of His incarnation, He had powers and knowledge that ordinary human beings did not. From all of eternity, His vision had included, well, all of eternity! He knew where everything was going, and why, and how it all fit together. We humans stumble around in the dark just trying to understand what is happening around us.

Add to that our fallen nature; it is not enough that, compared with the Supreme Being who created, sustains, and governs the entire universe, we're extremely limited in our intelligence. Because of the Fall, we are damaged goods, flawed, defective ... we can look right at something God is doing and not see or understand it. It's no surprise, therefore, that the disciples of Jesus frequently just didn't get it.

Jesus knew their limitations, as He knows ours. Yet for those of us who have seen Him work, He does expect a certain amount of understanding and faith.

How many times has God done miracles on our behalf and then, the next problem we face, we act as if we don't know what to do or where to turn? At those times, Jesus says, "Don't you remember anything at all?"

Are you doubting God today? What reminder from the
past can help you trust Him for your current need?

HOW TO GET AHEAD

He sat down, called the twelve disciples over to him, and said, "Whoever wants to be first must take last place and be the servant of everyone else".
MARK 9:35

Jesus not only taught humility, He practiced it. It was not enough for Him to keep reminding His rabidly ambitious disciples to stop quarreling over their respective positions in the hierarchy of the Kingdom. The Master Himself had to show them, repeatedly, that He was willing to do the dirtiest jobs Himself.

Thus, when He came down off the mountain where His dazzling glory had been briefly visible, the serenity was rudely dispelled by the noise of religious teachers arguing with His disciples. The latter had failed at casting out an evil spirit from a boy. It was a horrifying picture: The child was foaming at the mouth, grimacing and shrieking wildly, writhing and convulsing. When the spirit saw Jesus, things only got worse (Mark 9:20).

Any person in his right mind would put as much distance as possible between himself and such an abhorrent scene. But Jesus didn't turn down the job or consider it beneath His dignity. He stepped right into the mess to "mop it up," as it were, directly confronting and defeating the evil spirit, then raising the boy up by the hand to restored normalcy.

Later, Jesus took another child in His arms, telling His disciples that service to such little people is equivalent to serving the Lord Himself.

Are you willing to do "the dirty jobs" in the Kingdom?

ARE YOU ABLE TO DO THIS?

But Jesus said to them, "You don't know what you are asking! Are you able to drink from the bitter cup of suffering I am about to drink? Are you able to be baptized with the baptism of suffering I must be baptized with?".

MARK 10:38

The sons of Zebedee wanted high positions in the coming Kingdom, and they were not afraid to come right out and ask for them. Like many twenty-first-century aspirants for greatness and power, they knew it was all about "who you know." James and John figured if they wanted to rise to the top, they had to go to the one who could make it happen – and fortunately, they had an inside track with Him. When asked, as James and John were by Jesus, whether they thought they would really be able to do what was required for the posts they were seeking, they confidently chirped, "Oh yes, we are able!"

You can almost see Jesus shake His head at their glib naiveté. They had no idea what was in store for them; yet they brashly sought preeminence. Jesus replied that they would indeed drink from the bitter cup of suffering, but even then, places of honor were not up to Him. It is strange that in God's Kingdom, as much as in the business world, overblown ambition often blinds people to their own frailty. Moreover, as Jesus explained, such ambition disqualifies candidates because they will be unable to exercise true leadership according to His standards.

Soon after the church was founded, James would indeed be first in line – to be killed by a government sword (Acts 12:2). John would end up in exile (Rev. 1:9). God will honor His followers, but sometimes in ways we might not expect – or choose.

Are you seeking to be served or to serve?

Day 53

IN NEED OF JESUS

When the leading priests and teachers of religious law heard
what Jesus had done, they began planning how to kill him. But they
were afraid of him because the people were so amazed at his teaching.

MARK 11:18

What's up with the constant antagonism of the religious establishment toward Jesus? Pharisees were the most devoted of all Jewish people to personal piety; priests spent their days attending to worship in the Temple; teachers of religious law poured over God's Word with care, seeking to understand its minutest ramifications. Why, then, all this hostility toward Jesus?

It was coldly deliberate in its intention, too. What happened to Jesus on the Friday of Passover was not an impromptu mob riot that accidentally got out of hand; instead, it was the realized goal of a long-premeditated plan stemming from the religious leaders' animosity. It is jarring to read so often in the Gospels phrases like "they began planning how to kill him." Often, running alongside such grim reports, the contrasting attitude of the common people forms a sort of artistic counterpoint in the mood of the sentence: "but they were afraid of him because the people were so amazed at his teaching."

Why does one group so fervently want to do away with Jesus while the other just as ardently loves Him? Perhaps it is a question we can only answer by looking deep into our own hearts. Even then we might be misled, however. Like the religious leaders of old, too many are able to fool themselves into thinking that they are religious people and therefore have no need of Jesus.

Is Jesus Lord of – or a dangerous threat to –
your carefully constructed personal religion?

WHAT IS MOST IMPORTANT?

"And you must love the LORD your God with all your heart,
all your soul, all your mind, and all your strength".
MARK 12:30

Things really couldn't be clearer than this. No one can accuse Jesus of teaching an esoteric doctrine; no one can claim to not understand. This crystal clear summary of all that is important in God's Law is pronounced, significantly, right at the end of an extended contest between Jesus and a whole slew of His religious opponents.

One after another representatives of the various Jewish religious orders of the day had approached Jesus and tried to beat Him in rabbinical debate. Their jousting consisted of questions ranging from the mundane to the arcane, but one after another they were toppled off their high horses by Jesus' lucid answers.

Now, one final religious scholar, this one perhaps more sincere than the rest, asked Jesus, "Of all the commandments, which is the most important?" Jesus answered, succinctly but thoroughly, and the tournament was over. "And after that, no one dared to ask him any more questions" (Mark 12:34).

Love God. This simple, transitive imperative tells us all we need to find satisfaction and joy in life. Focus all of our energy – emotive, spiritual, intellectual, and physical – on loving God. That's all there is to it. Nothing fancy, nothing esoteric; just love God.

How much do you love God?
How do you show it?

A REQUEST FOR HIS ABIDING PRESENCE

In me there is darkness, but with You there is light;
I am lonely, but You do not leave me;
I am feeble in heart, but with You there is help;
I am restless, but with You there is peace.
In me there is bitterness, but with You there is patience;
I do not understand Your ways,
but You know the way for me.
Lord Jesus Christ, You were poor and in distress,
a captive and forsaken as I am.
You know all man's troubles; You abide with me.
When all men fail me; You remember and seek me;
it is Your will that I should know You and turn to You.
Lord, I hear Your call and follow; help me. Amen.

Dietrich Bonhoeffer

Day 56

MY PRAYER FOR JESUS' ABIDING PRESENCE

_____
_____
_____
_____
_____
_____
_____
_____
_____
_____
_____

Let this be your whole endeavor, this your prayer,
this your desire, that you may be stripped
of all selfishness, and with entire
simplicity follow Jesus only.

Thomas à Kempis

GET READY

"I say to you what I say to everyone: Watch for him!".
MARK 13:37

Like everyone else, Jesus' disciples wanted to know about the "end times." So when He let drop certain hints, they pressed Him to be more specific. Sometimes He obliged their curiosity and spoke directly of dangers and trials that they would eventually have to go through in His name, of subsequent generations' further persecutions and woes, of apocalyptic events still eons distant in time, and finally of His own triumphant personal return, a universally visible event that would bring human history to climactic conclusion.

But then He would revert to the language of enigma, speaking of reading the signs of the times like buds on a tree in springtime, and that sort of thing. He said, "This generation will not pass from the scene before all these things take place," but in the next breath admitted that not even the Son knows when these things will happen. He would switch back and forth from detailed descriptions to metaphors. What can we really learn from this?

The message always comes down to the same thing: The Lord will one day appear, and when He does, we had better be ready, waiting and watching for Him.

Are you ready? Stay alert and keep watching.

DISCOVERING WHO WE REALLY ARE

*"No!" Peter declared emphatically. "Even if I have to die with you,
I will never deny you!" And all the others vowed the same.*
MARK 14:31

How little we know ourselves! When we hear of villainy or cowardice, we are confident that if placed in similar circumstances we wouldn't act as this or that one did. Peter, too, thinks himself a cut above the rest – "even if everyone else deserts you, I never will" (Mark 14:29).

We are blind to how flawed we really are. It is in fact an essential part of our sinful nature that we do not take into account our sinful nature! A vast majority of convicted criminals believe they didn't do anything to deserve to be behind bars.

On the other hand, a crisis can provoke us to see the truth: that we are just like all the others. The Russian writer Solzhenitsyn tells how when he was horribly abused by gulag prison guards, the evil in others became a mirror that reflected back at him a true picture of himself. He came to a state of repentance when he realized that if the tables were turned, he would act exactly as did his tormentors.

Jesus is not surprised by our weakness or our sin. He actually knows them beforehand. So when He calls attention to some looming disappointment, whether a spectacular debacle or some small shameful act we hope never comes to light, we should heed His caution, rather than, like Peter, blindly insisting on our immunity to failure.

What is the Lord saying to you today?

SEEING IS BELIEVING

When the Roman officer who stood facing him saw how he had died,
he exclaimed, "This man truly was the Son of God!".

MARK 15:39

*F*ace-to-face with Jesus' sufferings, no one can remain indifferent or neutral. His miracles one may doubt, His teachings one may debate, but His sufferings – those hours of agony on the cross following a night of beatings and scourging – what can anyone do but look on in awe and, eventually, reverence?

There is no reason to think that the Roman officers charged with the duty of torturing Jesus to death had any previous faith in Him, as did a few other Roman officers we meet in the Gospels. On the contrary, everything in the story leads us to understand that the whole Roman cohort had been tormenting Jesus cruelly for hours – this was just part of their job, and perhaps they took a rather morose enjoyment from it. They were to assure the condemned man's death, and to do so as viciously as possible as a preventative example to other potential wrongdoers.

Yet, this particular officer had been watching Jesus at close range for many hours. He had watched dozens, perhaps hundreds, of other human beings die slowly and cruelly. But Jesus was different, and this moved him … changed him. When it was all over, this Roman officer blurted out what the Jewish religious elite refused to acknowledge: "This man truly was the Son of God!"

If extended contemplation of Jesus' agony had such an effect
on a hardened executioner, what might it do in my heart?

Day 60

GONE AHEAD OF YOU

But the angel said, "Don't be alarmed. You are looking for Jesus of Nazareth,
who was crucified. He isn't here! He is risen from the dead!
Look, this is where they laid his body".

MARK 16:6

Looking for Jesus where last you saw Him can be futile; often He has moved on. Jesus' followers were accustomed enough to His habit of rising early in the morning and taking off before anyone knew it. Crowds would come looking for Him where last He was seen only to find that He had already moved on. But no one thought this would happen now, after they'd seen His body wrapped and placed in a tomb three days ago.

It's no wonder the women "fled from the tomb, trembling and bewildered," startled speechless, when a shining angel told them, "He isn't here! He is risen from the dead! ... Now go and tell his disciples, including Peter, that Jesus is going ahead of you to Galilee" (Mark 16:6-8).

What?! This is the one day they expected no surprises. They'd followed Jesus for three years as He strode vigorously forward to His next station of call with the rest of them stretched out in a thin line behind him, out of breath, trying to keep up. But Friday they'd seen Him stopped. They'd seen Him dead. How could He possibly have gone ahead anywhere?

Yogi Berra famously said about the game of baseball (and life), "It ain't over 'til it's over." But with Jesus, one may modify the maxim: "It's not over, even when you think it's over!"

Are you giving up on something? Jesus calls you
to press on and follow Him. It may not yet be over.

ABOVE AND BEYOND

But the angel said, "Don't be afraid, Zechariah! God has heard your prayer.
Your wife, Elizabeth, will give you a son, and you are to name him John".
LUKE 1:13

Zechariah had fulfilled the chores of the priesthood rather uneventfully for years. Today, however, was his once-in-a-lifetime opportunity to enter the Temple and offer incense on the altar. Professionally, it was the apex of his career. And it came none too soon – Zechariah was getting old, almost finished with life, and he felt it.

He slipped into the dark interior, burned the incense, and prayed on behalf of his nation. Surely he prayed that the promised Messiah would soon come, as had every priest before him. But then something happened – there beside the altar stood the angel Gabriel with an astonishing message: "You thought you'd reached the pinnacle of your career ... that your life was complete? Well, your life's just beginning. You're going to be a father – of a son who will be someone spectacular! You prayed for the Messiah to come – well, He's on His way, and your son will prepare the way." God answered the prayer for a nation by giving a barren couple a son. Talk about an above and beyond answer to prayer!

God is at work in your life today and, through you and your prayers, in the lives of those you love. Nothing in your life is wasted; nothing in your prayers is impossible; you're never too old to be used by God.

Pray for your children and those you love
that God will use them to do great things for Him.

LIVING LIFE TO THE FULL

Lord, I commit my failures
as well as my successes into Thy hands,
and I bring for Thy healing
the people and the situations,
the wrongs and the hurts of the past.
Give me courage, strength and generosity
to let go and move on, leaving the past behind me,
and living the present to the full.
Lead me always to be positive
as I "entrust the past to Thy mercy,
the present to Thy love,
and the future to Thy providence".
Amen.

St. Augustine

Day 63

MY PRAYER FOR
A LIFE WELL LIVED

_____

_____

_____

_____

_____

_____

_____

_____

_____

_____

_____

The secret of contentment is the
realization that life is a gift, not a right.

Day 64

NO ROOM HERE!

*She gave birth to her first child, a son. She wrapped him snugly in strips of cloth
and laid him in a manger, because there was no lodging available for them.*

LUKE 2:7

*A*h, the poor, much-reviled innkeeper! In countless nativity plays we've all seen bathrobe-clad Mary and Joseph knock at a door, tired from their trip, only to be rebuffed by the meanest person who could be found for the part. That actor usually embellishes his role a bit, not only refusing the humble couple lodging but also throwing in a few coarse insults as he sends them on their way.

Who knows if he was really so mean? Yet such a personality is not difficult to imagine. Who among us hasn't had to deal with such personalities as we travel? Rude, inconsiderate, sarcastic – some people seem emboldened by the knowledge that they'll not see us again and so treat us shamefully. Our natural response at such effrontery is defensiveness and anger.

But when we read the rest of Luke 2 and see how much joy everyone *else* was having – the angels, the shepherds, Simeon, Anna, and especially Mary – celebrating the appearance of the Christ child, we actually begin to feel a little sorry for the people who missed out on all the fun because they had refused to receive the needy couple.

The next time you run across those "innkeeper-type" people, realize that their personal misery may be even greater than the misery they cause others. Their unhappiness may stem from "not having lodging" in their hearts for Christ.

*Have patience today for the miserable people. Say a
prayer that they will make room in their hearts for Christ.*

WHAT DOES GOD WANT ME TO DO?

Annas and Caiaphas were the high priests. At this time a message
from God came to John son of Zechariah, who was living in the wilderness.

LUKE 3:2

While Luke situates his narrative in precise historical relationship to the civil powers of his day, he also seems to relish posing an ironic contrast between those emperors, governors, rulers, high priests ... and the humble figure of John who was "living in the wilderness," to whom "a message from God came."

The message of the promised Messiah's arrival came not through the high and mighty, but rather through a recluse living on the periphery of society. Yet tax collectors, Roman soldiers, and the general populace came to ask him, "What should we do? How shall we live?"

His answers consistently reference a standard of justice and righteousness far above the expectations common to civil society. "There is One coming," he intones, "who is going to make everything wrong *right*. If I were you, I'd do everything possible to get squared away now before He gets here."

It's still good advice for us today. To know what we should do we must look beyond the minimal ethics of government regulations for direction. The message came, not to the powers that be, but to the humble man in the wilderness. You may need to set yourself apart from the noise of society for a while and listen for that word from God.

Where can you go today – without the attractions and distractions
of the bustling, busy world – that is quiet enough to hear from God?

THE "HOMETOWN PROPHET" DILEMMA

"But I tell you the truth, no prophet is accepted in his own hometown".
LUKE 4:24

Why is it so difficult to live a consistent Christian life before those who know us best? Usually it's because they see to our inner core – the sin nature that still, at times, rears its ugly head.

Jesus didn't have that problem. He lived a perfectly consistent and sinless life, yet the people in His hometown *still* didn't believe in Him! If He, being perfect, could not gain the confidence of those who knew Him before He entered into His spiritual calling and ministry, how much less might we expect to do so?

We ache to see those closest to us won over to the sweetness of Christ, and we hope that, somehow, it will be through our own ministry and example. But the way things seem to work in the spiritual realm is that it is often through the witness and nurture of *others* that those for whom we care the most are brought to Christ. This actually should be a relief for us, both lessening the burden, and also freeing us to be "prophetic" in someone *else's* hometown.

We sense, intuitively and correctly, that our lives should always and in every place reflect what we say we believe. May we seek to live consistently before all people, trusting God to work His way, His time.

Wherever you are today, be the light of Christ. Who knows?
You may be influencing someone else's loved one!

Day 67

JOIN THE PARTY

One day some people said to Jesus, "John the Baptist's disciples
fast and pray regularly, and so do the disciples of the Pharisees.
Why are your disciples always eating and drinking?".
LUKE 5:33

What is more important, good theology or good works? Did Jesus come to save people from hell or to make their lives better here on earth? Which is more spiritual and Christ-like, an ascetic life of self-denial or a perpetual "party-on" lifestyle of effusive celebration? Such questions, perennially debated, are shown by Jesus to simply be the wrong questions.

In Luke 5 we find Peter and his fishing companions working all night and coming up with nothing, a horribly-disfigured leper, a totally dependent paraplegic, and a despised tax collector – all finding that Jesus reaches out and generously removes their most harrowing personal embarrassment and impediment. Even while He fixed material dysfunctions, He talked about repentance and forgiveness and cleansing and wholeness. He miraculously healed, He said, specifically to demonstrate His greater power to release them from sin. The result is exuberant celebration.

As people from a wider and wider spectrum of backgrounds kept attaching themselves to this joy-maker, there was a lot of rowdy whooping and hollering and eating and drinking wherever Jesus went. Dowdy religious gatekeepers grumbled at the alleged inappropriateness of such festive carrying on, but Jesus leaned in close and said, "Listen, you don't fast during the wedding party, and you don't put new wine in old wineskins. They are happy because *I* am here."

Does your life in Christ look like a party going on?
Would others observing you think you are
full of joy because of His presence within you?

LOVING FIRST

"Give to anyone who asks; and when things are taken away from you,
don't try to get them back. Do to others as you would like them to do to you".

LUKE 6:30-31

Love requires more risk than security. Jesus pointed out the reason when He described love as the decision to take the first step. His words were so simple and direct that they have been called the Golden Rule.

Once we decide how we would like to be treated, we are not to wait until someone comes along who meets those expectations; instead, we are to treat others that way. Loving back is easy compared to loving first. God's kind of love acts without guaranteed response.

The knowledge that we are loved makes it easy to show love! The life of Jesus can be read as the greatest example of how to love others, but it should be read first as God's demonstration of His love for us.

Our love for God will always be responding love, but loving others as Christ has loved us is our golden opportunity to actually imitate God.

To whom can you show love today?

A PRAYER FOR PEACE

Lord, make me an instrument of Thy peace.
Where there is hatred, let me sow love;
where there is injury, pardon;
where there is doubt, faith;
where there is despair, hope;
where there is darkness, light;
where there is sadness, joy.
O Divine Master, grant that I may not so much seek;
to be consoled as to console,
to be understood as to understand,
to be loved, as to love;
for it is in giving that we receive,
and it is in pardoning that we are pardoned,
and it is in dying that we are born to eternal life. Amen.

St. Francis of Assisi

Day 70

MY PRAYER FOR PEACE

_____

_____

_____

_____

_____

_____

_____

_____

_____

_____

If God be our God, He will give us peace in trouble:
when there is a storm without, He will make music within.
The world can create trouble in peace,
but God can create peace in trouble.

Thomas Watson

WHEN YOU WONDER

John's two disciples found Jesus and said to him, "John the Baptist sent us to ask, 'Are you the Messiah we've been expecting, or should we keep looking for someone else?'".
LUKE 7:20

I t surprises us that even John the Baptist had his moment of doubt. Such wavering on the part of that bold prophet who constantly proclaimed that Messiah was coming seems incongruous. But see it his way: He had been deep in Herod's dark dungeon hearing about Jesus' brilliant ministry – but not seeing any benefit himself. After many months, he was still incarcerated and, rumor had it, headed for worse.

Given what was expected of the Messiah, this just didn't make sense.

At the same time, Jesus *was* very active in behalf of lots of other people: curing many diseases, preaching hope to the poor, forgiving notorious sinners, raising a widow's dead son, bringing relief to, of all people, an officer of the occupying Roman army. Yet for John, His most loyal and devoted fan, He did nothing. No political string-pulling, no miraculous intervention, no setting free of this particular captive.

No wonder John wondered.

Jesus' answer to John's – and to our – question is, "Look at the big picture, what I'm doing for others, not just what you are experiencing in this moment. Oh, and if you resist being offended by the way I operate, God will bless you."

Where is God at work in your life today?
If you're having trouble seeing it,
ask Him to give you at least a glimpse.

BEHIND THE SCENES

Joanna, the wife of Chuza, Herod's business manager;
Susanna; and many [other women] were contributing their
own resources to support Jesus and his disciples.

LUKE 8:3

O f all four Gospel writers, only Luke mentions the women who apparently supplied the principal infrastructure of Jesus' itinerant ministry. Their task of providing for Jesus and His twelve disciples must have been daunting. There were no economy hotels, no fast-food chains, no electronic communication systems to assure reservations. Somehow, at each place Jesus would stop for the night, they had to hustle around and put together provisions for everybody. And they paid for it all out of their own pockets.

Such heroic service would seem to merit more than incidental mention, but it is not the first time that support ministry has been given short shrift in the recounting of great works. Could it be simply because they were women? It might; but even in today's more enlightened social context, those who do all the behind-the-scenes work, be they male or female, are seldom praised, or even recognized, the way the more visible up-front people are.

So if the women weren't doing this for people's praise, what motivated them to devote themselves to this arduous task? Luke provides a clue when he describes them as "women he had healed and from whom he had cast out evil spirits" (Luke 8:2).

Evidently they served purely out of gratefulness.

Do you?

RADICAL COMMITMENT

As the time drew near for him to ascend to heaven,
Jesus resolutely set out for Jerusalem.

LUKE 9:51

Many students of Luke's Gospel see this verse as the pivotal point of the whole narrative. Up to now, Jesus had cast the net wide and the range of His followers ran the gamut from the curious to the committed. Thousands came to enjoy stimulating discourse, the visceral thrill of the miraculous, and sometimes even a free meal.

But Jesus sifted through the varying responses to His ministry, asking His disciples, "Who do people say I am? Who do you say I am?" (Luke 9:18, 20).

Then suddenly He began to raise deliberate hurdles before those who claimed they wanted to follow Him. To superficial, would-be disciples, He warned them that this was going to be no walk in the park. He pointedly predicted that His followers would be rejected by some to whom He would send them. He spoke repeatedly of His own imminent sufferings and death, and of the parallel necessity of His disciples to shoulder their crosses and give up their lives to follow Him.

And to all, Jesus manifested a single-minded purposefulness – to march to Jerusalem and fulfill His destiny. From this point on there was no turning back, either for the Messiah or for those who would follow Him.

Are you ready for this? Can you set your face
resolutely to fulfill your calling, as Jesus did?

GOD'S BEST

"There is only one thing worth being concerned about.
Mary has discovered it, and it will not be taken away from her".
LUKE 10:42

Luke 10 is filled with contrasts. Towns that welcome Jesus and the disciples are contrasted with towns that do not.

Simple, childlike people to whom the Father reveals His truth are contrasted with self-styled wise people from whom the truth is hidden.

Prophets and kings of old who earnestly longed to see the Messiah are contrasted with Jesus' disciples who are given the privilege of understanding.

The outward appearance of serious piety by the expert in religious law is contrasted with his actual inner state, seen as he tries to wiggle out of the implications of the Good Samaritan story.

As the day concluded, Jesus settled down for the evening in the home of two beloved friends where one last contrast is drawn. The sisters welcome Him, each in her own way: Mary, by listening to Jesus devotedly; Martha, by preparing a big meal. When the latter emerges from the clutter and clank of kitchenware to express resentment that Mary isn't helping, Jesus cut to the heart of the matter. He pointed to Mary's single-minded devotion to Himself as the "only one thing worth being concerned about."

We cannot escape the contrast between just *doing* for Jesus and *knowing and loving* Him. There are times when we must discern the contrast between the good and the best.

With all the things in life that scream for attention,
how can you choose God's best today?

PERSEVERANCE IN PRAYER

*"And so I tell you, keep on asking, and you will receive
what you ask for. Keep on seeking, and you will find.
Keep on knocking, and the door will be opened to you".*

LUKE 11:9

The incomparable value of sheer, dogged persistence is elevated by Jesus to a spiritual principle. Any salesman understands what Jesus was talking about when He made the point that for some things, you just have to keep coming back and coming back, pressing your case, until you convince the client and make the sale. If you want it bad enough, the common wisdom holds, you just have to hang in there until you get it.

Luke humorously recorded Jesus' folksy illustrations of the principle at work: The man hopes to silence the loud knocking of his neighbor before he wakes up the kids, so he gets out of bed in the middle of the night to lend the three loaves of bread. Fathers are reminded of how natural it is for them to give good, not bad, things to their children who ask. Jesus pressed home the analogy: "How much more will your heavenly Father give the Holy Spirit *to those who ask him*" (Luke 11:13, emphasis added).

For some reason we tend to be timid and conservative in our prayers, not asking for much compared to how much God *wants* to give us. And when we do ask for great things, we easily relent if they are not immediately forthcoming. Jesus urges us to persist.

*Are you weary in prayer over a seemingly ignored request?
Keep on knocking.*

PRAISE FOR GOD'S LOVE
AND FAITHFULNESS

I have talked about Your faithfulness and saving power.
I have told everyone in the great assembly
of Your unfailing love and faithfulness.
Lord, don't hold back Your tender mercies from me.
Let Your unfailing love and faithfulness always protect me.

Psalm 40:10-11

MY PRAYER OF PRAISE FOR GOD'S LOVE AND FAITHFULNESS

_____

_____

_____

_____

_____

_____

_____

_____

_____

_____

The great thing in prayer is to feel that we
are putting our supplications into
the bosom of omnipotent love.

Andrew Murray

WHO ME, WORRY?

"Seek the Kingdom of God above all else,
and he will give you everything you need".

LUKE 12:31

Jesus, who knows the Father intimately, goes to great lengths to get us to understand that God watches over us very carefully and is going to take care of us. He doesn't want us to focus on material matters but rather to devote ourselves to the Kingdom. Yet He saw all around Him, as we do today, that human beings either worry and fret if they think they won't have enough or else boast and indulge themselves to excess if they do feel successful. Either way, they're missing the point.

Jesus keeps trying to get us to look around at the natural world, to see that sparrows and ravens, flowers and food crops, all are nourished and cared for directly by God's hand. They do not have to calculate or plan in order to flourish; God just makes their life sweet out of His own goodness. And then He drives home His point: "You are far more valuable to him than any birds! Can all your worries add a single moment to your life?" (Luke 12:24-25).

"So," Jesus admonishes us, "don't keep knocking yourself out about whether you'll have enough tomorrow. You *will*! My Father takes care of that. Free yourself from worry and pay attention to more important matters." When we seek the Kingdom of God above all else, He will give us everything we need.

Can you really live free from worry?
How would that affect your life?

WHOSE SIDE ARE YOU ON?

This shamed his enemies, but all the people
rejoiced at the wonderful things he did.

LUKE 13:17

It didn't take long (and still doesn't!) for Jesus' teachings and actions, His message and ministry, to divide groups of people squarely down the middle. On one side there always seem to be throngs of delighted well-wishers who rejoice at the wonderful things He does. But on the other side are the resentful critics, people of such stubborn ill will that they are indignant rather than elated by the good things Jesus does for others.

Jesus went to great lengths – even violating certain traditional religious rules – to free His beloved ones from evil. Each time He intervened in some suffering sinner's life, those looking on either rejoiced or ground their teeth.

For the recalcitrant, Jesus had nothing but warnings, articulated in bloody, violent language. Judgment is near, the escape door is very narrow, only a few will be saved, and they will come from around the world, not from the local inner circle of pompous religiosity. Repentance is the only hope. "Unless you repent, you will perish" (Luke 13:5).

For those who do repent, however, there is the promise of new life and of greatness in God's eternal Kingdom.

Which side are you on? If you've repented of your sin, you're in Jesus' camp. Too many Christians, however, still carry around a certain amount of ill will. How do you react when others are blessed? Do you rejoice at the wonderful things God does for others?

What are you doing today?
Rejoicing or complaining?

HOW MUCH IS THIS GOING TO COST ME?

"Don't begin until you count the cost. For who would begin construction of a building without first calculating the cost to see if there is enough money to finish it?".

LUKE 14:28

Once again Jesus brought the parade of His followers to a halt. Wanting to clarify this "following Jesus" phenomenon, He began with the words, "If you want to be my disciple," and explained that He alone must be the most important and valued focus of a true disciple's life (Luke 14:26). He went on with a principle: One does not embark on a major endeavor – the examples He cited are a building project and a war – without first calculating whether you have the resources to finish what you started. To do otherwise – to plunge ahead with a highly visible venture and then fall short of completing it because there wasn't enough of whatever it takes to finish the job – is to invite the ridicule of everyone watching.

"So," He tells His followers, both then and now, "you'd better stop and count the cost *first*, before you go any further with this intention of being My disciple." And the cost turns out to be ... *everything*: our wealth, our social standing, our families, our very lives. All of it must be submitted to Him.

But it's not so bad. What we give up can't begin to compare with what awaits us in eternity!

Discipleship: The cost is "everything."
But Jesus promises: "God will reward you."

R.S.V.P.

*"In the same way, there is more joy in heaven over one lost sinner
who repents and returns to God than over ninety-nine others
who are righteous and haven't strayed away!".*

LUKE 15:7

Jesus tells three parables in a row that all have the same point. Whether it's a sheep, a valuable coin, or a wayward son, when something valuable is found that had been lost, the natural reaction to finding it again is joy. Jesus says the happiness of the shepherd, the woman, and the father of the prodigal all reflect the atmosphere of heaven where joyous clamor breaks out every time a sinner repents.

That celestial joy contrasts starkly, however, with the strange resentment of many earthly persons. Like the angry older brother in the prodigal son story, religious leaders of Jesus' day were irritated, rather than pleased, by the repentance of notorious sinners. Like that elder brother, they felt that their years of constantly walking the straight and narrow was what should be celebrated and praised, not the erratic flip-flopping of recovered drifters.

Jesus, who had spent all but the previous thirty years of His existence in the festive atmosphere of heaven, is both puzzled and pained by this unseemly rejection of salvation and restoration. He urged His mean-spirited hearers to understand how right it is to celebrate. But, esteeming their "never strayed" status above the joy of grace, they persist in their gloomy snobbery and refuse to join the party.

*You've gotten the invitation.
Have you sent your R.S.V.P.?*

Day 82

MONEY PROBLEMS

"And if you are untrustworthy about worldly wealth,
who will trust you with the true riches of heaven?".
LUKE 16:11

Some people are surprised when they discover that Jesus doesn't always pose money and spirituality as direct antitheses. "I always thought He was *against* rich people," they admit, "or even against making a healthy profit. But in one of these parables He actually holds a dishonest business manager up to be admired for His shrewdness!"

It's true. Jesus corroborates the amused admiration of the rich man in His story, whose canny – albeit totally dishonest – manager saves His own skin by cooking the books. He even sets the clever rascal before His disciples as an example of the kind of resourcefulness necessary to those who have great responsibilities. Then Jesus continues with a discourse on how to make money work for your benefit.

"But," He warns, "you can't have it both ways. It's one thing to make money work for you – but if you don't watch out, *you* could become the servant of money." That seems to be the real problem: Who is the master? Cheating, dishonestly acquiring riches, the kind of callous indifference to the poor depicted in the Lazarus story (Luke 16:19-31) – all seem to have their root in this substituting of money for God. You serve one or you serve the other.

Money is not the problem; it's what you do with it.

Who is your master?

A PRAYER FOR GODLY LIVING

Almighty and most merciful Father,
we have erred and strayed
from Thy ways like lost sheep.
We have followed too much the devices
and desires of our own hearts;
we have lèft undone those things
which we ought to have done;
and we have done those things
which we ought not to have done;
and there is no health in us.
But, Thou, O Lord, have mercy upon us miserable offenders;
spare Thou those, O God, who confess their faults,
restore Thou those who are penitent
according to Thy promises declared unto mankind
in Christ Jesus our Lord;
and grant, O most merciful Father, for His sake;
that we may hereafter live a godly, righteous, and sober life,
to the glory of Thy holy name.
Amen.

Book of Common Prayer

Day 84

MY PRAYER FOR
A GODLY LIFE

_____

_____

_____

_____

_____

_____

_____

_____

_____

_____

_____

By His divine power, God has given us
everything we need for living a godly life.

2 Peter 1:3

WHEN JESUS COMES BACK

*"Yes, it will be 'business as usual' right up to
the day when the Son of Man is revealed".*

LUKE 17:30

When will the end come? We'd all like to have insider information on that day to end all days. The people of Jesus' era were no different. They wanted to know what to watch for, what portents would signal the coming of the Son of Man, perhaps so they could "get ready" in time and thereby avoid too much personal calamity.

But Jesus replied that outward circumstances won't be much help to herald the event. Rather, He says, it'll be just like when the cataclysms of Noah's and Lot's days hit: one moment people were going about their daily business routines and the next moment universal catastrophe struck. That's the way it will be when the end comes, Jesus affirmed.

So how do we live, knowing it could be any moment as easily as the next? You live, Jesus taught, as those who know that the Kingdom is already here among you. That is, we should live moment by moment in service to the King – in thankfulness, like the healed leper (Luke 17:11-19), in faithfulness, like the dutiful servant (Luke 17:7-10), forgiving one another over and over, in short, simply doing what we know we are supposed to do.

We don't have to wait until the Kingdom becomes fully visible. In fact, to do so would be truly disastrous.

Are you living today as though, at any moment, Jesus could return?

HAUGHTY OR HUMBLE?

Then Jesus called for the children and said to the disciples,
"Let the children come to me. Don't stop them!
For the Kingdom of God belongs to those who are like these children".

LUKE 18:16

The simplest and lowliest of people – children, widows, social outcasts, the poor, the disabled, and habitual, occupational sinners – are cared about deeply by Jesus.

A widow bereft of power or social status appears together in an anecdote with a proud magistrate so highly placed he doesn't care about anyone, yet it is the woman whom Jesus tells His disciples to imitate (Luke 18:1-8). When a strictly righteous-living Pharisee and a dishonest but sorrowful tax collector are placed side by side in the Temple, you know almost before you finish reading the story who's going to receive Jesus' thumbs up (Luke 18:9-14).

When a wealthy religious leader comes to Jesus wondering what he must *do* to inherit eternal life, Jesus sends the man away with the understanding that he loves his earthly possessions more than he could ever love Jesus. The sad but true lesson is that it is difficult for the affluent to enter God's Kingdom (Luke 18:18-30).

Squeezed in between these latter two stories is the account of little children rushing into Jesus' arms. They receive His affection but more, His blessing, as exemplars of the simple faith of which the Kingdom of God is comprised. To His disciple Peter who ventures, "We have left all to follow You," Jesus replies approvingly, "Yes! And you will get *so much* in return!"

What have you given up in order to follow Jesus?
What have you received?

WHY AM I HERE?

"For the Son of Man came to seek and save those who are lost".
LUKE 19:10

Many of us, particularly if we travel a lot as part of our job, come to know a peculiar vagueness as part and parcel of our existence. Not only the bewildered grasping around to orient ourselves when we wake up in a new hotel room but the ongoing feeling that we're not sure why we're here today or where we're going next. We politely greet completely new and strange people and set right into doing business with them, though we haven't a clue as to who they really are.

Jesus did the same thing, though He obviously knew far more about the people around Him than we usually do. When He called Zacchaeus down from his tree to take Him home for dinner, the little man was astonished and thrilled that Jesus not only knew him, but wanted to know him better (Luke 19:1-10). The encounter resulted in his complete turnaround, and Zacchaeus was giddy with joy.

The onlookers were disgruntled by Jesus' choice of hosts, but He says, matter-of-factly, "This is what I've come here for, to reach such people and save them."

We may be surprised by the people Jesus urges us to reach out to on His behalf throughout the day, or even *that* He calls our attention to them. But He knows why we're here, even if we don't.

Jesus knew exactly why He had come
and what He was about. Do I?

BALANCING ACT

*"Well then," he said, "give to Caesar what belongs to Caesar,
and give to God what belongs to God".*

LUKE 20:25

I t's an age-old question, how much and what to give to God and what to give to earthly authorities. Whether it has to do with money, time, or allegiance, we're seldom confident that we've got the balance right. For that reason Jesus' enemies were pretty sure they had Him with the question of taxes to an unpopular government.

It's never easy trying to balance the various responsibilities and opportunities that present themselves. We have to work; we want to succeed at work; we need and want to spend time with our family; we want to give of our time to our church and other worthwhile organizations; we have meals to fix, a lawn to mow, a house that constantly needs to be fixed in one place or another; we want to take our family on vacations and send our children to good colleges; in order to do that we have to work. And we're right back where we started. We're running in circles and getting nowhere fast.

As always, Jesus had it right. The balance is right in front of us if we'll just take the time to think about it. Do what is best with what is right in front of you. When you're at work, work. When you're at play, play. "And give to God what belongs to God." Ask God to give you wisdom to set wise priorities in your particular season of life.

Talk to God today about setting His priorities for your life.

THE END IS NEAR

*"So when all these things begin to happen,
stand and look up, for your salvation is near!".*
LUKE 21:28

Jesus declared that worldwide cataclysmic upheavals will erupt just before He brings history to a close. Not only will society dissolve into chaos, but the elements of the physical universe will go awry: terrible earthquakes, tidal confusion, and the stability of the very heavens will be broken up. He says that the courage of many people will falter because of the fearful fate they see coming upon the earth. It's perfectly understandable. As the only world they've ever known falls apart, they too will fall apart emotionally and psychologically, wrenched from dependency on the material universe they have always taken for granted.

The creation, even spoiled by our sin, has been for the most part so benign that some like to affectionately call it Mother Nature. Many human beings hold the cosmos in awe so reverently it can be called idolatry. So to be there when the whole thing goes haywire and crumbles to dust will be the most traumatic shock anyone has ever experienced.

Yet Jesus – apparently incongruously – tells His followers, "That's your cue! Straighten up in hopeful anticipation of My imminent appearance because with that event the old heaven and earth will finally disappear. What you've been waiting for all this time will come into existence."

Are you waiting eagerly for Jesus to return?

A PRAYER FOR SERENITY

God, grant me the serenity to
accept the things I cannot change;
courage to change the things I can;
and the wisdom to know the difference.
Living one day at a time;
enjoying one moment at a time;
accepting hardships as the pathway
to peace; taking, as He did,
this sinful world as it is, not as I would have it;
trusting that He will make all
things right if I surrender to His will;
that I may be reasonably happy in this life
and supremely happy with Him forever in the next.
Amen.

Reinhold Niebuhr

Day 91

MY PRAYER FOR
SERENITY AND PEACE

_____

_____

_____

_____

_____

_____

_____

_____

_____

_____

_____

_____

A great many people are trying to make peace,
but that has already been done. God has not
left it for us to do; all we have
to do is to enter into it.

Dwight L. Moody

WHEN DARKNESS REIGNS

"Why didn't you arrest me in the Temple? I was there every day.
But this is your moment, the time when the power of darkness reigns".
LUKE 22:53

In the last hours before Jesus was captured and condemned, everyone seemed to be sneaking around, arranging matters surreptitiously. The betrayer Judas agreed with the Temple elite to betray Jesus – first by locating a suitable time and place devoid of crowds that could wreck the plot. Peter and John, following a prearranged secret signal, quietly slipped into the upstairs room of a private home to prepare the Master's last supper with the twelve disciples. Just when it was ready, Jesus and the others arrived and sat down. In the privacy of the quiet room, He gave last instructions – something terrible was about to happen.

Later they went out together to the dark silence of a garden where the Master entered into serious agony, preparing to face the coming ordeal. But the disciples, overcome by darkness of spirit, were not ready, so when the blazing torches, gleaming swords, and grimacing faces invaded the garden, they panicked. Jesus, however, was completely composed. He spoke ironically, actually scoffing at Judas and his gang, taunting them with their cowardice – that they refused to arrest Him in the Temple, preferring instead to sneak around in the dark and brandish unnecessary weapons!

"But," He acknowledged, "this is your moment, the time when the power of darkness reigns." What a terrible thing to hear, to realize about themselves, if they were really listening!

In the secrecy, in the darkness, do you let the
power of darkness reign in your heart?

HE DID IT FOR YOU

The crowd watched and the leaders scoffed. "He saved others," they said,
"let him save himself if he is really God's Messiah, the Chosen One".
LUKE 23:35

We normally think of Jesus' physical sufferings – so graphically depicted in many sculptures, paintings, and dramas – as the worst part of His experience. Yet another aspect of that day may have been even more difficult to bear: the scornful mocking of His enemies, taunting Him, daring Him to prove His messianic claims ... by simply saving Himself.

I doubt whether we can ever empathize with how great a temptation that must have been. Ground under the mill wheel of pain, listening to the hoots of derision from the crowd, but worst of all listening to these self-assured religious leaders calling out for everyone to hear what must have seemed irrefutable logic: "All He has to do to prove that He is God's Chosen One, as He claims, is to simply come down from there. Exercise Your power, Messiah, if that's who You are, and we'll all believe in You."

He must have thought about how divinely easy it would be: to suddenly, dramatically rip the nails from the cross, step down with a miraculously restored, powerful, scar-free body and smile smugly right into the centurion's, and then the priests', blanched faces. "*See?*"

But He didn't. If He had saved Himself, you and I would still be lost and unforgiven, without a shred of hope. But He knew that He came to save others, so He ignored the taunts and bore it to the end.

Thank Jesus for the pain He endured – for you.

WHAT DOES HE HAVE TO DO FOR ME TO BELIEVE?

And just as they were telling about it, Jesus himself was suddenly standing there among them. "Peace be with you," he said.

LUKE 24:36

Jesus' followers were flabbergasted by the bits of news they kept hearing. They listened to far-fetched tales of an empty tomb, folded grave clothes, and imposing bright angels, and tried to piece together and understand this unheard-of phenomenon, comparing it with ancient prophecies and with things Jesus had said, mulling it all over. But it was just too extraordinary to understand, let alone believe.

On several occasions, at the very moment they were discussing the matter with one another, Jesus Himself was suddenly there with them. Yet their grief-induced stupor prevented them from recognizing Him. Jesus at first played with the two disciples walking to Emmaus.

"Are you the only person in Jerusalem who hasn't heard about all the things that have happened there these last few days?" they asked.

"What things?" Jesus innocently replied.

He let them demonstrate the limits of their comprehension, then He filled in the blanks and connected the dots. They suddenly realized that it was *He* and dashed back to the gathered disciples in Jerusalem to tell them that Jesus was alive.

Once again, He appeared at the very moment He was being spoken of, but He grew impatient with the unbelief of people who had actually seen, spoken with, and even eaten with the risen Lord. "I've already told you this so many times. Why do you keep on doubting?"

What would it take for you to believe Jesus' promises,
finally leaving your doubts behind?

IN FOCUS

In the beginning the Word already existed.
The Word was with God, and the Word was God.
JOHN 1:1

John doesn't waste any time but dives purposefully into his subject right from the opening words. The other Gospels argue for Jesus' divinity by way of genealogies and stories, revealing evidence from the unfolding of Jesus' life so that we might conclude, as did the centurion at the foot of the cross, "This man truly was the Son of God!" (Mark 15:39). John states right from the beginning that the Word (whom he will eventually identify as Jesus) was from everlasting before time *with* God, and moreover was Himself God.

In these opening words of his Gospel, John characterizes Jesus as the Word, the deliberate rational and personal expression of God for human eyes. Jesus is also Light and Life, two of the most dynamic forces known to us. If John tells us this much up front, what more will be revealed within? Reading these opening words of the fourth Gospel, we realize that this is going to be a very different ride.

Jesus had intimate fellowship with God the Father, so He is uniquely qualified to tell us about Him, as John reiterates in chapter 1:18. Yet Jesus is more than a witness; He carries within Himself the very nature of divinity. As we look at the man Jesus in action, we actually see the Father.

Do you wonder what God is like? Then read about Jesus. He is God brought into focus. He is God in the flesh.

*What do you believe about God, really? As you read this Gospel,
look for new things to learn about God through the lens of Jesus.*

Day 96

SAVING THE BEST FOR LAST

"A host always serves the best wine first," he said.
"Then, when everyone has had a lot to drink, he brings out
the less expensive wine. But you have kept the best until now!".
JOHN 2:10

Saving the best for last is a little trick many of us learned as children. We grimaced and gulped down the vegetables *first* so that we could savor the better parts of the meal afterward, with no hassles from Mom!

The master of ceremonies in this story was quite surprised, however, at his host's tactic, for with wine it is quite the opposite: You normally serve your guests the very best tasting wine at the beginning while their palates are still fresh and clear. Later, when an abundance of the wine itself has made fuzzy the ability of tasters to discern best from good ... or pretty good from really cheap ... one brings out the latter, knowing it won't make much difference to those who've already had plenty.

In the Bible wine often symbolizes gladness of heart and celebration, so those who read this story have usually understood it to represent the joyous arrival of Jesus Himself in relation to all that preceded Him in earlier Judaism. It is no mere coincidence, for example, that the vessels in which the rich wine suddenly appeared were normally used for traditional Jewish ceremonies—until they became vessels for *something better*.

Throughout this Gospel, John will return again and again to images of Jesus fulfilling in His own personal familiar but worn out Jewish paradigms, as if to suggest *God saved the best for last.*

Do you think of Jesus as bringing gladness and celebration into your life? How can you leave behind stale alternatives in order to fully embrace and savor that which He offers?

A PRAYER FOR GOD'S GRACE

Plenteous grace with Thee is found,
grace to cover all my sin;
let the healing streams abound;
make and keep me pure within.
Thou of life the fountain art –
freely let me take of Thee;
spring Thou up within my heart;
rise to all eternity.
Amen.

Charles Wesley

Day 98

MY PRAYER FOR
GOD'S GRACE

_____

_____

_____

_____

_____

_____

_____

_____

_____

I am not what I ought to be. I am not what I want to be.
I am not what I hope to be. But still, I am not what I once
used to be. And by the grace of God, I am what I am.

John Newton

JESUS: JUDGE OR SAVIOR?

"God sent his Son into the world not to judge the world,
but to save the world through him".

JOHN 3:17

Most people think Jesus came to earth to clean things up, to scold wrongdoers and warn recalcitrant sinners of a painful fate that awaits them. Moreover, He is seen to be the Judge who will carry out that sentence upon the obstinate and disobedient. In this perception, those holding it are half-right. He will return to earth a second time not only as the Savior of those who trust Him but also as the Judge of all who continue to reject Him.

But His purpose in coming the first time was not to condemn the world but to save a world already under condemnation. What He offered Nicodemus, and all the rest of us who eavesdrop on their conversation, is a new start – a chance to begin all over again as a newborn babe, born of the Spirit. He didn't say, as we would expect, "You have made so many mistakes! Your sins are so overwhelming it's going to take the rest of your life to fix up this mess. You'd better get busy; you'll never undo all the damage you've done before I have to judge you as having failed."

Rather, He says, "Like the bronze serpent Moses lifted up to save the Israelites, *I* will be lifted up, so that everyone who believes in me will have eternal life" (John 3:14-15). He doesn't say we "will *earn* eternal life," but that we "will *have* eternal life" because of Him.

How do you see Jesus, as your Judge or as your Savior?
What does that tell you about your present relationship with Him?

Day 100

LIVING WATER

"Anyone who drinks this water will soon become thirsty again.
But those who drink the water I give will never be thirsty again.
It becomes a fresh, bubbling spring within them, giving them eternal life".
JOHN 4:13-14

It was a hot afternoon in Samaria – the no-man's land for the Jews located between Judah in the north and Galilee in the south. The Samaritans were considered to be half-breeds. After the northern kingdom, with its capital at Samaria, fell to the Assyrians, many Jews were deported to Assyria and foreigners were brought in to settle the land and help keep the peace. The intermarriage between those foreigners and the remaining Jews resulted in a mixed race, impure in the opinion of Jews who lived in the southern kingdom. Thus, the pure Jews hated this mixed race.

When Jesus spoke with the Samaritan woman at the well, He crossed over several cultural lines. He was a man speaking to a woman; He was a holy man speaking to a woman of impure reputation; He was a Jew speaking to a Samaritan. And yet, to this woman He offered *eternal life*. Relating His offer to physical thirst, He described *His* "water" as a perpetual spring that would quench her thirst forever. Jesus could make this promise because He was God in the flesh – the author of life and the giver of eternal life. And when Jesus makes a promise, we can be sure that He will fulfill it – all those who drink *will* live forever.

Are you thirsty for meaning, purpose, and significance? Have you visited numerous "wells" in your search? Remember, water from Jesus will quench your longings and deepest needs.

Are you feeling alone in the world, facing difficult personal struggles? Are you frustrated with this world, its pain and injustice? Jesus, the living water, can quench your thirst.

WOULD YOU *LIKE* TO GET WELL?

"I can't, sir," the sick man said, "for I have no one to put me into the pool when the water bubbles up. Someone else always gets there ahead of me".
JOHN 5:7

Excuses, excuses. Some of us have a whole litany of reasons for why we can't be expected to respond to life with healthy enthusiasm and vigor. Like the man in this story who had been lying around for thirty-eight years and had apparently gotten rather accustomed to his condition, we usually begin by blaming others when asked if we *want* to get well.

If we are stuck in a paralyzed mode, we may believe that it is because no one has helped us when we needed it. Or worse, others have competitively jumped in ahead of us when there were advantages to be gained. Ah, poor us! No one cares about us. We'd like to do more, but these other people got in our way. The fact that Jesus had to actually ask this man if he really wanted to be well says it all. Jesus didn't reason with the man, or even acknowledge His proposed agenda for their discussion. He just said, "Stand up, pick up your mat, and walk!"

Jesus sees deeper into our real condition than we do ourselves. He offers healing for many of our pains and hurts, but we must first candidly answer the question, "Do you want to be well?" Too many hold onto those hurts in order to harbor bitterness or to gain pity. Jesus says, "I can heal you, but you first must *want* to be well."

What pains and hurts do you harbor?
Do you truly want to be well?

STICK AROUND

Simon Peter replied, "Lord, to whom would we go?
You have the words that give eternal life".
JOHN 6:68

*Y*ea, Peter! Don't you just want to hug him when he says this to Jesus? If ever Jesus needed someone to bolster His sagging spirits, this was one of those moments. The steadily flagging popularity of Jesus as this chapter unrolls is impossible to miss. Masses of fickle fans followed Jesus everywhere, expecting to be fed and entertained. But Jesus would not be a party to such superficial motives for following Him.

Instead, He launched into theological and metaphysical discourse that is difficult to comprehend. He talked of being the Bread of Life; He talked of raising people to eternal life; He talked of eating His flesh and drinking His blood – hard sayings that made Him sound like a crazy man.

The vast majority of His would-be disciples found His words complex, even offensive. The result? They trickled away, disappointed. Jesus apparently wasn't going to be what they all wanted Him to be. He was just another nutty preacher.

At that point, as He gazed at the dust from the sandals of retreating former followers, Jesus turned to His few remaining faithful and asked them, "Are you also going to leave?" And good old Peter knew exactly what He needed to hear: "Are you kidding? Where else would we go? You are the only One who knows the answers we need. Nope, we're not going anywhere. We're sticking with you."

*How can you show Jesus today that you're sticking with Him
because He alone has the words that give eternal life?*

JOY LIKE A FOUNTAIN

"Anyone who believes in me may come and drink!
For the Scriptures declare, 'Rivers of living water will flow from his heart'".
JOHN 7:38

At the climax of the festival when thousands of people were milling around in the highest expectation and in the most animated of spirits, Jesus *shouted* this open and generous invitation. "Listen, all of you!" He called out to the throng of religious celebrants. "If you are thirsty, come to me! *This* is what you've been looking for all your life. *This* is what will finally and forever satisfy you. It will be like a spring of water bubbling up from within you. *Living* waters, always flowing, fresh and new every day. Never stagnant, never brackish, always sweet and refreshing."

His raised voice and the extraordinary content of what He offered immediately called the attention of the crowd – and stopped the guards dispatched to arrest Him, who returned to their chagrined masters empty-handed. While the crowd, and even the religious leaders, were divided over the question of who Jesus was (and what He was talking about), the writer and we who peer over his shoulder know that Jesus was no carnival huckster selling a magic potion or advocating self-help regimes or disciplines. He was speaking, the writer tells us, of the Spirit of God that is given to those who believe in Jesus, a Spirit who thereafter keeps bubbling up from within, an endless source of delight and refreshment.

This is what Jesus offers to those who come to Him. He gives us not just forgiveness, and salvation, and teaching, but also joy – like a living, bubbly fountain.

In what ways can you be a living,
bubbling fountain of joy in your world today?

A PRAYER OF PRAISE

I will praise You with my whole heart;
before the gods I will sing praises to You.
I will worship toward Your holy temple,
and praise Your name
for Your lovingkindness and Your truth;
for You have magnified Your word above all Your name.
In the day when I cried out, You answered me,
and made me bold with strength in my soul.
All the kings of the earth shall praise You, O LORD,
when they hear the words of Your mouth.
Yes, they shall sing of the ways of the LORD,
for great is the glory of the LORD.

Psalm 138:1-5

Day 105

MY PRAYER OF
PRAISE TO GOD

_____

_____

_____

_____

_____

_____

_____

_____

_____

_____

When you enter His presence with praise,
He enters your circumstances with power.

IN THE DARK

"I am the light of the world. If you follow me, you won't have to walk in darkness, because you will have the light that leads to life".
JOHN 8:12

Remember when you were a child and didn't like the darkness. You wanted a night-light, or to have your room door left open just a crack so you could see the light from the living room and hear the comforting voices of your parents. Darkness hid slimy things under the bed and slimier things in the closet. Darkness evoked fear.

We're older now, but few of us like total darkness. Like a child imagining monsters in the shadows, we may begin to hear and see threats in the dark. Darkness can discourage and depress. Closed off from light and hope, we may wonder if there is any way out. Darkness can foster doubt. Unable to see the realities we knew in the light, we may begin to wonder if they even exist. Darkness can cause us to stumble … and fall. Darkness comes in many forms: economic reversals, personal loss, devastating sorrow, crippling illness, incriminating sin, persistent opposition.

But Jesus is the Light, the Light of the World. His presence will brighten the day. His words will give understanding and hope. His sacrifice will bring forgiveness and eternal life. His promises and love will provide certainty and security.

You don't need to be in the dark. All you have to do is turn on the Light!

What darkness envelops your life today?
How could Jesus' light drive that darkness away?

HOW DOES IT LOOK TO YOU?

Some of the Pharisees said, "This man Jesus is not from God, for he
is working on the Sabbath." Others said, "But how could an ordinary sinner
do such miraculous signs?" So there was a deep division of opinion among them.

JOHN 9:16

*F*rom the raw data – Jesus did miracles in behalf of hurting people – His contemporaries extrapolated in one of two directions. Either He was a sinner – a lawbreaker – because what He did conflicted with strict interpretation of Moses' Law, or else He was from God, for how else could one explain His power to do so much good? Several characters debated the question, but it was the principal individual, the healed blind man, who exhibited rapid growth in understanding.

He started out that day overhearing voices speculating on whether he was in this miserable condition because of his own fault or some major sin of his parents. No doubt he often asked himself the same question. Then for the first time he heard an alternative, a hope-inspiring explanation: "Neither one. He was born this way so that the power of God could be seen in him." Now *there's* a new, a better way to think! The next thing he knew, he was returning from washing his face and for the first time in his life, *seeing*!

He was soon the center of admiring attention, then of hostile interrogation. To the latter he responded with increasing boldness as he perceived the Pharisees' stubborn refusal to believe in Jesus. "Why, who is really blind here? If this man weren't from God, He couldn't do what He has done. Don't you see that?"

The blind man saw the truth; those who could see, however, were blind indeed.

*Could it be that some of the undesirable circumstances
of your life are not God's lack of care but rather His way to show
His glory? Ask God to open your eyes and help you truly see.*

A FAMILIAR VOICE

"My sheep listen to my voice; I know them, and they follow me".
JOHN 10:27

Do you recognize the voice of the Good Shepherd? A hubbub of other voices washes over us each day. From the time our radio alarm issues some cheery announcer's voice into our subconscious, yanking us to wakefulness, we are besieged with voices clamoring for our attention, our business, our loyalty. It is tiring, confusing, often annoying. Among all of these competing for our attention, to whom should we really listen?

Jesus says that while other shepherds pretend for a while to be interested in the welfare of the sheep, they really are not. When difficulty approaches, they are out of there quickly. Jesus, on the other hand, proclaimed (and later proved) His willingness to lay down His life for His sheep. Such love draws the loved; the sheep *know* that the true Shepherd loves them, so when they hear His voice, they naturally follow.

Voices shout at us from everywhere. They promise a lot but deliver little. They pretend to care, but when the going gets tough ... well, you know the story. As Jesus' followers, His sheep, we are known by Jesus and we should, in turn, know His voice. Only then can we follow where He leads.

Listen for the voice of the Shepherd.
Where is He leading today?

THE WHY QUESTIONS

"I am the resurrection and the life. Anyone who believes in me will live,
even after dying. Everyone who lives in me and believes in me will never ever die".
JOHN 11:25-26

L ife often has more questions than answers. We don't understand the loss of the young mother, or the tiny baby, or the energy-filled teenager. We grieve that death can squelch our dreams or the dreams we have for others. *Why God? Why?*

In John 11 we see Mary and Martha standing at their brother's tomb, grieving their loss. Martha questioned Jesus' timing. "If only you had been here," Martha said, "my brother would not have died" (John 11:21).

If only, Lord. We question God's timing, God's seeming lack of concern, His seeming refusal to answer.

But Jesus is never late. Jesus is never unconcerned. Jesus never refuses to answer. Gently He reminded Martha of His awesome power and limitless love. "I am the resurrection and the life," He said. Then He called to Lazarus, the dead man, and commanded that He come forth. And Lazarus did, still wrapped in his burial clothes.

Are you asking the *why* questions? Does Jesus seem to have been distracted and therefore unconcerned or simply late? Remember, Jesus is always exactly on time. We don't understand, but maybe that's the point. We aren't supposed to understand. Instead, we must have faith. Whatever happens has a reason that can reveal His glory if we let it. But of course, that's the hard part.

What questions are you asking God today?
How can you trust Him to do things His way,
in His time, for His glory?

EXTRAVAGANT DEVOTION

*Then Mary took a twelve-ounce jar of expensive perfume
made from essence of nard, and she anointed Jesus' feet with it,
wiping his feet with her hair. The house was filled with the fragrance.*

JOHN 12:3

What a beautiful scene! A woman pouring out a generous quantity of wonderful-smelling perfume on one whom she loves, then tenderly wiping His feet with her hair. John must have vividly remembered the scene, for he wrote that "the house was filled with the fragrance." Judas thought this was too much, and he self-righteously suggested that the gift could have been better spent.

Jesus responded to those offended at Mary's extravagance by saying, "She did this in preparation for my burial" (John 12:7). Mary's act of devotion and love was lavished upon Jesus just days before the vile hatred of His enemies would culminate in His torture and death. This moment of sweet adoration would contrast with nearly every other moment of the week as Jesus' enemies bitterly hardened their hearts to reject and kill Him.

Jesus knew this, but no one else did. Sure, Jesus had warned them three different times what would happen to Him, but they didn't hear. They didn't want to know. Mary may not have understood the significance of what she was doing; all she intended was to offer the very best to One who had done so much for her. And Jesus honored her for it.

*Are you lavish and extravagant in your adoration of Jesus?
What difference might it make to those around you if the fragrance
of your love for Him were to fill every room you're in?*

A PRAYER FOR FELLOWSHIP WITH GOD

Fill Thou my life, O Lord my God,
in every part with praise,
that my whole being may proclaim
Thy being and Thy ways:
So shall no part of day or night
from sacredness be free;
but all my life, in every step,
be fellowship with Thee.
Amen.

Horatius Bonar

Day 112

MY PRAYER FOR
FELLOWSHIP WITH GOD

_____

_____

_____

_____

_____

_____

_____

_____

_____

_____

_____

God is faithful, by whom you were called into
the fellowship of His Son, Jesus Christ our Lord.

1 Corinthians 1:9

DO AS I SAY *AND* AS I DO

"I have given you an example to follow.
Do as I have done to you".
JOHN 13:15

J esus didn't just talk the talk; He walked the walk. He didn't just lecture His disciples; He modeled the behavior called for, whether it was a matter of turning the other cheek, loving God with all one's heart, or serving others with humility. The context here is that He had just washed the disciples' feet, a menial chore none of them would ever stoop to doing for anyone.

But that's exactly why He did it. Jesus was always able to surprise His disciples, and it seems that He was able to do so right up to the end. As they sat around the room, Jesus quietly disrobed, wrapped a towel around His waist, and proceeded to do the job of a slave. Imagine twenty-four dirty feet; removing twelve pairs of sandals; washing and drying. What was He thinking as He came to the feet of Judas Iscariot – feet that would soon run to betray Him? What was Judas thinking as Jesus lovingly washed and dried? Did he feel a tinge of guilt? Or did this just solidify his concerns about Jesus, that this was no king at all? A servant-king? Unheard of. And that's certainly not the kind of king Judas wanted.

But Jesus understood that for His followers to be able to reach out to a world in dire need of the message of salvation, they must be willing to serve their Lord and one another. And He showed them how.

How are you at serving others?

THE ONLY WAY

"I am the way, the truth, and the life.
No one can come to the Father except through me".
JOHN 14:6

When the disciples asked how they would get to the Father and His home, Jesus answered that He was the only way.

This fact that Jesus is the only way to heaven isn't popular in our age of "it doesn't matter what you believe as long as you're sincere" and "all faiths lead to the same destination" ways of thinking. People argue that having just one way is too narrow and limiting.

In reality, it is wide enough for all who believe. Instead of arguing and worrying about how limited it sounds, people should be grateful that there actually is *one* way to God. He didn't have to provide a way. He could have made us figure it out on our own. It is as if we are standing at a precipice and wishing to get to the other side of the great divide.

God could have left us stranded or told us to make our own bridge. But He didn't. Instead, He made the bridge Himself and then sent us the directions to get there. If we listen, we can travel to the bridge, the only bridge, and make our way across.

Jesus is *the way – follow* Him. Jesus is *truth – believe* Him. Jesus is *life – live* in Him. There is no other way to the Father but through Him.

What can you say to those who think that all roads lead to God?

BEING FRUITFUL

"I am the vine; you are the branches. Those who remain in me, and I in them,
will produce much fruit. For apart from me you can do nothing".
JOHN 15:5

The purpose of an apple tree is to bear apples. The purpose of a cherry tree is to bear cherries. The purpose of a grapevine is to bear grapes. And the branches apart from the tree or the vine will bear no fruit at all.

Christians are also expected to bear fruit: love, joy, peace, patience, kindness, goodness, faithfulness, gentleness, and self-control (Gal. 5:22-23). Here, Jesus says He is the vine and believers are the branches. Thus, the secret to our bearing fruit is staying attached to the vine. Jesus' point is that we are totally dependent upon Him. Just as we could not become God's children through our own efforts but only through faith in Christ, so too we cannot bear fruit by wishing and hoping for it or by working hard at it on our own. Instead, we must allow Christ to produce His fruit through us. The secret is in "remaining."

So how do we remain in Him and Him in us? We communicate with Him, do what He says in His Word, live by faith, and relate in love to the community of believers. As the branches draw nourishment from the vine, so we draw our nourishment to live the Christian life from the source of that life.

Do you want your life to be fruitful? Then remain attached
to your life source – the Vine, Jesus Christ Himself.

YOU CAN OVERCOME

"I have told you all this so that you may have peace in me. Here on earth you will have many trials and sorrows. But take heart, because I have overcome the world".
JOHN 16:33

Jesus was about to be arrested, tried, convicted, and crucified. Soon His disciples would be left to carry His message throughout the world. Jesus knew that they would be tested, tempted, and persecuted. So in these final instructions, He warned them and gave them a promise.

Note that Jesus didn't say the disciples "might" or "could" have trouble; He said they "will" – it was a certainty. They would be hated and persecuted. In truth, most of them would eventually be martyred for their faith. They would indeed "have many trials and sorrows." Yet in their troubles they could have peace and be encouraged.

Until Christ returns, Christians will always conflict with the world. We stand out with a different allegiance, different values, and a different lifestyle. We threaten the status quo by refusing to compromise our faith, living for Christ, and calling people to turn from their sins and to give their lives to the Savior.

That doesn't make us popular. We *will* have trouble. With all this trouble, however, we can have peace. Knowing that our Lord has defeated sin, death, and all of the temptations and attacks of Satan gives us courage to face adversity with calmness of spirit during any trial.

Whatever trouble you face, take heart! You can be an overcomer because Jesus has "overcome the world."

"JUST LIKE YOU AND ME, FATHER"

"I pray that they will all be one, just as you and I are one – as you are in me, Father, and I am in you. And may they be in us so that the world will believe you sent me".
JOHN 17:21

Jesus' last hours with His disciples culminated in their overhearing His final prayer concerning themselves, addressed to His Father but spoken aloud for their intended ears. What they heard Him say was, essentially, that above all else, He wants them to be unified.

More than that, He prayed for believers down through the ages. In essence, He was praying for us. We are right there in the Bible as Jesus prayed for all believers, "all who will ever believe in me through their message" (John 17:20), to be one, to be unified.

This is far more than mere agreement or harmony among people, for Jesus described this oneness as being "just as you and I are one – as you are in me, Father, and I am in you." This kind of oneness shows to the world the reality of God and His love.

Think about it. Isn't it amazing when you travel to another part of the world and find a Christian? Immediately you have a connection. You may dress differently, eat differently, and worship differently, but you are united in the deepest part of your souls because you both believe in Jesus as Savior.

That's the kind of unity that makes the world wonder. That's the kind of unity Jesus wanted.

The next time you meet a fellow believer in your travels,
rejoice in the fact that Jesus prayed for the unity
and connection that you feel with that person.

A YEARNING FOR GOD

Jesus, Thou Joy of loving hearts,
Thou Fount of life, Thou Light of men,
from the best bliss that earth imparts,
we turn unfilled to Thee again.
Our restless spirits yearn for Thee,
wherever our changeful lot is cast;
glad when Thy gracious smile we see,
blessed when our faith can hold Thee fast.
Amen.

St. Bernard of Clairvaux

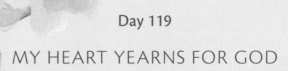

Day 119

MY HEART YEARNS FOR GOD

_____

_____

_____

_____

_____

_____

_____

_____

_____

_____

_____

_____

God, You have made us for Yourself,
and our hearts are restless
till they find their rest in You.

St. Augustine

WHAT IS TRUTH?

Pilate said, "So you are a king?" Jesus responded, "You say I am a king.
Actually, I was born and came into the world to testify to the truth.
All who love the truth recognize that what I say is true".

JOHN 18:37

ow many people "love the truth"? If we extrapolate from what Jesus said here to Pilate, the number must be rather small, for the number of people who recognize that what Jesus says is *true* is relatively small. This seems to be corroborated by our everyday experience.

Many people appear to expend an enormous amount of energy fooling themselves about their own lives, about the significance of circumstances around them, about the ultimate meaning of the universe. Most people do *not* love the truth.

Blaise Pascal, the brilliant mathematician and astute observer of the human condition, said that most human beings, rather than seeking truth, devote their energies to diverting themselves. He believed that most people, in order not to recognize the truth of Christianity, divert themselves with amusing pastimes that keep them distracted and prevent them from having to face the otherwise imposing nature of truth. After all, truth requires a decision, a choice to believe or not. Most people would prefer to play both sides, to sit on the fence and not have to stand for anything.

Perhaps Pilate was one of those; even when face-to-face with the Truth he didn't want to believe. He preferred to maintain his usual skepticism; thus, he did not profit from his encounter with the one man who was the embodiment of truth.

What does it mean to you to love the truth?

IS THIS YOUR KING?

Then Jesus came out wearing the crown of thorns and the purple robe.
And Pilate said, "Look, here is the man!".
JOHN 19:5

At the moment of His greatest personal triumph, Jesus was presented as an object of mockery. When His claims to be the true Davidic king prophesied for ages – the Anointed One, the Messiah – were investigated and rejected by the Jewish leaders, they mocked Him and sent Him to the Romans who flogged Him and sentenced Him to die.

Then the bleeding thorn-crowned figure dressed in a purple robe was brought out onto Pilate's balcony and presented to the waiting throng with Pilate's solemn introduction, "Here is the man!" The instantaneous effect upon the members of the religious establishment, who had been waiting for Jesus to reappear after His long interview with Pilate, was to evoke wild shouts for Him to be crucified.

It has nearly always been so – those who consider the claims of Jesus and then reject them often turn to ridicule. If one doesn't acknowledge His sovereignty, the only other option is to make light of it and to mock Him and those who believe in Him. But not for long. Although He suffered humiliation, He will return one day as undisputed ruler, in all His regal glory – the one true eternal King, the Messiah. Then, we're told, every knee will bow.

If you've faced ridicule because of your faith, trust that
Jesus will Himself one day make all things clear. One day everyone
will acknowledge that Jesus is Lord – whether they want to or not.

SEEING (AND HEARING) IS BELIEVING

Then Jesus told him, "You believe because you have seen me.
Blessed are those who believe without seeing me".
JOHN 20:29

Poor Thomas! He has become for hundreds of generations the quintessential doubter, the poster child for misgiving and distrust, the synonym for weak faith – "a doubting Thomas." Most of us can readily relate to his story; we probably would have reacted the same way he did when, three days after Jesus' burial, the other disciples started babbling about having seen the resurrected Lord.

But then he saw Jesus, and Jesus graciously brought Thomas back within the believing fold. At that teachable moment, Jesus made an important point. Many more people after Thomas would believe in Jesus without any tangible evidence at all. They (meaning us) would not have the advantages Thomas had of being able to actually verify Jesus' resurrected state with their (our) own eyes and hands. They (we) would just have the proclaimed testimony of others ... who had believed after hearing the message from still others, who in turn had heard it from believing *others* ...

Starting fifty days later, at Pentecost, and right through to the present moment, the means by which God proclaims Jesus to the world is through the testimony regarding Him that His followers give. And on it goes. We are blessed because we have not seen and yet we have believed.

How will you explain your belief in Jesus to the doubters around you?

A BIG SPLASH

Then the disciple Jesus loved said to Peter, "It's the Lord!"
When Simon Peter heard that it was the Lord, he put on his tunic
(for he had stripped for work), jumped into the water, and headed to shore.
JOHN 21:7

Twice before, since the resurrection, Jesus had appeared, but now enough time had elapsed that Peter, always the one to take the initiative, had gone back not just to Galilee but also to his old profession. These disciples went fishing, but their luck was bad. Terrible, in fact. Repeatedly they threw the nets out and repeatedly they dragged them back again, dripping wet, rough on the hands – and empty, every time. They must have felt pretty amateur, wondering where their skills had gone during the years they'd been following Jesus around. And now nobody had seen Him in over a week. It was a dismal night.

When the stranger on the shore directed them to an enormous catch, they suddenly realized that it was Jesus. Peter remembered a time, a few years before, when Jesus had done the exact same miracle – telling them to simply put their nets out in a different spot and try again (Luke 5:1-11).

In his excitement at Jesus' appearance on this morning, Peter plunged overboard in order to swim to Jesus! This time, instead of saying, "Oh, Lord, please leave me – I'm too much of a sinner to be around you" (Luke 5:8), Peter splashed wildly in the cold sea rushing to be with Jesus again. Peter had sinned and denied his Lord, but he had discovered the forgiveness Jesus gives. And *that* filled him with overwhelming joy!

Joy doesn't come from having success in your professional efforts,
but from being forgiven by Jesus and being with Him.
Do you have that joy today?

AN INSTRUMENT OF GRACE

"But you will receive power when the Holy Spirit comes upon you.
And you will be my witnesses, telling people about me everywhere – in Jerusalem,
throughout Judea, in Samaria, and to the ends of the earth".

ACTS 1:8

In this last statement to His disciples, Jesus promised that the Holy Spirit would come to them, that they would receive power through the Spirit, and that this power would enable them to be His witnesses throughout the world. A few verses (and days) later, we see the fulfillment of that promise (Acts 2:1-47). Filled with the Holy Spirit, the disciples courageously preached the gospel, and thousands responded. The church began to spread from Jerusalem into Judea and Samaria and then around the world.

Notice the progression of Christ's promise: Power to witness comes from receiving the Holy Spirit through us. Too often we try to reverse the order, witnessing in our own power and authority. When we do that, we are trying to win converts and build our "kingdom" rather than bringing people to the Savior. Witnessing is not showing what we can do for God; it is showing and telling what God has done for us. It is the outpouring of the Holy Spirit's work in our lives.

When we submit to Christ, yielding completely to His control and allowing the Holy Spirit to fill us, we become God's instrument to speak His words in His place at His time. The Holy Spirit works ahead of time, preparing the hearts of those to whom we are called to speak. Then we have the privilege of watching God work through us, changing lives for eternity.

It's not all up to you. If you're yielded to the Spirit,
God will prepare the hearts of those to whom
He wants you to speak. Salvation is, after all, His work.

A PRAYER OF REJOICING

Lord, I rejoice that nothing
can come between me and Your love,
even when I feel alone or in difficulty,
when in sickness or am troubled.
Even if attacked or afraid,
"no abyss of mine is so deep
that Your love is not deeper still".
Amen.

Corrie ten Boom

MY PRAYER OF REJOICING

_____

_____

_____

_____

_____

_____

_____

_____

_____

_____

_____

There is not one blade of grass, there is no color
in this world that is not intended to make us rejoice.

John Calvin

NOW WHAT?

"So let everyone in Israel know for certain that God has made this Jesus,
whom you crucified, to be both Lord and Messiah!" Peter's words pierced their hearts,
and they said to him and to the other apostles, "Brothers, what should we do?"
Peter replied, "Each of you must repent of your sins, turn to God, and be baptized
in the name of Jesus Christ to show that you have received forgiveness for your sins.
Then you will receive the gift of the Holy Spirit".

ACTS 2:36-38

"What should we do to be saved?" The question rings down through the ages – asked by sincere seekers and uncertain doubters. Salvation is available; how do we obtain it?

The disciples learned the hard way. They went from being fearful men who fled from Jesus in His time of need to becoming powerful preachers of the gospel message. During those days in the upper room as they had talked and prayed together, they must have shed a few tears realizing what they had done. But they also knew what had to happen – repentance and turning back to God for forgiveness. They had done that, and then the Holy Spirit had come upon them in power. In this first sermon, Peter explained that repentance and turning to God is the way of salvation for all people.

And so it is for all time. We come to God by repenting of our sins. There are no shortcuts, no buyouts, no complex flowcharts. You just need to come to Him and ask to be saved.

In fact, that's one of the problems people have with the gospel message: It's too simple. They want complexity; they want twelve steps; they want to feel like they've somehow earned what Jesus offers for free. It can't be done. A gift is free. And that's what salvation is. A gift. It just needs to be accepted.

Salvation is not a complex set of rules or rituals; it's a gift.
Have you accepted it? How can you express
the wondrous simplicity of this gift to others?

Day 128

GLORIOUS OPPORTUNITIES

As they approached the Temple, a man lame from birth was being carried in.
Each day he was put beside the Temple gate, the one called the Beautiful Gate,
so he could beg from the people going into the Temple.

ACTS 3:2

*C*onsider the "gates" you traverse. Wherever you go and whomever you come in contact with, you can share a word of encouragement and kindness that strengthens the weak and weary. You might even have the opportunity to share the message of salvation as Peter and John did with the beggar at the Beautiful Gate.

But usually we're in a hurry – we have places to be, people to meet, things to do. Peter and John were, after all, on their way to the three o'clock prayer service. Maybe they were running a little late. Maybe the traffic jam of people was unusually heavy. We might excuse them for dashing past the beggar (as they may have done many times before) to get to the service on time.

This time something made them stop (most likely, it was the Holy Spirit, who had prepared the heart of this beggar for this special day). The beggar wanted money, but he got so much more!

You pass through many gates in your travels – the security guards at the airport, the toll collectors on the highway, the receptionists at the hotel registration desk, the security guards at the conference center. Often those are seen as an irritation. Think instead how those gates might provide an opportunity to share God's love with the gatekeepers.

Take time to smile and say a kind word
to the people at the "gates" today.

BOLDNESS

*When they heard the report, all the believers lifted their voices together
in prayer to God: ... "O Lord, hear their threats, and give us,
your servants, great boldness in preaching your word".*
ACTS 4:24, 29

Before His ascension into heaven, Jesus told His followers: "You will receive power when the Holy Spirit comes upon you. And you will be my witnesses, telling people about me everywhere" (Acts 1:8). On the day of Pentecost, they did receive that power, but they still faced opposition – such as threats from the Jewish council against preaching the Good News.

So the believers met together to pray. But this was no prayer of worry or fear. These believers didn't ask for the destruction of the opposition or for an easier task or for an excuse to just keep silent. Instead, they prayed for "great boldness" in sharing the Good News and for God to demonstrate His power through them. They reported to God the threats they had received and reminded themselves of the way religious leaders had opposed Jesus, their Savior.

While it's certainly fine to bring all of your requests to God – even the worried and fearful ones – remember that "the Spirit who lives in you is greater than the spirit who lives in the world" (1 John 4:4). Let's just not let our prayers be too "small"; after all, we have a very big God. The opposition may be fierce, but we can pray for boldness to face it. That's a prayer God loves to answer! Be prepared to be surprised at what you can accomplish when God's boldness shines through you!

In what part of your life do you need God to give you boldness?

Day 130

CONFIDENCE IN CONFLICT

*But Peter and the apostles replied,
"We must obey God rather than any human authority".*
ACTS 5:29

I t's tough out there in the business world. The pressure is intense – make the sale, get ahead, climb the ladder, break the glass ceiling, make the margins, do whatever it takes.

In the wake of various scandals in the business world and prison sentences for various executives, you start to wonder when it was exactly that those people sold out. When did they turn the corner and decide that it would be okay to cook the books or act illegally or just lie outright? What circumstances led them to think they had no other choice?

You probably recall an adult advising you as a child, "Stand up for yourself!" when you faced the bullies on the playground. Easier said than done when it is a corrupt authority who also happens to employ you. God tells us to obey those He has placed in authority over us; however, when leaders' behavior conflicts with the righteous behavior commanded by God, we must obey God rather than people.

God is able to protect His children. He will intercede for you when you must confront unrighteousness. When the pressure is intense to act in ways contrary to what you know is God's will for you, don't take the bait – no matter what is offered, threatened, or promised. Remember that, when faced with conflicting choices, you must obey God.

Where do you need to make a stand for God today?

THE MAIN THING

So the Twelve called a meeting of all the believers. They said, "We apostles
should spend our time teaching the word of God, not running a food program.
And so, brothers, select seven men who are well respected and are full of the
Spirit and wisdom. We will give them this responsibility. Then we apostles
can spend our time in prayer and teaching the word".

ACTS 6:2-4

When it comes to succeeding at work, you know that prioritizing,
doing what you do best, and delegating are linchpins. You know
from experience what happens when priorities get out of whack, when you
have to work in an area you know nothing about, or when you try to do it
all yourself. You know that your time is best spent on the things you do well.

The apostles found that they had to prioritize and delegate if they were
going to be able to focus on their main responsibilities of "prayer and
teaching the word." Even though they surely desired to be servants, they
found that they couldn't run the food program *and* pray and teach as they
had been called to do. So in this early lesson about the body of Christ, they
found other people to carry the responsibility of the food program. The
twelve apostles retained the proper focus and were free to do what they
were called to do. In addition, this allowed other believers to step into roles
of responsibility in the church.

Prioritize, do what you do best and have been called to do, and delegate
the rest. Keeping God's calling as your focal point provides wisdom to help
you make those decisions – both at work and at home.

Pray to know your priorities, your calling,
and when and what you should delegate
in order to share both the load and the glory.

INTERCEDING FOR OTHERS IN LOVE

Lord, save us from being self-centered in our prayers,
and teach us to remember to pray for others.
May we be so bound up in love
with those for whom we pray
that we may feel their needs
as acutely as our own
and intercede for them with sensitivity,
with understanding
and with imagination.
We ask this in Christ's name.
Amen.

John Calvin

Day 133

TODAY, I INTERCEDE FOR ...

_____

_____

_____

_____

_____

_____

_____

_____

_____

_____

Since love grows within you, so beauty grows.
For love is the beauty of the soul.

St. Augustine

EXTRAORDINARY IN THE ORDINARY

As they stoned him, Stephen prayed, "Lord Jesus, receive my spirit."
He fell to his knees, shouting, "Lord, don't charge them with this sin!"
And with that, he died.
ACTS 7:59-60

Stephen wasn't one of the twelve apostles. In fact, he was chosen as a relief worker so the apostles could get back to praying and teaching instead of serving food. Acts 6 describes the situation. The apostles wanted to choose "seven men who are well respected and are full of the Spirit and wisdom" (Acts 6:3) to help with food distribution in the early church. Stephen is first on the list, described as "a man full of faith and the Holy Spirit." Just a kitchen worker ... yet Stephen "performed amazing miracles and signs among the people" (Acts 6:8) and was so persuasive in his arguments for the faith that no one "could stand against the wisdom and the Spirit with which Stephen spoke" (Acts 6:10).

That's what got him arrested and dragged before the high priest and the Jewish council (incidentally, the same set of people who had condemned Jesus). And before these self-proclaimed religious leaders, Stephen courageously proclaimed the true identity of Jesus and the purpose of His death and resurrection. For his forceful and persuasive proclamation of the Good News, he was stoned to death.

Stephen, the kitchen worker, stands tall in the annals of faith as one of those men who did much for God's Kingdom. Clearly, God doesn't need everyone to be preachers and teachers; He just needs ordinary people who will learn from Him and be willing to be used in extraordinary circumstances.

Do you ever feel that you're not qualified to do
great things for God? Think again. Even if you feel ordinary,
tell God you're ready to do the extraordinary for Him.

Day 135

TIME FOR EVALUATION

When Simon saw that the Spirit was given when the apostles laid their hands on people, he offered them money to buy this power. "Let me have this power, too," he exclaimed, "so that when I lay my hands on people, they will receive the Holy Spirit!".

ACTS 8:18-19

The story has happened in many places in various permutations: The employee spends extra time at work. He or she seems to be willing and able to do anything. Later, when this person's desk is suddenly empty, you're shocked to discover that he or she had been sneaking sensitive information out of your company and selling it to the competition. The employee had gotten into everyone's good graces but had impure motives.

Simon the sorcerer had quite a following, for he astounded people with his magic. When the rest of the apostles laid hands on the believers and the Holy Spirit came – well, this was a trick he'd *never* seen! He wanted to know the secret, the trick behind the trick, and he offered the apostles money for it. Simon followed not out of faith, but out of fascination. He didn't want God; he wanted more ideas for his bag of magic tricks. The apostles made it clear that God's power cannot be bought.

While we may be blindsided by people's wrong or evil motives, God never is. And that should give us pause. What exactly are your motives – for going to church, tithing, serving? You may not be selling out to the competition, but are you truly focused on what is important to God? Now there's a question worth pondering.

Ask God to search your heart and to help your motivations be honoring to Him.

GOD'S AGENTS

When Saul arrived in Jerusalem, he tried to meet with the believers,
but they were all afraid of him. They did not believe he had truly
become a believer! Then Barnabas brought him to the apostles ...

ACTS 9:26-27

Saul of Tarsus was in the process of abusing Christians – men, women, even children – and was complicit in their murders when God stopped him in his tracks on the Damascus Road and rerouted his life. God had plans for Saul, calling him "my chosen instrument to take my message to the Gentiles and to kings, as well as to the people of Israel" (Acts 9:15). The change was radical and happened literally overnight.

Given human nature, however, the believers in Jerusalem were unconvinced. What would stop Saul from pretending to be a believer in order to infiltrate their ranks and cause even more havoc? It was an understandable suspicion and something Saul had difficulty overcoming. That is, until a respected believer took him under his wing. Barnabas knew that Saul was the real deal – truly converted, called, and on fire for God. Acting almost like an agent, Barnabas "sold" Saul to the believers. Because they trusted Barnabas, they trusted his word about Saul.

Sometimes people just need someone to come alongside and be an encouragement. We should see people afresh when they join God's Kingdom – whatever their past. We need to allow people to change and grow, as we have done. When we are willing to step in and make the introduction, we may see God turn the world upside down.

Who needs your encouragement today?

IN EVERY NATION

Then Peter replied, "I see very clearly that God shows no favoritism.
In every nation he accepts those who fear him and do what is right".

ACTS 10:34-35

We're used to people playing favorites. Teachers have "pets," bosses have "fast-track employees," and just about everyone has a "best friend." And remember those days when kids would choose sides for playground games? The "good" players were chosen first; no one wanted to be chosen last.

Considering our experience, we might assume that God acts the same way – that He favors certain people because of ability, personality, physical attributes, social standing, or another identifying characteristic. (Peter certainly felt that way – he was sure that Gentiles were unclean.) This assumption may lead us to wonder about God's feelings toward us and, perhaps, even to doubt our relationship with Him.

But God revealed the truth to Peter: God doesn't act that way. That is, "God shows no favoritism." Instead, He accepts people "in every nation." The only qualification for acceptance is that they honor and revere ("fear") Him and obey Him.

Know that God accepts you, affirms you, and stands by you. And through His Son, Jesus, He gives you eternal life, regardless of your height, beauty, weight, strength, gender, talent, ability, or nationality. You may be fortunate enough to meet believers all over the world. As you do, rejoice that God has people in every nation who fear Him and do what is right. God has no favorites; He loves all His people all over the world. What an amazing family is the family of God!

What believers have you met in your travels?
Say a prayer for them as they minister
in their part of the world.

BEYOND BOUNDARIES

Meanwhile, the believers who had been scattered during the
persecution after Stephen's death traveled as far as Phoenicia, Cyprus,
and Antioch of Syria. They preached the word of God, but only to Jews.
However, some of the believers who went to Antioch from Cyprus
and Cyrene began preaching to the Gentiles about the Lord Jesus.

ACTS 11:19-20

Thank goodness for these early Christians! They were unwilling travelers,
to be sure, scattered from their homes in Jerusalem because of the
fear of persecution. They gathered what they could carry, boarded up their
homes, and left – traveling to locations far and wide.

Perhaps some went to the homes of relatives in nearby towns; perhaps
others took the opportunity to go to the island of Cyprus or to visit friends
in Phoenicia. Maybe others just decided to start over in Antioch of Syria.
They carried with them not just their belongings but their new faith in a
Savior named Jesus Christ.

When Jesus promised that His people would be His "witnesses, telling
people about me everywhere – in Jerusalem, throughout Judea, in Samaria,
and to the ends of the earth" (Acts 1:8), He had been fuzzy on exactly how
that would happen. As always, God worked in an unexpected way – shaking
the believers "to the ends of the earth" by way of persecution. Little did
those persecutors know that they were only causing the spread of the very
message they sought to squelch!

As a modern-day woman, what are you carrying – your briefcase,
backpack, laptop, the latest novel? Remember your most important carry-
on of all – your faith in your Savior.

How can you leave a bit of Christ in every place you visit?

WORSHIPFUL PRAYER

For You are great and do marvelous deeds;
You alone are God.
Teach me Your way, LORD,
that I may rely on Your faithfulness;
give me an undivided heart,
that I may fear Your name.
You, Lord, are a compassionate and gracious God,
slow to anger, abounding in love and faithfulness.

Psalm 86:10-11, 15

Day 140

MY PRAYER OF
HEARTFELT WORSHIP

_____

_____

_____

_____

_____

_____

_____

_____

_____

_____

There is not in the world a kind of life
more sweet and delightful than that of a
continual conversation with God.

Brother Lawrence

WHEN GOD ANSWERS

Meanwhile, Peter continued knocking. When they finally opened
the door and saw him, they were amazed. He motioned for them
to quiet down and told them how the Lord had led him out of prison.
"Tell James and the other brothers what happened," he said.
And then he went to another place.
ACTS 12:16-17

Have you ever been surprised by an answer to prayer? You prayed and suddenly there it was! *How can this be?* So often we get used to having to wait (albeit impatiently), having to keep persevering in prayer (albeit begrudgingly), then when God just says yes, we don't know what to do! Like Rhoda, we shut the door and run back to the inner room, needing to convince ourselves that the answer is real.

When angels miraculously delivered the apostle Peter from Herod's jail, Peter hardly could believe it himself. Then the circle of believers who were calling on God for Peter's release had difficulty believing that their prayer had actually been answered. Rhoda brought the report that Peter was standing at the door, and the believers, who raised their heads from prayer at her intrusion, told her she was out of her mind (Acts 12:6-17).

Out in the street, Peter kept knocking until they finally stopped praying long enough to rejoice over the answer!

Many of our prayers seem to be on hold – up there in God's "In-box" awaiting His attention. Once in a while, He sends those yes answers, reminding us that He is there and He is listening. Don't be shocked; just rejoice!

What recent answer to prayer has surprised you?

Day 142

TRAVEL PLANS

One day as these men were worshiping the Lord and fasting,
the Holy Spirit said, "Dedicate Barnabas and Saul for the special work
to which I have called them." So after more fasting and prayer,
the men laid their hands on them and sent them on their way.

ACTS 13:2-3

They "sent them on their way." Sounds so easy. Once this meeting was over, however, Paul and Barnabas surely had their share of preparations to make in order to be ready to set out on a lengthy road (and ship) trip.

Preparing for travel is never easy. There's so much to do to get ready to go. Packing everything we think we'll need (how will the weather be? do I have enough pairs of underwear and shoes?), then planning ahead for someone to collect the mail, water the lawn, and feed the pets. Travel itself is never easy. We wait in lines, we get peanuts on the plane, we slog our luggage from place to place (if it arrives, that is!).

What must it have been like for Paul and Barnabas? Sure, they had no security checks and people digging through their luggage, but they certainly had less than luxurious travel accommodations. And it's not like they had been making plans for this trip. Instead, God said go and they went. They had a mandate from God and a message to share, and nothing would stop them.

Every place you go – whether for business or pleasure – is part of God's plan for your life. See it as a potential place to plant seeds of salvation with the people you meet. You never know what a kind word, a smile, or a piece of encouragement might do in someone's life.

What "seeds" can you plant today?

PSST!

*Some of the Jews, however, spurned God's message and
poisoned the minds of the Gentiles against Paul and Barnabas.*
ACTS 14:2

Have you faced gossip on the job or at church? It's painful to find that people have talked about you behind your back and not given you the opportunity to respond. It is indeed like poison.

When Paul and Barnabas traveled to Iconium, some unbelievers rallied opposition against them by planting mistrust among the people, poisoning their minds with lies. Paul and Barnabas stood against it for a long time until eventually a riot broke out and they literally had to flee for their lives.

Lies have been around since the garden of Eden, and gossip has existed since two people could talk about a third. The Old Testament book of Proverbs has much to say about the danger of gossip: "A gossip goes around telling secrets, but those who are trustworthy can keep a confidence ... A troublemaker plants seeds of strife; gossip separates the best of friends ... Fire goes out without wood, and quarrels disappear when gossip stops" (Prov. 11:13; 16:28; 26:20).

Clearly, gossip is harmful when it happens to us – but are we just as careful to not be party to gossip about others? It can be difficult, but it must be done. Let's not be known as gossips who foment strife and quarrels; instead, let's be people who can keep a confidence.

*How often do you talk about others behind their backs?
What would God have you do?*

OUTSIDE IN

*"And so my judgment is that we should not make it difficult
for the Gentiles who are turning to God. Instead, we should write and
tell them to abstain from eating food offered to idols, from sexual immorality,
from eating the meat of strangled animals, and from consuming blood".*

ACTS 15:19-20

I n Judaism, Moses' Law was the standard, and good Jews adhered to it. Suddenly, along came this new faith, grown out of Judaism. Christianity opened its doors wide to Jews and Gentiles alike, blending them into the family of God. We take it for granted, but for these early believers, the issue of Gentiles becoming believers was hotly debated and questioned. Many Jewish believers thought that Gentiles needed to become Jews first before they could become Christians – in other words, they needed to follow Moses' laws, including the requirement of circumcision.

Fortunately, the leaders of the church didn't see it that way. Gentiles could become believers without having to follow all the rules of the Jewish law, particularly the requirement of circumcision. They saw beyond the letter of the law to the spirit of the law, and what could have torn the church apart was handled with finesse and wisdom.

Because of Christ, the gospel is for everyone. All believers will have their variations in how they worship or what they believe about various doctrines. But as long as we agree on the basics, we are all children of God and should treat each other with respect and love. Apart from upholding godliness in each other's lives, we must not judge one another according to our own sets of rules.

*In what ways can you overlook nonessential differences
among believers – even rejoice in how God uses
so many people to accomplish His purposes on earth?*

SACRIFICIAL LIVING

Paul wanted him to join them on their journey. In deference to the Jews
of the area, he arranged for Timothy to be circumcised before they left,
for everyone knew that his father was a Greek.

ACTS 16:3

Many Christians practice sacrificial giving: submitting more of their money, time, and talents than Scripture prescribes. These individuals believe that everything belongs to God, and they trust God to provide for their needs. Here we see an example of sacrificial *living*.

When the apostle Paul met Timothy and chose to have the young man join the missionary journeys, Paul did something unusual. Although the Jerusalem council (Acts 15) had specifically stated that new believers did not have to be circumcised, Paul made sure that Timothy was. And Timothy submitted because he was totally devoted to God.

Timothy's father was Greek and his mother was Jewish. Had Timothy been raised in the religion of his mother, circumcision would have been performed not long after his birth. Yet he was raised as a Gentile and so had never been circumcised. In part, Timothy decided to endure circumcision according to his Jewish heritage. Beyond this, he submitted himself in the flesh in order to be a *blessing* – to do the work of Jesus Christ. Because not being circumcised would have hindered the message, he chose to be circumcised in order to remove any question of his faith.

Timothy didn't have to do it; he chose to do it. According to God's Word, Timothy's sacrificial living – total submission to God – resulted in others being "strengthened in their faith" (Acts 16:5).

*Might there be an area of your life where
you need to practice more sacrificial living?*

A PRAYER TO AN ALMIGHTY GOD

You are holy, Lord, the only God,
and Your deeds are wonderful.
You are strong. You are great.
You are the Most High. You are Almighty.
You, Holy Father are King of heaven and earth.
You are Three and One, Lord God, all Good.
You are Good, all Good, supreme Good, Lord God, living and true.
You are love. You are wisdom. You are humility.
You are endurance. You are rest. You are peace.
You are joy and gladness. You are justice and moderation.
You are all our riches, and You suffice for us.
You are beauty. You are gentleness.
You are our protector. You are our guardian and defender.
You are our courage. You are our haven and our hope.
You are our faith, our great consolation.
You are our eternal life,
Great and Wonderful Lord, God Almighty, Merciful Savior.
Amen.

St. Francis of Assisi

Day 147

MY PRAYER OF ADORATION
TO THE ALMIGHTY GOD

_____

_____

_____

_____

_____

_____

_____

_____

_____

_____

Praise His glorious name forever!
Let the whole earth be filled with His glory.

Psalm 72:19

WORKING THE NET

*He went to the synagogue to reason with the Jews and the God-fearing Gentiles,
and he spoke daily in the public square to all who happened to be there.*

ACTS 17:17

An Internet search of the term *marketplace Christian* delivers dozens of organization, periodical, book, and blog websites that teach Christians to uphold their faith at work. These sites also provide tools to encourage workplace evangelism. Their central message is that the spiritual life is not divorced from practical, daily decision making and living, but wed to the milieu of the marketplace – boardroom discussions, business-to-business transactions, cubicle tasks, and water-cooler conversations. The marketplace-Christian thrust spurs evangelism and missions that span the global community.

In the early centuries of the Christian community, the apostle Paul formed his own network as he traveled from Philippi to Thessalonica to Berea to Athens and beyond. It was his custom to preach and teach about Christ regularly in the synagogues. Paul and those who traveled with him also evangelized aboard sailing vessels, in prisons, by the river-side, in homes, as well as in the "public square" – speaking to anyone and in whatever manner was necessary to deliver the Good News of Jesus Christ's resurrection.

Paul's tools did not include a computer or handheld device. He simply sought opportunity to speak to those who would listen. Whether by e-mail, website, one-on-one, or group conversation, we can do the same in the marketplace today.

How does your faith make a difference in your "marketplace"?

ON THE MOVE FOR CHRIST

*Paul stayed in Corinth for some time after that, then said good-bye
to the brothers and sisters and went to nearby Cenchrea. There he shaved
his head according to Jewish custom, marking the end of a vow.
Then he set sail for Syria, taking Priscilla and Aquila with him*

ACTS 18:18

Relocation has its share of challenges. Even with a corporate allowance, relocation requires us to collect, organize, pitch, pack, truck, and ship belongings. If family members are involved, it means more work. If our move involves leaving the country, other complications arise. Of course, relocation also can bring welcome change: when we take a great new job, move into a new home, or relocate to a new part of the country or into a foreign country where new sights, foods, and experiences await.

Yet imagine the moves endured by the early Christians. Priscilla and Aquila were put out of their hometown, ordered by Emperor Claudius to leave Rome along with all other Jews. This couple ended up relocating themselves, their tent-making business, and their ministry to Corinth. That is where they met Paul, who stayed with the couple. Only eighteen months later, Priscilla and Aquila relocated again, from Corinth to follow Paul and do ministry at Ephesus. Two dramatic moves in less than two years! In each place, God used them mightily for His work. While it may have seemed inconvenient to them, God had a plan.

Change isn't easy, but when we're willing to see God in it – and anxious to see His plans unfold – change becomes an adventure of walking into the unknown with Him.

*What changes are taking place in your life?
How can you see them as an adventure with God?*

BLOOMING FROM WITHIN

Then when Paul laid his hands on them, the Holy Spirit came on them,
and they spoke in other tongues and prophesied.

ACTS 19:6

Roses attract particular pests, including deadly aphids and worms, and fungi-attacking diseases that curl, blotch, and blacken leaves. Attentive gardeners can ward off destruction with specially prepared plant foods. Gardeners sprinkle this all-purpose plant food around roots so that roses draw in water laced with nutrients and disease-fighting agents. The result: The plant protects its health from within.

Paul questioned these disciples in Ephesus to see if, since they had believed in God, they had the necessary "ingredient" inside them – the Holy Spirit. Paul realized that these believers had accepted Christ intellectually and had submitted to the exterior prescription of John: water baptism and radically changed behavior. However, only Jesus' Spirit *inside* of them could nourish their souls and guard their hearts from temptations and persecutions.

Paul laid hands on these believers' heads and the Holy Spirit entered them, as evidenced by their praises to God. No longer were they merely following Jesus outwardly, but they were following from within their hearts and souls.

Some people are believers only outwardly – they look good and say all the right things, but their hearts are far from Jesus. True believers, however, are not dependent on how they look or what they do; instead, they trust in what Jesus did for their salvation and depend on the Holy Spirit for daily guidance. Those who do that, like the roses, are protected from within and can fight off all manner of "bugs."

How healthy is your inner life? How much do you
depend on the Holy Spirit for your daily living?

Day 151

LIFE-GIVING WORDS

*Then they all went back upstairs, shared in the Lord's Supper, and ate together.
Paul continued talking to them until dawn, and then he left.*

ACTS 20:11

In many churches today, sermons are timed to our busy culture that dictates brevity. Time-conscious congregants impatiently eye the clock when speakers' remarks exceed thirty minutes. Eyes roll as pew sitters silently communicate, *Time to close!* Yet, in the scheme of priorities, what is more important: arriving home in time to retrieve food from the oven and turn on the TV, or listening to the words of life spoken from the pulpit?

The apostle Paul had spoken at great length one day in Troas. One listener, Eutychus, was sitting on the windowsill. "As Paul spoke on and on" (apparently long-winded preaching is not a new invention), Eutychus fell asleep and spiraled down three stories to his death. Paul ran down and took Eutychus in his arms, and the young man revived! You'd think everyone would have had enough, but back upstairs they all went, and "Paul continued talking until dawn" (Acts 20:9-11). So hungry were these people for the Word of God that staying up all night was not an inconvenience.

How hungry are we for God's Word? True, we have more Bibles than we know what to do with and more Christian books than we ever have time to read. Yet those who minister to us from the pulpits of our churches have a calling, and we should listen attentively to what God lays on their hearts to share – even when they preach "on and on."

*What are you communicating when you sit
in the pew on Sunday morning – impatience,
or a desire to hear what God might say to you?*

WHAT A FELLOWSHIP

*When we returned to the ship at the end of the week,
the entire congregation, including women and children, left the city
and came down to the shore with us. There we knelt, prayed,
and said our farewells. Then we went aboard, and they returned home.*

ACTS 21:5-6

Lyricist Elisha A. Hoffman and composer Anthony J. Showalter penned a hymn titled "Leaning on the Everlasting Arms," which eloquently sings of the divine joy derived from fellowship with Jesus. Our vertical relationship with God, of course, rings true in our interpersonal relationships: As we love God above all else, we can love one another. We express this love toward all believers, crossing familial, cultural, generational, and eternal boundaries. What a witness to those who feel disconnected, isolated, and disenfranchised.

The beach scene at Tyre may have been observed by the onlookers curious at the sight of Jesus' followers who were heading toward the sands and kneeling by the sea to pray. How long the Christians were on their knees is not stated, but imagine the throng, possibly weeping as the Ephesian elders had at Paul's departure (Acts 20:36-38). The believers no doubt hugged as they said their good-byes. What blessings might they have yelled as they waved at Paul boarding the awaiting ship?

As Christians, our prayer and fellowship with one another witnesses to the unique relationships we have in Christ. Onlookers, who note that our fellowship crosses all human-made boundaries, may be moved to wonder, *What a fellowship!* We can hope that they will be pricked in their hearts with a desire to join us.

*What onlookers – acquaintances or neighbors –
would benefit from your invitation to visit
the fellowship of your Christian friends?*

A PRAYER FOR THE
HELPLESS AND HOPELESS

Thou, O Lord, art the Help of the helpless,
the Hope of the hopeless,
the Savior of the bestormed,
the Haven of the voyager,
the Physician of the sick.
Be all things to all mankind,
for Thou knowest everyone and their request,
every home and its needs.
Amen.

St. Basil the Great

Day 154

MY PRAYER FOR THE
HELPLESS AND HOPELESS

_____

_____

_____

_____

_____

_____

_____

_____

_____

_____

No good work is done anywhere without
aid from the Father of Lights.

C. S. Lewis

THE TRUTH REMAINS UNCHANGED

"Brothers and esteemed fathers," Paul said, "listen to me as I offer my defense."
When they heard him speaking in their own language, the silence was even greater.

ACTS 22:1-2

Many people are interested in what we think and feel. Corporate advertisers, politicians, teachers, and preachers share an interest in understanding audiences. Demographers and other researchers compile data that paints a picture of us and then develop subsequent strategies to achieve a desired impact. Their goal is to reach us with a message. The right message can compel us to purchase a product, vote for a candidate, or embrace a new idea.

Oddly enough, God doesn't work that way. He doesn't stick His finger in the wind and figure a way to change His message in order to make it palatable to a new audience or a new generation. In preaching his message, the apostle Paul simply told about Jesus. Except for speaking in Aramaic to the rowdy crowd at Jerusalem in order to hold the people's attention, Paul was not concerned with the crowd's acceptance. In fact, God already had told him what the outcome would be – rejection – yet Paul unabashedly shared the gospel with the angry crowd anyway.

Jesus does not need to do research to connect and communicate with us. He doesn't change His message to fit our desires. The truth is the truth – and God has delivered the same truth to people for thousands of years. Whether people listen and respond or angrily reject it, truth remains unchanged.

Is the truth of the gospel message the final truth to you?
How can you defend that truth to others?

THE STORMS OF LIFE

That night the Lord appeared to Paul and said, "Be encouraged, Paul.
Just as you have been a witness to me here in Jerusalem,
you must preach the Good News in Rome as well".

ACTS 23:11

An anonymous statement reads: "Sometimes the Lord calms the storm; sometimes He lets the storm rage and calms His child." Christians face persecution, injustice, discrimination, poverty, chronic illness, pain, divorce, childlessness, and much more. We need God's strength to overcome our struggles, and He provides assurance through Jesus Christ. He is our Comforter in the midst of life's storms. The knowledge that God is in control and watching over us empowers us to endure the trials this life inevitably brings.

Paul faced many fierce storms. He endured the stiff winds of persecution in Jerusalem before the Sanhedrin. A horde of Jews thundered their anger against him and plotted his murder. But God was watching. God stood near Paul and encouraged him, promising that there was a greater purpose in his ordeal. God promised that Paul would preach the Good News in Rome, the center of the empire. "And by the way, Paul, don't worry about how you're going to get there. I've got it under control." God not only rescued him from the murderers, he also arranged for Paul's passage all the way to Rome – courtesy of the Roman empire!

God's sovereignty over our lives should encourage us greatly when the storms of life rage around us. He's got it under control.

In whatever situation you face today,
you can rest in the sovereign care of Almighty God.

WORLDVIEW ON TRIAL

"I am on trial before you today because I believe in the resurrection of the dead!".
ACTS 24:21

Some people say there are no absolutes, no one's approval is needed, what's truth for you is truth. This worldview allows people to live as they please. Then, when those same people cheat, lie, steal, and commit heinous crimes, the world wonders what went wrong.

Christians have a different worldview, however. For believers, there is an absolute standard of truth – God Himself as revealed in His Word. We look not to the world for approval, but to God. Such a worldview provides for consistency that allows for peace and order. As much as the "no-absolutes" people like to believe that their way of thinking can bring utopia, they are asking only for anarchy. A world cannot function without truth, without absolutes, without right and wrong.

In Acts 24, as Paul stood trial before Roman governor Felix, the apostle realized his standard was not the approval of Felix. Nor did Paul need the approval of the Jews, who labeled Paul a troublemaker for disturbing their self-proclaimed power base. Paul made it clear that he taught only the truth and he sought only God's approval.

Disturbing the peace and living in opposition to world standards that negate the truth of Jesus Christ – *that* should be the job description of all believers. We live by a different worldview, and we ought not apologize for it.

What shift in values and goals can you make
to become more compatible with a biblical worldview?

WHO'S WATCHING?

*But Paul replied, "No! This is the official Roman court,
so I ought to be tried right here. You know very well I am not guilty
of harming the Jews. If I have done something worthy of death,
I don't refuse to die. But if I am innocent, no one has a right to turn
me over to these men to kill me. I appeal to Caesar!".*

ACTS 25:10-11

As we follow the trials of the apostle Paul – before the Sanhedrin, Roman governor Felix, then Festus, and King Agrippa, the ordeal is reminiscent of the illegal trials and trumped-up charges made against Jesus. Paul was a victim of false accusations and mistreatment, and in today's legal system, he probably could have sued for damages. He didn't deserve this treatment, but he bore it patiently. As each new monarch came in to talk to him, he retold the story. He waited two years in prison and then told the story again. Chances are, it made no difference in the lives of the government leaders. Such a waste of time ...

Or was it? Who knows what people may have been standing on the sidelines, listening as Paul defended the faith before the rulers? Who knows what impact Paul's testimony may have had on the scribe, or the lady-in-waiting, or a lowly servant? We may never know who went home saved that day – even if the kings didn't. We do know that this whole ordeal set the stage for Paul to be able to go to Rome and spread the gospel from the very center of the empire.

Who's watching you go through your personal "trials"? What kind of example are you of trust in your Lord, even in the most difficult and unfair circumstances? You may not know whose life will be changed simply because they silently watched you.

*How can you turn a situation of difficulty into an
opportunity to glorify the Lord and make Him known to others?*

Day 159

LOST PEOPLE IN HIGH PLACES

Agrippa interrupted him. "Do you think you can
persuade me to become a Christian so quickly?".

ACTS 26:28

It is a misunderstanding to think that missions and evangelism are restricted to impoverished peoples in nations around the world. Though Jesus made it a point to minister to the poor, He died so no one would perish.

Among Jesus' acquaintances were the rich and the influential. In fact, the Gospels retell the interactions between Jesus and several wealthy people. Nicodemus was a wealthy religious leader, and many women of means, healed of their sins, faithfully supported Jesus and the disciples' ministry.

In speaking with King Agrippa, Paul shared the gospel with a mighty individual who was as lost as Paul had been before his encounter with Jesus. Agrippa was present in order to give respect to a corrupt politician, Festus. The king also was accompanied by his sister, with whom he was involved in an incestuous relationship. An assembly of power-drunk dignitaries filled the chamber where Paul began to speak. All were blinded by self-will and sophistication. Still, Paul shared the gospel.

People who think they are powerful and sophisticated need Christ too. The firm, calm recollection of how Jesus has changed the lives of Christians is meant for the well-to-do as much as for those who are not so well-off.

We should not dismiss the lost in high places as unreachable or unworthy of the Savior.

*Think of someone in power who you know
is a lost soul. Pray for that person today.*

A PRAYER FOR A STEADFAST HEART

Grant us, O Lord, a steadfast heart,
which no unworthy affection may drag downwards;
give us an unconquered heart,
which no tribulation can wear out;
give us an upright heart,
which no unworthy purpose may tempt aside.
Bestow upon us also, O Lord our God,
understanding to know Thee, diligence to seek Thee,
wisdom to find Thee, and a faithfulness that may
finally embrace Thee; through Jesus Christ our Lord.
Amen.

St. Thomas Aquinas

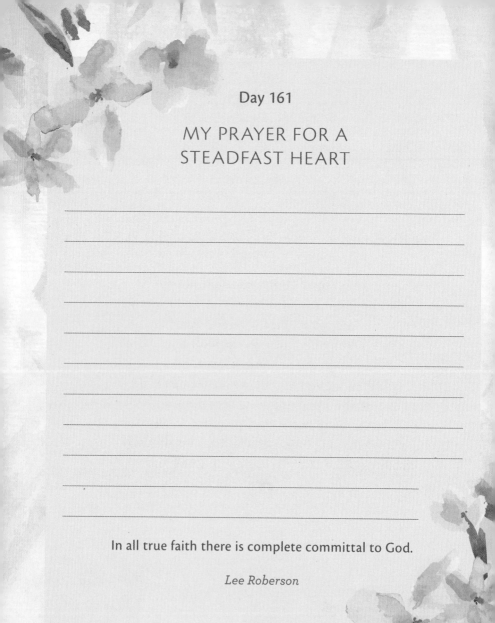

Day 161

MY PRAYER FOR A
STEADFAST HEART

In all true faith there is complete committal to God.

Lee Roberson

A RIGHT WORD AT THE RIGHT TIME

*"So take courage! For I believe God. It will be just as he said ... Please eat
something now for your own good. For not a hair of your heads will perish".*

ACTS 27:25, 34

The right words can make all the difference. They can close a deal, help a friend, save a life. In Acts 27, as the sailors struggled to keep the ship afloat, they didn't need a sermon. They needed encouragement – and God gave it to Paul, and Paul passed it along to everyone on the ship.

Though the men in charge of the ship had dismissed Paul's warnings, he gave the men the encouragement they desperately needed in the face of what appeared to be certain death. Though they would be forced to abandon the ship, Paul confirmed that no one would perish. Then he proposed that everyone eat a good meal so as to be able to swim out of the rough seas to safety on Malta. "It's going to be alright," Paul said, "so let's eat something and prepare for the task ahead."

Sometimes you just need wisdom to say the right thing, the simple thing, the helpful thing. Sometimes, the most helpful thing is to say nothing at all, but just to be present with someone in his or her time of need.

When you don't know what to say, ask God to give you the right words that will offer grace and encouragement.

*Ever feel at a loss for the right words to say? Next time it happens,
send a prayer up to God for the right words to say at the right time.*

WHEN THEY JUST SAY NO

Some were persuaded by the things he said, but others did not believe.
ACTS 28:24

Paul had been through much to bring the Good News to his Jewish brethren in Rome: angry mobs, floggings, murder plots, lengthy imprisonment, official injustices, shipwreck, snake bite, and insults. Finally, he was able to share with them. A time was set and a large number of people came to where Paul was imprisoned. Brimming with words of life, Paul spoke all day, pointing Jewish listeners to Moses' words and the prophets' proofs in order to persuade them to believe. Yet the Bible says that some believed, but others did not.

When it comes to sharing our testimony with unsaved loved ones, the reality is that some will believe and others will not. Maybe they remember our pre-salvation antics and think this is just another phase. Or maybe they just don't want to think you know or have something that they need. Or maybe they don't want to be told what to do. In any case, we want so much for our loved ones to find what we have in Jesus, yet they can present the most difficult audience.

Paul concluded that he had done all that he could to persuade the Jews and that his energies were directed by God elsewhere – to the Gentiles who might embrace Christ. We, too, must entrust unsaved and seemingly unwilling-to-be-saved loved ones to our sovereign God. While we continue to pray that they might receive the testimony of someone other than us – and remain ready to share the reason we hope in Christ when they inquire – we can move on.

*Pray for your unsaved loved ones and ask God,
"With whom else can I share the gospel today?"*

CHOSEN AND SENT

This letter is from Paul, a slave of Christ Jesus, chosen by God
to be an apostle and sent out to preach his Good News.

ROMANS 1:1

*P*aul had never been to Rome, but a church had been planted there by believers who were present when the Spirit came upon the believers who gathered together on the day of Pentecost (Acts 2:10). In this letter to those Roman believers, Paul laid out the case for Christianity. Going step by step, he walked his readers carefully along the foundation stones of the Christian faith, wanting them to understand *what* they believed and *why*.

Paul was specially chosen by God as His "chosen instrument to take my message to the Gentiles and to kings, as well as to the people of Israel" (Acts 9:15). After his conversion experience, he stayed in Damascus for three years and began his ministry. Paul then returned to Jerusalem, sponsored by Barnabas. After some attempts on his life, however, the apostles sent him back to Tarsus for his own safety where he stayed for fourteen years (Acts 9:21-30; Gal. 1:18; 2:1). Paul ministered in Antioch for about eight more years before he and Barnabas were commissioned for their first missionary journey.

God prepared Paul for a great ministry over the course of several years. Eventually, this man who had pursued Christians to their deaths would help to change the world for Christ. No time is wasted with God. If you feel like you're in a waiting period, He's probably just preparing you for the next step. Be patient. Obey right now, right where He has placed you.

God is preparing you, even today, for tasks He has for you.
Are you learning the lessons so you'll be ready?

BY GRACE ALONE

*Don't you see how wonderfully kind, tolerant, and patient God
is with you? Does this mean nothing to you? Can't you see
that his kindness is intended to turn you from your sin?*
ROMANS 2:4

Paul talks much about the law in Romans 2. The believers who came out of a Jewish background already had certain understanding of the law of their heritage – the Law of Moses. Believers who came out of a Gentile Roman background had no knowledge of God's law through Moses. How could the Christian faith possibly blend these two distinct types of people into one cohesive unit?

Paul dealt with this issue head-on, explaining that all the believers, Jews and Gentiles alike, needed to understand that the law really made no difference when it came to salvation. The Jews had the law but, in order to be saved by it, they would need to keep it perfectly (which is impossible). So no matter how good they tried to be (and as a former Pharisee, Paul knew whereof he spoke), they could never be good enough to be saved. That left them on the same footing as the Gentiles who didn't have the law at all. All people are sinners. The law cannot save because people cannot keep it. The only hope anyone has of salvation is the "wonderfully kind, tolerant, and patient God."

Our salvation is by God's grace alone. We obey Him not because we are *trying* to be saved, but because we *have been* saved and want to show our love for Him and all He has done for us.

Are you still trying to be "good enough" to be saved?

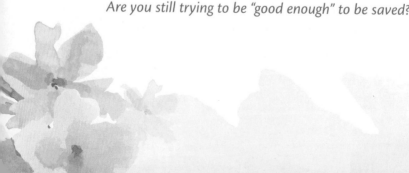

JUSTIFIED FREELY BY HIS GRACE

For everyone has sinned; we all fall short of God's glorious standard.
Yet God, with undeserved kindness, declares that we are righteous. He did
this through Christ Jesus when he freed us from the penalty for our sins.

ROMANS 3:23-24

Let's face it: We can become complacent in our Christian walk. Because we have been rescued from the domain of darkness and transferred to the Kingdom of God's beloved Son, there is reason for joy and contentment. But contentment sometimes turns to complacency, and complacency can breed smugness and, even worse, self-righteousness. Once we come to God and He begins to bless us with successful strides in the faith, victories over temptation, and the good works that He has prepared for us, we puff up in pride or somehow think we've "arrived" and stop doing what we need to do to keep growing and maturing in the faith.

No matter how much good we do, we still fall short of the glory of God. Even the most righteous men and women of faith have failed to achieve the glory of God, whose standard is perfect obedience. We may try – we may even think that we get close – but we are still just sinners saved by grace. There is no room for complacency and pride in the Christian life.

Instead, we should remember daily that although we are sinners who fall short, by God's great love we are "freed from the penalty for our sins." Our obedience should then flow out of thankfulness for all that God has done for us.

In what ways are you making sure that you're still growing in the faith and not lapsing into complacency or self-righteousness?

FILL THY EMPTY VESSEL

Behold, Lord, an empty vessel that needs to be filled.
My Lord, fill it. I am weak in faith; strengthen Thou me.
I am cold in love; warm me and make me fervent
that my love may go out to my neighbor.
I do not have a strong and firm faith;
at times I doubt and am unable to trust Thee altogether.
O Lord, help me. Strengthen my faith and trust in Thee.
In Thee I have sealed the treasures of all I have.
I am poor; Thou art rich and didst come to be merciful to the poor.
I am a sinner; Thou art upright.
With me there is an abundance of sin;
in Thee is the fullness of righteousness.
Therefore, I will remain with Thee
of who I can receive but to whom I may not give. Amen.

Martin Luther

Day 168

MY PRAYER FOR A
STRONG AND FIRM FAITH

_____

_____

_____

_____

_____

_____

_____

_____

_____

_____

_____

_____

Christ will always accept the faith
that puts its trust in Him.

Andrew Murray

HOPE AGAINST HOPE

Abraham never wavered in believing God's promise. In fact,
his faith grew stronger, and in this he brought glory to God.
ROMANS 4:20

Hopelessness. What dreaded finality is contained in that word. You may have encountered situations that seemed hopeless, times when the cold wind of despair rushed over you. Abraham faced just such a situation. He and Sarah were well beyond childbearing years. But God had made a promise, saying, "You will have a son of your own who will be your heir" (Gen. 15:4). Even at that time, Abraham and Sarah were old – but then 25 more years passed with no son in sight. What was God doing?

With some missteps along the way (that is, a child through his servant Hagar, whom God made clear was *not* the promised heir), Abraham kept on believing God's promise, taking Him at His word. Despite the apparent futility of the situation, Abraham's hope was firm and secure, an anchor for his soul. "Even when there was no reason for hope, Abraham kept hoping— believing that he would become the father of many nations" (Rom. 4:18).

Abraham believed God, and his belief was credited to him as righteousness (Rom. 4:22). In the same way, your belief is credited to you as righteousness.

During seemingly hopeless situations, when you've prayed and prayed for years for something that has not yet come to pass, trust God, hope against hope, believe even when you don't see. That, after all, is what faith is all about.

Feeling hopeless? Ask God to give you faith to believe,
to hope against hope, to keep on praying.

RIGHT WITH GOD

Therefore, since we have been made right in God's sight by faith, we have peace with God because of what Jesus Christ our Lord has done for us. Because of our faith, Christ has brought us into this place of highest privilege where we now stand, and we confidently and joyfully look forward to sharing God's glory.

ROMANS 5:1-2

Remember when your mother caught you disobeying one of her orders? You were guilty, caught red-handed, and you knew it. And you had to accept your punishment.

Over the years the situations have changed drastically, but the results are the same – when we do something wrong, we experience guilt. Our adult sins take many forms: hatred, gossip, lying, lust, pride, self-centeredness. And we know that we have offended someone more important even than Mom. In fact, we stand guilty before God, for every sin is a defiance of His laws and an affront to His holiness. The reality is that the deserved punishment for our sins is death – eternal death, separation from God forever.

Now for the true Good News: This passage says, "we have been made right in God's sight by the blood of Christ" (Rom. 5:9). Being made right with God means that we have been declared "not guilty." No matter what we have done, we have been acquitted and forgiven because of Jesus. "He was handed over to die because of our sins, and he was raised to life to make us right with God" (Rom. 4:25). Thus we have peace with God and stand in a place of highest privilege. Not only has God declared us not guilty, He has drawn us close to Himself. Instead of being His enemies, we have become His friends – in fact, His very own children.

Reflect on what it means to be "right in God's sight"
and to have peace with Him. How should that
affect your outlook and actions today?

TRULY FREE

Sin is no longer your master, for you no longer live under the requirements of the law. Instead, you live under the freedom of God's grace.

ROMANS 6:14

What was Paul thinking when he asked the question that opens Romans 6: "Should we keep on sinning so that God can show us more and more of his wonderful grace?" Paul's question sounds peculiar – even absurd – because we know from Scripture that God hates sin and desires us to live holy lives. Paul posed this question because he anticipated that the believers in Rome might ask it based on his words at the end of chapter 5: "As people sinned more and more, God's wonderful grace became more abundant" (Rom. 5:20).

Understanding the abundance of God's grace lies not in sinning more and more, but in simply living our daily lives and seeing that, no matter how hard we try, we just can't be sinless. We don't need a challenge to keep on sinning – it comes rather naturally!

The promise of God's wonderful grace in spite of our continual sin allows us to keep moving in life, free from the constraints of guilt and fear of condemnation. In the meantime, grace abounds. Sin no longer is master over us; the law no longer constrains us. Instead, we live under the freedom of God's grace. And, as Jesus said, "So if the Son sets you free, you are truly free" (John 8:36).

Rejoice that you are under grace and have been set free from the tyranny of sin.

FORGIVEN

And I know that nothing good lives in me, that is, in my sinful nature.
I want to do what is right, but I can't. I want to do what is good, but I don't.
I don't want to do what is wrong, but I do it anyway.
ROMANS 7:18-19

Don't you just sigh with relief when you read these verses? Thank goodness Paul was so willing to be transparent. We read all of his other letters and start to wonder if he was superhuman; here we get a glimpse that he was not. He was just a sinner saved by grace like the rest of us. Sin was a daily struggle for him. He wanted to do right but couldn't. He wanted to do good things but didn't. He didn't want to do wrong but did it anyway. Doesn't that sound just like you on some days?

It's a mystery, this Christian life. God could have made us perfect the moment we were saved – it seems like He could have saved Himself a lot of trouble. We'd have perfect churches, perfect families, perfect marriages. Instead, He chose to bring His Spirit into our lives and yet allow us to move slowly toward holiness – step by step, daily battling with sin. We make mistakes, say hurtful things, and do any and all manner of wrong.

We're saved, but we need every day to seek forgiveness and cleansing. Sin is there, but it no longer has mastery over us. We need to depend on God's grace in us to help us live holy lives. We have been set free to live for God the best we know how – today and every day.

You're not perfect, you're forgiven. Rest in that incredible promise.

GOD'S ARTWORK

*Can anything ever separate us from Christ's love? Does it mean
he no longer loves us if we have trouble or calamity, or are persecuted,
or hungry, or destitute, or in danger, or threatened with death?*
ROMANS 8:35

Neither of these questions by Paul was merely rhetorical. The second one lists the very experiences people often use as evidence that God has abandoned them! But anyone who follows Jesus soon discovers what Jesus meant when He said, "You can enter God's Kingdom only through the narrow gate. The highway to hell is broad, and its gate is wide for the many who choose that way. But the gateway to life is very narrow and the road is difficult" (Matt. 7:13-14). Just because we know and trust Christ does not remove the possibility from our lives of any or all of these listed problems.

God weaves our lives like fine linen. His work is not finished until our last breath. He includes the broken and frayed threads that represent the difficulties and hurts of life so that they become part of His pattern. In short, He "causes everything to work together for the good of those who love" Him (Rom. 8:28). Viewed alone, the troubles and difficulties often make no sense. But the longer we trust God, the more we will see the sheer beauty of His artwork in us.

Our difficulties cannot separate us from God's great love. Not only that, but our difficulties actually are working together for our *good*. Only our loving heavenly Father could accomplish that!

*What difficulties are you facing today?
Trust that God is working all things together
for your good – even if you can't see it right now.*

SEEKING THE LORD GOD

O God, You are my God; earnestly I seek You;
my soul thirsts for You;
my flesh faints for You,
as in a dry and weary land where there is no water.
So I have looked upon You in the sanctuary,
beholding Your power and glory.
Because Your steadfast love is better than life,
my lips will praise You.

Psalm 63:1-3

MY DESIRE TO EARNESTLY SEEK GOD

_____

_____

_____

_____

_____

_____

_____

_____

_____

God is found by those
who seek Him with all their heart.

Samuel Chadwick

GOD'S AMAZING MERCY

So it is God who decides to show mercy.
We can neither choose it nor work for it.

ROMANS 9:16

We will never understand some things this side of eternity: Why do children suffer? Why are whole cities wiped out in natural disasters? Why does a sovereign God allow calamity?

Romans 9 presents us with similarly unsettling questions while revealing God's sovereignty. Right after Paul comforted the church in Rome by assuring them that nothing would separate them from God's love(Rom. 8:38), he here began to discuss issues of God's sovereign choice regarding to whom He will show mercy. *That sure doesn't seem fair,* we think. We hear of God hardening hearts and ask, as Paul did here, "Why does God blame people for not responding? Haven't they simply done what he makes them do?" (Rom. 9:19).

If we're honest, we'll never be comfortable with the thought that God seems to control people like pawns on a chessboard. In reality, however, we must look at *all* that we know about God. For instance, we know that God is just (Rom. 9:14); He does not want anyone to perish (2 Pet. 3:9); He is love (1 John 4:8). In addition, we should be thankful that God decided to show mercy at all – in fact, He showed us so much mercy that He sent His Son to die for us (John 3:16).

We mere human beings will never plumb the depths of God's justice or mercy. Instead of thinking God is unfair, we should instead rejoice at the incredible lengths He went to in order to show mercy to us.

How can you thank God today for the great mercy He shows you?

BEAUTIFUL FEET

And how will anyone go and tell them without being sent?
That is why the Scriptures say, "How beautiful are the feet
of messengers who bring good news!"

ROMANS 10:15

You probably don't think of your feet as beautiful – if you think of them at all. Most of the time we don't think about our feet unless they're tired from a long walk through the airport or when the new shoes are pinching just a bit. Feet are just feet. They get us where we need to go – painfully or not. But we usually don't use the adjective *beautiful* to describe them.

But Paul would beg to differ – as would the prophet Isaiah, from whom Paul quoted these words: "How beautiful are the feet of messengers who bring good news!"

The Good News is that salvation is not a complex process. It's not filled with initiation rites or application fees. Confess with your mouth and believe in your heart and you will be saved (Rom. 10:9). In fact, anyone who calls on the Lord will be saved. What wonderful promises!

But people can't call on someone they don't know about. The message needs to be taken to people by people. Paul asked the rhetorical questions, "How can they call on him to save them unless they believe in him? And how can they believe in him if they have never heard about him? And how can they hear about him unless someone tells them?" (Rom. 10:14).

So beautiful feet need to go. The message is simple: Confess and believe and you will be saved.

As you make your travels, to whom can your
beautiful feet take the Good News today?

IT'S A MYSTERY

Did God's people stumble and fall beyond recovery? Of course not! They were
disobedient, so God made salvation available to the Gentiles. But he wanted his
own people to become jealous and claim it for themselves. Now if the Gentiles
were enriched because the people of Israel turned down God's offer of salvation,
think how much greater a blessing the world will share when they finally accept it.

ROMANS 11:11-12

The mysterious words of this chapter make us wonder, in some ways,
what God is up to. Paul wrote of his fellow Jews and his concern for
their salvation. Even though Jesus Christ came as their promised Messiah,
so few Jews – then and now – accepted Him as such. Paul was a Jew who
believed; therefore, he understood that God had not completely rejected
His people.

The metaphor of branches being grafted into the vine is a picture of
Gentiles being offered the gift of salvation, accepting it, and becoming
part of God's family tree. Paul warned the Gentile believers not to become
arrogant but to understand that their salvation was a gift from God. The
Jews were and always will be the covenant nation and God will keep His
promises to them.

While we may not understand the mystery of how God will cause that to
happen, we can take from this chapter the warning that we must not ever
think that we deserve the favored treatment God has given, nor should we
ever take it for granted. Israel's unbelief was in trying to attain their own
righteousness instead of depending on the righteousness that comes from
God. If we take God's mercy and grace for granted and somehow think we
deserve such favor, we are in danger of similar unbelief.

Ask the Lord to help you never to take
His gift of salvation for granted.

RIGHT LIVING

Don't just pretend to love others. Really love them. Hate what is wrong.
Hold tightly to what is good. Love each other with genuine affection,
and take delight in honoring each other. Never be lazy, but work hard
and serve the Lord enthusiastically. Rejoice in our confident hope.
Be patient in trouble, and keep on praying. When God's people are in need,
be ready to help them. Always be eager to practice hospitality.

ROMANS 12:9-13

Do you want to know how to live the Christian life in your rough-and-tumble world? Take to heart these five simple verses.

Our love for others should be genuine and unmasked. We should take delight in honoring others. That can be difficult in the workplace, where we often feel that we don't get the credit we deserve; it can be difficult at home, where we know all too well the flaws of those with whom we live. But when we love genuinely, we should also be delighted to give honor.

We should hate wrong and hold tightly to the good. Never be lazy; work hard; serve the Lord enthusiastically. If we combine these phrases with another command to "work willingly at whatever you do, as though you were working for the Lord rather than for people" (Col. 3:23), we see that whatever job we have – our occupation, our church commitments, our family plans, our board involvements – whatever is on our schedule should be done enthusiastically as if we are doing it for the Lord. In addition, we should willingly help others and be hospitable.

We can rejoice and be confident – our hope is in God who has promised salvation and eternal life! What could possibly pull us down? So be patient in trouble and stay in close communication with God in prayer.

Five verses. Make these a priority and you'll find that other things will fall into place.

Which of the commands in these verses
do you need to most take to heart today?

THE DEBT OF LOVE

Owe nothing to anyone – except for your obligation to love one another.
If you love your neighbor, you will fulfill the requirements of God's law.

ROMANS 13:8

Not bad advice – "owe nothing to anyone." You may have plenty of debt and want to pay all of it off and be debt-free. Apart from a discussion of money, however, is Paul's point that we should continue to owe the obligation of loving one another. The debt of love ought to be a debt we cannot ever pay in full. Just as we continue to need love from others, so others need us to continue to love them.

Paul repeated what Jesus had said regarding love. When Jesus was asked, "Teacher, which is the most important commandment in the law of Moses?" Jesus answered that people should love God and love their neighbors because "the entire law and all the demands of the prophets are based on these two commandments" (Matt. 22:36, 40). Hence Paul's words in Romans 12:10 to "love each other with genuine affection." Genuine love, given freely with no strings attached, fulfills the entire law because we will not hurt, murder, steal from, lie to, or do anything evil to those we genuinely love. It's easy to keep those commands when we first show love.

So keep this debt of love outstanding. After all, we can never repay to Jesus the love that He has shown us. The best we can do is to love Him and to love others. And is that really so much to ask?

Thank God for the love that He has shown you.
Look for opportunities to express His love to others today.

A PRAYER FOR CONTENTMENT

Almighty God, who knows our necessities before we ask,
and our ignorance in asking:
Set free Thy servants from all
anxious thoughts about tomorrow;
give us contentment with Thy good gifts;
and confirm our faith that
according as we seek Thy kingdom,
Thou wilt not suffer us to lack any good thing,
through Jesus Christ our Lord.
Amen.

St. Augustine

Day 182

MY PRAYER FOR
CONTENTMENT

_____

_____

_____

_____

_____

_____

_____

_____

_____

_____

_____

_____

_____

True godliness with contentment
is itself great wealth.

1 Timothy 6:6

BUILD UP ONE ANOTHER

So let's stop condemning each other. Decide instead to live in such
a way that you will not cause another believer to stumble and fall.
ROMANS 14:13

Differences among believers can be quite astounding. Our theologies, music tastes, and ways of worship vary widely. We are wise when we recognize that as long as we agree on the essentials (for example, who Jesus is and what He did for us), then the nonessentials can be as different as the many people who are part of this big Christian family.

Paul had already spent much of this letter establishing the equality before God of the Jewish and Gentile believers. In this chapter, however, Paul focused on two very sensitive issues that had to be worked out in practical ways in order for them to have true unity: (1) dietary restrictions and (2) the observance of special days. The Jews were concerned about eating certain foods according to their law, as well as the continued observance of certain special Jewish holidays. Gentiles, on the other hand, didn't have the rules about certain foods and knew nothing about the special Jewish days, but had other concerns about meat in the marketplace and whether it had been offered to idols.

These might seem like small matters, but in the practical outworking of the early church, these issues caused great concern. Paul counseled the believers to maintain unity by living in the freedom they had in Christ but always being willing to look out for those with weaker faith. In the end, the bottom line was to love and to build one another up in the faith.

In what ways can you be mindful of those who are weaker in faith?

COMPLETE HARMONY?

*May God, who gives this patience and encouragement, help you live
in complete harmony with each other, as is fitting for followers
of Christ Jesus. Then all of you can join together with one voice,
giving praise and glory to God, the Father of our Lord Jesus Christ.*

ROMANS 15:5-6

Worshiping in a congregation whose members are excited about what God is doing is thrilling. Jesus told His disciples, "Your love for one another will prove to the world that you are my disciples" (John 13:35). In his letter to the Romans, Paul prayed that the believers in Rome would "live in complete harmony with each other." Only when believers live that way will they "join together with one voice, giving praise and glory to God, the Father of our Lord Jesus Christ."

Think what an impact the church could have on a skeptical – but watching – world if we could live in harmony as the Bible teaches. In Jesus' final prayer for His followers, He had prayed for unity, saying, "May they experience such perfect unity that the world will know that you sent me and that you love them as much as you love me" (John 17:23).

Perfect unity – or complete harmony, as Paul called it – doesn't mean that, like automatons, all Christians will agree on everything. Try getting everyone at your church to agree on anything – it won't happen. But too many Christians are caught up in so much nitpicking and infighting that they can't accomplish anything for God in the world. We must learn to pick our battles and seek first and foremost to live in harmony. Only then can we truly give praise and glory to God.

*Pray for your church – that its members (including you)
will learn what it means to have complete harmony
in order to be a positive witness in your community.*

HOLD ON TO TRUTH

*Watch out for people who cause divisions and upset people's faith
by teaching things contrary to what you have been taught. Stay away from them.
Such people are not serving Christ our Lord; they are serving their own personal
interests. By smooth talk and glowing words they deceive innocent people.*

ROMANS 16:17-18

*A*t the same time that we should be willing to allow for variety in the nonessentials of the faith, we should be very firm about what constitutes the essentials. Paul warned the believers in Rome of this very thing. Teachers would come in causing divisions and upsetting people's faith. The key issue? The teaching would be "contrary to" what the Roman believers had been taught.

It's popular nowadays to be open-minded. Many teachers want to claim that new knowledge has been discovered, that new gospels have been found, that Jesus really wasn't who we originally thought. They will make those who believe God's Word as it has stood for two thousand years feel like idiots for being so narrow and blind to this new truth.

Don't fall for it. Paul saw it coming and warned the believers to stay away from those teachers and to hang on to the truth. Indeed with tears he had warned the leaders of the church in Ephesus, "I know that false teachers, like vicious wolves, will come in among you after I leave, not sparing the flock. Even some men from your own group will rise up and distort the truth in order to draw a following. Watch out!" (Acts 20:29-31). False teachers have been around since the church was first formed, and they will continue to cause trouble until Jesus comes back and shows them for who they are.

Hang on to the truth in Scripture. Then you won't have to worry about being deceived.

*You hold the truth in your hands.
Let it always be your guide.*

Day 186

TIME OUT!

*I appeal to you, dear brothers and sisters, by the authority of our
Lord Jesus Christ, to live in harmony with each other. Let there be no divisions
in the church. Rather, be of one mind, united in thought and purpose.*

1 CORINTHIANS 1:10

Paul wrote this letter in response to questions brought to him by a delegation from Corinth while Paul was at Ephesus. Clearly this was a gifted church (as noted by Paul's commendation in verse 7 that they had every gift they needed), but their conflicts centered around those very gifts. Instead of using their gifts to evangelize and stand strong for the faith in their pagan surroundings, the Corinthian believers were caught up in arguing about who had the more important gifts. Not only that, they were choosing their favorite teachers and, like so many groupies, were following after the one they favored. Paul called a halt to the infighting.

The rest of this letter focuses on helping the believers to see that gifts mean nothing without love, that all gifts are valued and needed, and that the teachers themselves were not in competition; instead, they had a united message.

The Corinthian church doesn't sound all that different from some churches today. Too many are so busy arguing among themselves that they're no good for building the Kingdom. Paul appeals to us all to be in harmony, to let there be no divisions, to be of one mind, united in thought and purpose. It's a tall order, but if we want to be effective for Christ in this world, we need to fulfill it.

*Is your church unified or divided by infighting?
What can you do to be a part of the solution?*

THE MIND OF CHRIST

For, "Who can know the Lord's thoughts? Who knows enough to teach him?"
But we understand these things, for we have the mind of Christ.
1 CORINTHIANS 2:16

I f you've ever traveled to a foreign country, you know why it's "foreign" – at least to you. The language is incomprehensible. Bills and coins seem like play money. You can easily find yourself embarrassed by messing up on a particular custom. You might shake hands with the wrong hand, or not eat your food correctly, or drive on the wrong side of the road. If you don't know the culture, you can't understand it. But once you immerse yourself in a new culture and learn about it, then all of those things don't seem strange anymore. Traveling back to that land is comfortable because everything makes sense.

Paul was saying something similar in 1 Corinthians 2. Becoming a believer is like entering a new culture – and it's foreign to us sinners. We don't know anything about the Lord or what He wants from us, so we have to immerse ourselves in this Christian culture and learn about it. We read the Bible in order to understand how we should live. We go to church and watch how others walk with Jesus.

Even more than that, the Holy Spirit gives us "the mind of Christ" so that our Christian walk is not in a foreign land, but is comfortable and familiar as we know God better and better. That precious gift helps us understand what God desires as we traverse through this world on our way to heaven!

What does it mean to you today
that you have "the mind of Christ"?

MOLDED BY THY HAND

Here, Lord, I abandon myself to Thee.
I have tried in every way I could think of to manage myself,
and to make myself what I know I ought to be,
but have always failed.
Now I give it up to Thee. Do Thou take entire possession of me.
Work in me all the good pleasure of Thy will.
Mold and fashion me into such a vessel as seems good to Thee.
I leave myself in Thy hands, and I believe Thou wilt,
according to Thy promise, make me into a vessel
unto Thine honor, sanctified, and meet for the Master's use,
and prepared unto every good work.
Amen.

Hannah Whitall Smith

Day 189

MY PRAYER FOR TRANSFORMATION

_____

_____

_____

_____

_____

_____

_____

_____

_____

The same Jesus who turned water into wine can transform
your home, your life, your family, and your future.
He is still in the miracle-working business,
and His business is the business of transformation.

Adrian Rogers

ARE YOU ACTING YOUR SPIRITUAL AGE?

I planted the seed in your hearts, and Apollos watered it, but it was God who made it grow.

1 CORINTHIANS 3:6

Did your mother ever tell you, "Act your age"? It was probably during your preteen years when you were struggling to understand what it meant to become an adult and leave childhood behind.

It seems like the Corinthians were having a similar struggle on a spiritual level. They just didn't get how to act their age spiritually. Paul used several metaphors to make it clear to them: Quit being babies. Stop drinking milk from a bottle. Move on to solid food. Paul was frustrated with their childish behavior. Instead of concentrating on evangelizing the city, the believers were arguing over who was the better evangelist: Paul or Apollos.

"Who cares?" Paul said. "We are both field workers for the Lord, each with his own task. I plant the seeds. Apollos waters them. Together, we both desire that these kernels of faith will sprout roots and mature into a great harvest. Then someone else will come along and nurture what God has caused to grow."

Just as infants develop into adults, so will new believers gain maturity if they are cared for properly. But how can they strengthen their faith, Paul asks, if others in the church fight like children? We would be wise to act our spiritual age toward believers and nonbelievers alike.

How mature are you as a believer? In what ways do you act (or not act) your spiritual age with those around you? What might need to change?

TO BE SERVED OR TO SERVE

*So look at Apollos and me as mere servants of Christ
who have been put in charge of explaining God's mysteries.*

1 CORINTHIANS 4:1

Servant. Most people don't like the sound of that word. It brings to mind notions of subservience and humiliation. Even Christians can bristle at the idea because they believe that to be a servant puts you in the category of "loser." If you have to serve, you just haven't made it in society. Those at the top get served; they have servants. That's where most of us want to be. This is exactly what the believers in Corinth were thinking. They were putting themselves on pedestals thinking they were wiser than one another, had better spiritual gifts than each other, and so sat in judgment of each other. Obviously this caused friction.

Along came Paul who echoed the attitude of Christ Jesus who had said, "For even the Son of Man came not to be served but to serve others and to give his life as a ransom for many" (Mark 10:45). Jesus turned everything upside down, suggesting that those who want to be leaders in the Kingdom should be the servants of all (Matt. 20:26).

Being a servant means simply allowing God to use you in whatever way He chooses. That very willingness to follow Him and do what it takes to help others toward salvation is true servanthood. When you can set aside your pride for the sake of the Kingdom, you have become a true servant.

*Do you desire to serve or to be served?
How can you become a true servant of the King?*

TABLOID NEWS

I can hardly believe the report about the sexual immorality going on among you – something that even pagans don't do. I am told that a man in your church is living in sin with his stepmother.

1 CORINTHIANS 5:1

Gasp! You would think that Paul had stumbled across a tabloid in the checkout line of the local street market. There, in large, bold letters, the headline read: "Christian Has Affair with Stepmother." It should have made everyone in Corinth blush, especially the Christians. But the man was continuing to worship in the church, and the believers didn't seem fazed in the slightest.

The godly response would have been grief, shock, and – yes – judgment of this sin. But the believers just let it happen. Perhaps they were so conditioned to their sinful society that it didn't seem to be that out of the ordinary. Perhaps they felt that with their own past indiscretions, they dared not make a big deal about this man's sin. Maybe they knew him personally and thought that, in his situation, being with his stepmother was a good thing. Who knows what they were thinking, but Paul told them, in no uncertain terms, what they needed to both think and do: Don't delay. Remove the offender from the fellowship in hopes that seeing the seriousness of his sin will cause him to repent.

By today's standards of tolerance and inclusion, Paul's behavior may seem extreme. Why was Paul so harsh? He wanted the believers to see that such sins among the believers, left unchecked, would both polarize and paralyze the church. A little yeast soon permeates the whole batch of dough. A small sickness can eventually kill the entire body.

Ask God to give your church leaders courage.
Pray that they can make the tough decisions
when God leads them to do so.

DON'T THEY GET IT?

And don't you realize that if a man joins himself to a prostitute,
he becomes one body with her? For the Scriptures say, "The two are united
into one." But the person who is joined to the Lord is one spirit with him.
1 CORINTHIANS 6:16-17

P aul was mad. Though he had established the Corinthian church and the believers there had gotten off to a good start, they were slipping into some pretty bad habits. It was time to respond with some pretty strong words.

Lawsuits were first on his agenda. Christians in Corinth were suing each other over personal disputes, taking the matter to court instead of to their own church leaders. You can almost hear the anger in Paul's voice: "Don't you get it? We need to settle our disputes like brothers, not in worldly courts. Otherwise, we are going to become even more divided, and our witness among the non-Christians in Corinth will suffer."

The believers' ongoing immoral sexual behavior was also on Paul's list. Sexual immorality was very prevalent in the Corinthian culture, and so he admonished believers to be different from those around them. "Run from sexual sin!" Paul admonished (1 Cor. 6:18). Nothing affects the body like such sin.

Believers should live differently from unbelievers. We should see our bodies as temples where God Himself dwells. When we do that, we see ourselves – and our activities and actions – in a whole new light.

Your body is God's temple.
How are you honoring God with your body?

Day 194

DEAR PAUL

*So I say to those who aren't married and to widows – it's better to
stay unmarried, just as I am. But if they can't control themselves, they
should go ahead and marry. It's better to marry than to burn with lust.*
1 CORINTHIANS 7:8-9

I f there had been such a thing as an advice column for believers in a daily
newspaper in New Testament times, and Paul was the columnist, he
might have received a letter like this:

*Dear Paul, I'm not sure that I want to get married, but I don't like the idea
of being alone. And all I can think about is being with my girlfriend.
What should I do?*
Signed, Confused in Corinth

Paul's response no doubt would have been as direct as any advice
columnist of our day. But it would have been better because he would have
gotten his inspiration from God. Paul might have answered the letter writer
this way:

*Dear Confused, It's better not to get married because you can do more
for the Lord. But if you find yourself thinking more about marriage than the
things of God, find yourself a spouse.*
Signed, Paul

According to Paul, it was better for the unmarried to remain that way because they could get more done for Christ without having concern for a spouse
and children. However, if they didn't have self-control, they should marry.

If you're single, don't devote all your energies toward finding a spouse.
Instead, devote your energies to God, but let Him know the desires of your
heart – and ask Him either to change them or to help you find a mate. If
you're married, then you know your responsibilities to God and to your
family, and you will need to keep those in correct perspective.

*Ask God to help you find contentment with your
current marital status and to serve Him as you should.*

A PRAYER FOR COURAGE

Even though I walk
through the darkest valley,
I will fear no evil,
for You are with me;
Your rod and Your staff,
they comfort me.
You prepare a table before me
in the presence of my enemies.
You anoint my head with oil;
my cup overflows.
Surely Your goodness and love will follow me
all the days of my life,
and I will dwell in the house of the LORD forever.

Psalm 23:4-6

Day 196

MY PRAYER FOR COURAGE

_____

_____

_____

_____

_____

_____

_____

_____

_____

_____

_____

Do not ask for fears to be removed;
ask for courage equal to the fears.

Jack Hyles

TO EAT OR NOT TO EAT

It's true that we can't win God's approval by what we eat. We don't lose anything if we don't eat it, and we don't gain anything if we do. But you must be careful so that your freedom does not cause others with a weaker conscience to stumble.

1 CORINTHIANS 8:8-9

Here Paul addressed the next question brought by the delegation from Corinth "about food that has been offered to idols" (1 Cor. 8:1). The issue was that meat purchased in the marketplace often came from animals that had been offered to an idol. Some Corinthian believers worried that their food was tainted and thought they shouldn't eat it. Paul told the believers not to worry. The gods to whom the meat was offered didn't even exist, and therefore they could have no effect on it.

However, the believers needed to begin to think beyond just themselves. As in any church today, the Corinthian church combined strong believers who could eat such meat without blinking, and other believers who really were bothered by the whole scenario. They might *know* intellectually that the meat was untainted, but they still couldn't feel comfortable eating it. So to those strong believers, Paul said, "Be careful. Go ahead and eat that meat from the marketplace. However, if you're having people over for dinner and among them is one of these weak believers, don't make it tough on that person. Be sensitive. Don't serve the meat. You don't want to cause the weaker one to go against his conscience and then stumble in his faith. By being sensitive, you're not hurting yourself any, and you're helping that person a whole lot."

We may know we're free, but we need to be sensitive to our fellow believers.

What would you be willing to forgo
so as not to trip up other weaker believers?

A FAIR WAGE

*Don't you realize that those who work in the temple get their meals from
the offerings brought to the temple? And those who serve at the altar get a share
of the sacrificial offerings. In the same way, the Lord ordered that those who
preach the Good News should be supported by those who benefit from it.*

1 CORINTHIANS 9:13-14

A fair day's wage for a fair day's work. It's an old saying, but earning an
income for our efforts is how we support ourselves and our families.
We expect to be fairly compensated for the work we do – or at least to get
paid what we agreed upon when we were hired!

Like anyone else, Paul needed money to live and pay for his missionary
journeys. Those trips by sea and by land weren't free! He didn't ask for
money when he preached and he didn't ask for money from the churches he
planted. He didn't want to appear to be "in it for the money." He didn't want
anything to hinder the gospel message. In fact, for much of his ministry, he
worked making tents in order to support himself (Acts 18:3). Later, Paul
counted on the churches he planted to help support his ministry. That was
the only way for the work to be done. In his letter to the believers in Philippi,
he thanked them for their generous support (Phil. 4:14-19).

And it continues today. Those who are called to full-time service need to
be cared for by those they serve. Your pastor needs to be fairly compensated –
and you need to regularly give to your church so that can happen. The
missionaries your church sends out need your help as well. Be willing to give
to those who minister to you and around the world for Christ.

*Are you regularly giving to your church?
As part of that body, you need to be part of
supporting it financially in order for it to function.*

ESCAPE ROUTE

The temptations in your life are no different from what others experience.
And God is faithful. He will not allow the temptation to be more than you can stand.
When you are tempted, he will show you a way out so that you can endure.

1 CORINTHIANS 10:13

Temptation comes in various forms: obvious enticements to break the law, cheat, or forsake a commitment; subtle pressure to flirt with wrong, bend the rules, or delay doing right; nearly invisible urgings to gratify self, shift values, or take the easy way. Through the constant pull of our sinful nature and the consistent attacks of our enemy, Satan, we find ourselves tempted all day, every day. Facing such powerful and continual influences, we may consider giving up and giving in.

Temptation – and sin – are very real. But God is more powerful ... and He is "faithful," promising to keep temptation from overwhelming us and to provide an alternative course of action, a way of escape, a "way out." It just takes willingness and self-control to look away from the temptation so that you can see where that "way out" is.

When you are tempted, thank God for trusting you that much – He knows you can bear it and He promises not to allow it to become more than you can withstand. So even if you feel overwhelmed, you're not. God knows you are strong enough not to succumb. Ask Him to show you His way out. And then run for it!

Take temptation seriously. When it occurs,
be ready for it by knowing that the way out
is right in front of you if you're willing to see it.

TAKE, EAT, AND REMEMBER

That is why you should examine yourself before eating the bread
and drinking the cup. For if you eat the bread or drink the cup without honoring
the body of Christ, you are eating and drinking God's judgment upon yourself.

1 CORINTHIANS 11:28-29

Picture this: There's a potluck at your church where those who bring the most food eat the most food. They behave as if they're guests of honor and indulge themselves. Meanwhile, the homeless have to wait until the end and eat whatever might be left over.

This is the modern-day version of what the Corinthians were doing at their gatherings to fellowship and remember Christ's death and resurrection. When the congregation met together for a feast in connection with the Lord's Supper, everyone was supposed to be loving and generous, sharing with one another. But the rich weren't sharing their food with the poor. Then the "haves" had the nerve to celebrate communion with the "have-nots," remembering Jesus' sacrifice for them without being willing to sacrifice for others.

Paul warned the wealthier believers to take the sacrament of the Lord's Supper seriously. While we don't generally have potluck dinners as part of celebrating Communion, the principles still apply. Whenever we take these sacraments, we must do so thoughtfully, examining ourselves for any unconfessed sin or bad attitude. We need to repent of those so that we can come to Christ with due reverence and respect. This is a solemn occasion, a time of remembering what Jesus did for us. When we take part in it, we are joining with believers all over the world who also are waiting in expectation "until he comes again" (1 Cor. 11:26).

The next time you celebrate Communion – the Lord's Supper –
do so with the respect and reverence that celebration deserves.

GIFT GIVING

A spiritual gift is given to each of us so we can help each other.
1 CORINTHIANS 12:7

Much discussion (and even more conflict) has surrounded the biblical doctrine of spiritual gifts. But this much is clear: God has given every believer at least one gift. And when those supernatural endowments are used to build up the rest of the body, God works in miraculous ways!

Unfortunately, in Corinth, the spiritual gifts had become cause for competitiveness and arguing. Paul wanted to make clear that the gifts were never meant for people to use for their own enjoyment or to draw attention to themselves. We don't have gifts so that we can feel good about ourselves or show up other people. God gives us gifts to use in building up one another and His Kingdom.

As a body needs all of its parts in order to function well, so the body of believers needs all its different people with all their different gifts to have maximum impact on the world. Whatever your gift is – be it large or small, extremely visible or behind the scenes – it is needed!

Instead of complaining about the gifts you do not possess or comparing yourself to others, thank God for graciously equipping you to serve a vital role in the building of His Kingdom. Ask Him to show you your gifts and then to show you opportunities to use them.

Gifts are for giving! Ask God where you need to be giving your gifts.

A PRAYER OF DEVOTION

Increase our faith, O merciful Father,
that we do not swerve at any time from Thine heavenly word,
but augment in us hope and love,
with a careful keeping of all Thy commandments,
that no hardness of heart, no hypocrisy,
no concupiscence of the eyes,
nor enticements of the world,
do draw us away from Thine obedience.
Amen.

John Knox

Day 203

MY PRAYER OF DEVOTION

_____

_____

_____

_____

_____

_____

_____

_____

_____

_____

_____

"Where your treasure is, there your heart will be also."

Matthew 6:21

TRUE LOVE

If I could speak all the languages of earth and of angels, but didn't love others,
I would only be a noisy gong or a clanging cymbal. If I had the gift of prophecy,
and if I understood all of God's secret plans and possessed all knowledge, and if
I had such faith that I could move mountains, but didn't love others, I would
be nothing. If I gave everything I have to the poor and even sacrificed my body,
I could boast about it; but if I didn't love others, I would have gained nothing.

1 CORINTHIANS 13:1-3

*A*fter discussing the spiritual gifts in 1 Corinthians 12, Paul moved into this chapter explaining that no matter how great our gifts, they are virtually worthless if we do not use them with love. While our gifts – verbal skills, breadth of knowledge, generosity, singing ability, computer skills, or even wisdom beyond our years – may impress others, they will accomplish absolutely nothing for God if they are not used with humility and with love.

When we use our gifts, we must be willing to love those to whom we minister. And what is the test of love? Paul went on to explain that when we're loving, we must be patient and kind, not jealous, boastful, proud, or rude. We don't demand our own way. We're not irritable. We're not keeping track when people wrong us. We don't rejoice about injustice, but we rejoice whenever the truth wins out. We don't give up or lose faith. We're always hopeful, enduring through every circumstance.

When you ask God for a place of service and gifts to exercise, ask Him also to help you express them out of love. If you are already aware of certain gifts or abilities that God has given, ask yourself how others have experienced the love of Christ when you have used your gifts. Make that your purpose.

Do the characteristics of love listed above describe you?
Where do you need to improve?

THE PROPER USE OF GIFTS

*It's the same for you. If you speak to people in words they
don't understand, how will they know what you are saying?
You might as well be talking into empty space.*

1 CORINTHIANS 14:9

The early church in Corinth was experiencing a communications meltdown. Some members were speaking in tongues and the rest of the congregation couldn't understand them. An interpreter wasn't in the assembly to interpret what was being said. Confusion reigned.

While speaking in tongues is a legitimate gift of the Holy Spirit, the Corinthians saw it as a sign of superiority. Those who had it felt that they were more spiritual than those who didn't. They would speak in the services, sort of showing off, but when no one could interpret, nothing was accomplished.

Paul explained that speaking in tongues was fine but that the believers should refrain from doing so in worship gatherings unless someone else with the gift of interpretation was also there and could interpret the words and so edify everyone else. Otherwise, that person is holding his own personal worship service with the Lord, and that is better done in private. In the end, it is far better for all of the believers if they seek to excel in the gifts that help others. Paul said that while he himself spoke in tongues, he "would rather speak five understandable words to help others than ten thousand words in an unknown language" (1 Cor. 14:19).

When spiritual gifts are properly used, they help everyone in the church.

*Do you know what your spiritual gifts are?
How are you using them to build up God's Kingdom?*

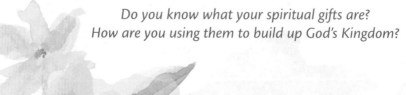

LIVE FOR TOMORROW

But let me reveal to you a wonderful secret. We will not all die,
but we will all be transformed! It will happen in a moment,
in the blink of an eye, when the last trumpet is blown.
For when the trumpet sounds, those who have died will be raised
to live forever. And we who are living will also be transformed.

1 CORINTHIANS 15:51-52

Can you imagine receiving a long and complicated letter like the one we call the book of 1 Corinthians? You've read answers to difficult questions – and some difficult answers to your questions. If you were a new believer living in Corinth, you might have wondered if this Christianity was really worth the trouble.

But Paul went on to explain the whole point of this Christian life. It's not about having a trouble-free life on earth (in fact, Christianity often seems to invite trouble). It's not about joining a club or secret society. It's not about setting yourself apart as superior to everyone around you. No, the bottom line is what eternity looks like – starting from the moment you received Christ as Savior. It's about the promise of the resurrection. After all, Paul wrote, "If Christ has not been raised, then your faith is useless ... And if our hope in Christ is only for this life, we are more to be pitied than anyone in the world" (1 Cor. 15:17, 19). But because Christ was raised from the dead (a historical fact) and because He Himself said that "since I live, you also will live" (John 14:19), we can look forward to eternity with Christ as an undeniable fact.

So as we live our days, we have more to look forward to than just "Let's feast and drink, for tomorrow we die!" (1 Cor. 15:32). We live to please our Savior, knowing that one day we will be with Him forever.

Live today with the knowledge that you
have already set your plans for eternity.

WIDE-OPEN DOOR

There is a wide-open door for a great work here, although many oppose me.
1 CORINTHIANS 16:9

Paul's attitude is commendable. While many of us would see opposition against us as indication that "the door must be closed to our ability to minister," Paul saw a wide-open door in spite of the fact that many people were opposing him and his ministry.

The "here" to which Paul was referring was the city of Ephesus, where Paul was preaching and teaching when he wrote this letter. We only need to take a quick read of Acts 19 to discover the type of opposition Paul was up against. Ephesus was not an easy ministry, but Paul felt called to stay because the door for great work was wide open.

What about you? Do you tend to see setbacks, difficulties, and opposition as clear indications that certain doors are closed to you? It takes great discernment and prayer to determine when such things mean to give up and when they mean to keep going with renewed perseverance.

You can be sure that whatever you do for the Lord will bring to bear the forces of evil against it. We are in a spiritual battle and must be willing to go where God sends us, even when it doesn't seem to make sense.

*Where is God sending you today? Where are the doors
wide open for you to bring the Good News?*

PASS IT ON

All praise to God, the Father of our Lord Jesus Christ.
God is our merciful Father and the source of all comfort.
He comforts us in all our troubles so that we can comfort others.
When they are troubled, we will be able to give them the same comfort
God has given us. For the more we suffer for Christ, the more
God will shower us with his comfort through Christ.

2 CORINTHIANS 1:3-5

How often have you noticed that soon after you receive comfort for some troubling situation, you encounter someone else facing a similar situation? God leads us to these people, for the comfort we provide for them seems more credible because they know we have "been there."

As Paul began this second letter to the church in Corinth, he knew he would need to say some extremely difficult things in order to get this church back on track. This church was not facing much external pressure, but inner turmoil abounded, as we discovered in Paul's first letter to the Corinthians – opposing sides vying for their viewpoints, Christians suing each other, problems during the fellowship meals, for example. The believers needed to deal with their problems, face their difficult situations, and ask forgiveness for their sins. Then God would comfort them. Paul had no doubt that the Corinthian believers would emerge strong and faithful and would, in turn, be able to pass along comfort to other believers.

How has God given you comfort in times of difficulty? Whom has He sent your way to help you through a difficult time? To whom have you given comfort? Thank God that you can give and receive comfort as part of His body here on earth.

How might you be able to comfort someone today?

TEACH ME TO PRAY

Lord, I know not what I ought to ask of Thee;
Thou only knows what I need;
Thou loves me better than I know how to love myself.
O Father! Give to Thy child that which
he himself knows not how to ask.
I dare not ask either for crosses or consolations;
I simply present myself before Thee, I open my heart to Thee.
Behold my needs which I know not myself;
see and do according to Thy tender mercy.
Smite, or heal; depress me, or raise me up;
I adore all Thy purposes without knowing them;
I am silent; I offer myself in sacrifice; I yield myself to Thee;
I would have no other desire than to accomplish Thy will.
Teach me to pray. Pray Thyself in me. Amen.

François Fénelon

Day 210

MY PRAYER FOR GUIDANCE IN PRAYER

_____

_____

_____

_____

_____

_____

_____

_____

_____

_____

Groanings which cannot be uttered are often
prayers which cannot be refused.

Charles Spurgeon

VICTORY MARCH

*But thank God! He has made us his captives and continues
to lead us along in Christ's triumphal procession. Now he uses us
to spread the knowledge of Christ everywhere, like a sweet perfume.*

2 CORINTHIANS 2:14

Ancient Roman generals returning from a victory in a distant land would parade down the main streets with the spoils of battle – including a throng of captives – in a great triumphal procession. The captives had been taken from the distant land and would be sold into servitude.

In this prayer of thanksgiving, Paul used this image to thank Christ for defeating the evil forces of this world. He portrayed Christ as the leader of the victory parade and believers, "his captives," being led along behind Him. Like those captives of Rome, we were once part of an enemy army but have been taken away and brought to a new home. For us, however, this is a happy place to be: We celebrate, for we have been taken from Satan's army and made captives of Christ. Our service? "To spread the knowledge of Christ everywhere, like a sweet perfume."

In the end, Christ will indeed lead a victory parade the likes of which the world has never seen. "Then I saw heaven opened, and a white horse was standing there. Its rider was named Faithful and True ... The armies of heaven, dressed in the finest of pure white linen, followed him on white horses" (Rev. 19:11, 14). The parade is coming! Don't miss it!

Thank God today that you are included in Christ's victory parade.

RECOMMENDATION LETTERS

Clearly, you are a letter from Christ showing the result of our ministry among you. This "letter" is written not with pen and ink, but with the Spirit of the living God. It is carved not on tablets of stone, but on human hearts.

2 CORINTHIANS 3:3

When you look for a new job, you need a standout résumé and glowing letters of recommendation. Obviously, you want to make a good impression, but you're also careful to be truthful. Unfortunately, that's not always the case in the world of job hunting. Sometimes, the résumé doesn't tell the whole truth and the recommendations don't give the full picture. Many an employer has been duped by employees who turned out not to be all that they (and others) claimed them to be.

In Paul's day, a letter of recommendation from a reputable source carried great weight for the person who wanted to travel and gain a hearing. Unfortunately, some false teachers were carrying such letters and had gained access to the Corinthian church.

Paul found himself having to defend himself against the false teachers to the church he had planted! So he pointed out that the letters the false teachers had shown were faulty; the letters Paul had were the Corinthian believers themselves – letters written "not with pen and ink, but with the Spirit of the living God." He needed nothing else to prove the truthfulness of his message; their very lives did it every day.

What does your life say about your faith? As a representative of your family, your church, your faith all over the world, what kind of "letter of recommendation" do you bring?

How will you represent Christ today?

LIKE POTS OF CLAY

*We now have this light shining in our hearts, but we ourselves
are like fragile clay jars containing this great treasure. This makes
it clear that our great power is from God, not from ourselves.*

2 CORINTHIANS 4:7

In the spring, you may decide to plant some flowers in containers for your porch or balcony. You go to the local garden shop to find stylish pots made from plastic or an array of ceramic pots beautifully hand painted. But your least expensive and still functional option is to choose pots made from clay. Such pots have been around for centuries. In Paul's day, these inexpensive containers held all kinds of items from the common to the very valuable.

That is what Paul says we are – fragile clay jars. Yet God has chosen to place all of His power and glory (so thoroughly described in 2 Corinthians 3) into us. We are the vessels that He has chosen to use to display Himself to the world.

Why would God do this? Why put His own great glory into such imperfect, flawed, breakable vessels? Why entrust us with the message of salvation when we might just mess it up in our imperfect, flawed, and broken manner? Why send us imperfect, flawed people into the world as His representatives?

Why? Because God loves to confound the wisdom of the world. He loves to do things that don't make sense to our imperfect and flawed minds. He loves to take weak vessels and make them strong, because then there is no doubt where that strength comes from!

*You are a clay jar filled with priceless treasure.
Thank God for what He can and will do through you.*

NEWS WORTH SHARING

Either way, Christ's love controls us. Since we believe that Christ died for all,
we also believe that we have all died to our old life. He died for everyone
so that those who receive his new life will no longer live for themselves.

2 CORINTHIANS 5:14-15

In what ways does the love of Christ control us? The key word here (*control*) can be translated "compel" or "urge on." The sense is almost "Christ's love *propels* us!" As Paul put it, the compelling force of Christ's love in us ought to have such a huge effect that we actually die to our old lives and no longer live for ourselves. We are people on a mission. When Christ's love controls us, we will be driven not by guilt or anxiety but by compassion. We will be so humbled that the news reached us that we will genuinely desire to share it with others as well as we can.

The news we share is that out of His great love, Jesus "died for everyone" so that we might know that there's more to life than what we see here and now. That's a message the world needs to hear – the neighbor who struggles with depression, the spouse who's been deeply hurt, the employee who's been downsized, the manager suddenly unemployed because of a company merger. Life brings joys and sorrows, and the people who focus only on those will find themselves empty indeed.

The Good News is that because Christ died, we are promised abundant lives here and a future in eternity with Him who died for us. That's news worth sharing!

So who are you living for? Is it all about you, or all about Him?

WHOSE TEAM ARE YOU ON?

*Don't team up with those who are unbelievers. How can righteousness
be a partner with wickedness? How can light live with darkness?*
2 CORINTHIANS 6:14

These difficult words may make us wonder how we can possibly live in our world. We're surrounded by unbelievers, by darkness. Are we supposed to hide within our Christian circles lest we be dirtied? That's not what Paul was saying. In fact, in other places he explained that Christians ought not be isolated from nonbelievers (1 Cor. 5:9-11) and that believers need to stay with their unbelieving spouses (1 Cor. 7:12-13). The only way to have an effect – in the world or in a marriage – is to be light shining in the darkness.

Paul's point was not separation from unbelievers; instead, he was advising against "teaming up" with them. Other Bible versions use the phrase "yoked together," which portrays a farmer harnessing two animals together to pull a plow or a cart. It was against God's law to yoke together completely different animals – such as an ox and a mule – because the plow would be pulled unevenly, the cart spilled, and perhaps the weaker animal hurt. Because believers and unbelievers are so different, to team up (in a business partnership, marriage, or other long-standing situation) will only lead to disaster, for their goals, aspirations, focus, and motives may be completely at odds.

Be in the world for that is your mission field, but do not "team up" with unbelievers in ways that would cause you to compromise your faith.

*Are you teaming up with unbelievers
in ways that are requiring you to compromise
your faith? If so, what do you need to do?*

A PRAYER FOR MERCY

O Jesus, poor and abject, unknown and despised,
have mercy upon me,
and let me not be ashamed to follow Thee.
O Jesus, hated, calumniated, and persecuted,
have mercy upon me,
and let me not be afraid to come after Thee.
O Jesus, betrayed and sold at a vile price, have mercy upon me,
and make me content to be as my Master.
O Jesus, insulted, mocked, and spit upon, have mercy upon me,
and let me run with patience the race set before me.
O Jesus, hanging on the accursed tree, bowing the head,
giving up the ghost, have mercy upon me,
and conform my whole soul to Thy holy, humble,
and suffering Spirit. Amen.

John Wesley

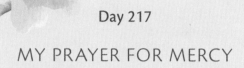

Day 217

MY PRAYER FOR MERCY

_____
_____
_____
_____
_____
_____
_____
_____
_____
_____
_____
_____

Taking up my "cross" means a life
voluntarily surrendered to God.

A. W. Pink

TRUTH CAN HURT – AND HELP

I am not sorry that I sent that severe letter to you, though I was sorry at first,
for I know it was painful to you for a little while. Now I am glad I sent it, not because
it hurt you, but because the pain caused you to repent and change your ways.

2 CORINTHIANS 7:8-9

The "severe letter" to which Paul referred was probably not 1 Corinthians, but another letter written between 1 and 2 Corinthians (now lost to us) that apparently included some severe reprimands. In fact, that letter had been so difficult that Paul had written "in great anguish, with a troubled heart and many tears" (2 Cor. 2:4). Paul had sent the letter on its way, but then must have second-guessed himself, probably going over lines in his head and wondering if he should have written some parts differently. But the letter had been effective and had caused the Corinthian believers to repent and change their ways, so now Paul was glad he had sent it, for change had come.

What do you do when someone challenges you, reprimands you, or points out some sin in your life? Do you get defensive or angry? Do you shut that person out? How about taking the time to think about what was said and truthfully look at your own life? Paul loved the Corinthians and couldn't let them continue in their wrong behavior; the Corinthians knew Paul loved them, and so they took his words to heart.

Few and far between are the friends who love us enough to be willing to help us to become better people. Thank God when such friends come into your life.

Which of your friends is the kind of person
you need to listen to? Which friend speaks words
of wisdom that will help you be the best you can be?

VAST RICHES

You know the generous grace of our Lord Jesus Christ. Though he was rich,
yet for your sakes he became poor, so that by his poverty he could make you rich.
2 CORINTHIANS 8:9

Jesus turns the values of the world upside down. He taught that those who lose their lives will find them (Matt. 10:39); the first will be last and the last, first (Matt. 20:16); and those who humble themselves will be exalted (Matt. 23:12). And this passage teaches that through Jesus' poverty, we can become rich.

In contrast, worldly values include winning, being first, and being exalted. In addition, the world's idea of being "rich" involves money, possessions, and power.

No wonder the world finds it difficult to understand and accept Christ. To Jesus, true riches include forgiveness, peace, purpose, and eternal life.

The Lord Jesus Christ left "riches" – His power and the glory of heaven – to become "poor" – living as a human being, suffering scorn and abuse, and dying on the cross. Now, because of what Jesus has done, we can share in God's wealth.

Comparing yourself to the world's standard, you may not measure up, and you may feel insignificant, a failure. Yet, according to God's standard, you stand tall, a glorious success. Regardless of the size of your bank account, house, or pile of earthly goods, you are rich in God's grace. Stack God's riches next to the world's – the difference is infinite.

Take inventory of your spiritual riches
and recognize that you are wealthy indeed!

GIVE CHEERFULLY

*Remember this – a farmer who plants only a few seeds will get a small crop.
But the one who plants generously will get a generous crop. You must
each decide in your heart how much to give. And don't give reluctantly
or in response to pressure. "For God loves a person who gives cheerfully".*

2 CORINTHIANS 9:6-7

Money can be a touchy topic, but Paul jumped into it with both feet as he reminded the Corinthian believers of a pledge they had made to help the suffering church in Jerusalem.

The Corinthians had gotten off to a good start. In fact, their enthusiasm had been contagious – and even had encouraged other churches in Macedonia to help (2 Cor. 9:1-2). But now the Corinthians' enthusiasm for the project had waned. Paul had advised in his first letter: "On the first day of each week, you should each put aside a portion of the money you have earned. Don't wait until I get there and then try to collect it all at once" (1 Cor. 16:2). Since that didn't appear to be happening, Paul was sending Titus and two other men to encourage the Corinthians to give cheerfully and to be ready with their gift when Paul arrived.

We don't like to think about it, but money is vital to Christianity – we need it to support our churches and our missionaries, to take care of our buildings, to pay those who serve us, and to simply give to those who are in need. If we have, we should give, for all that we have has been lent to us by God anyway. If we don't have much, we should still give even a little as a constant reminder of our dependence on God.

*Are you a cheerful giver? Do you feel that you're
giving in proportion to what God has given you?*

Day 221

TO WHOM SHOULD YOU LISTEN?

As the Scriptures say, "If you want to boast, boast only about the LORD."
When people commend themselves, it doesn't count for much.
The important thing is for the Lord to commend them.

2 CORINTHIANS 10:17-18

Often the best way to get a hearing when you have to say something difficult is to start out talking about everything that's gone *well* before you have to talk about what's gone *wrong*. In essence, that's what Paul was doing. The first nine chapters of this letter were encouraging and uplifting; here at chapter 10, the tone shifts. Paul found himself reduced to having to defend his authority because false teachers had infiltrated the church and were undermining Paul.

So Paul fired back, reminding the believers of who he was and what he had done for them. In this section of the letter, he pointed out that he was preaching with authority (2 Cor. 10:8) the gospel Christ had given him (2 Cor. 11:4); he wasn't preaching to become rich (2 Cor. 11:7) or popular (2 Cor. 11:23-25). His focus was on serving the Lord and doing what He called him to do. That alone was his measurement for whether he was a success.

Many voices clamor for our attention. How do we know to whom we should listen? Paul would say, "Stop listening to those who commend themselves based on the world's standards. Listen only to those whom the Lord commends."

Ask God for discernment to know who is worthy of your attention because he or she is speaking the gospel truth.

STANDING STRONG

Are they servants of Christ? I know I sound like a madman, but I have served him far more! I have worked harder, been put in prison more often, been whipped times without number, and faced death again and again.

2 CORINTHIANS 11:23

In marketing, there's such a thing as perceived value, and the more something costs the greater its apparent worth. If an item is free, it usually isn't worth much. False teachers in Corinth were saying that Paul's message wasn't worth anything because the Corinthians paid nothing for it. In those days, it was common to pay a teacher for the value of his teaching. Was Paul's teaching of no value because it was free?

Hardly. Paul loved the Corinthians and didn't want to be a financial burden to them or have them think he was preaching for the money. Would he have allowed himself to be put in prison so often, to be beaten so severely, or to be close to death time and again if he were doing it only for pay and not for devotion to his message? The false apostles had experienced nothing so drastic, yet they had the gall to criticize the real apostle.

Paul had to refute the false teachers, hence his harsh words in this chapter. He had worked too hard and suffered too much to let the church in Corinth be torn apart by them. His preaching about freedom from the law may have been free, but his sacrifices for others had cost him plenty.

Ask God to give you the willingness to stand strong for Him against those who would dilute or deny the Good News.

A PRAYER FOR HELP

Listen to my prayer, O God.
Do not ignore my cry for help!
Please listen and answer me,
for I am overwhelmed by my troubles.
My enemies shout at me,
making loud and wicked threats.
They bring trouble on me
and angrily hunt me down.
My heart pounds in my chest.
Fear and trembling overwhelm me,
and I can't stop shaking.
Oh, that I had wings like a dove;
then I would fly away and rest!
I would fly far away
to the quiet of the wilderness.
How quickly I would escape –
far from this wild storm of hatred.

Psalm 55:1-8

Day 224

MY PRAYER FOR GOD'S HELP

_____
_____
_____
_____
_____
_____
_____
_____
_____
_____
_____

Some people have the power but not the willingness
to help. Others have the willingness but not
the power. God has both.

Lee Roberson

GRACE AND POWER

I was given a thorn in my flesh, a messenger from Satan to torment me and keep me from becoming proud. Three different times I begged the Lord to take it away. Each time he said, "My grace is all you need. My power works best in weakness.".

2 CORINTHIANS 12:7-9

I t's a painful thing to make a request and be told no. It's especially difficult when we come to God with a request that seems to be perfectly in line with His will and we expect to get it. After all, Jesus had said, "Ask me for anything in my name, and I will do it!" (John 14:14).

Surely Paul felt that his request for healing was perfectly in line with God's will; this "thorn" was affecting his ministry. We don't know exactly what this problem was. Since he said it was "in the flesh," it was probably some kind of health issue.

A hint occurs in Paul's letter to the Galatian believers, where he refers to their willingness to give their own eyes to him if they could (Gal. 4:15) and mentions the big letters he wrote in his own hand at the end (Gal. 6:11). So when Paul begged the Lord to take it away, he probably felt that God would do so because that would make Paul much more effective.

But God said no. Through that negative response, Paul recognized heavenly greatness through earthly weakness. God let the thorn remain, telling Paul, "My grace is all you need. My power works best in weakness."

When God says no, He always has a reason and He willingly gives you His grace and power to deal with whatever situation you must face.

To what request has God said no?
Ask Him to make His power work through your weakness.

GOOD-BYE AND LIVE RIGHT

Examine yourselves to see if your faith is genuine. Test yourselves. Surely you know that Jesus Christ is among you; if not, you have failed the test of genuine faith.

2 CORINTHIANS 13:5

Paul was hoping for a special time with the Corinthians on his next visit to Corinth, but that wasn't a sure thing since the believers weren't living right. Legalism and immorality dominated their behavior. So Paul wrote to them before arriving, warning them to change their ways. "Examine yourselves to see if your faith is genuine. Test yourselves." In case there was any doubt, Paul explained the standard: "Be joyful. Grow to maturity. Encourage each other. Live in harmony and peace. Then the God of love and peace will be with you" (2 Cor. 13:11).

How often do we take time for self-examination? In our hurried days, we rarely quiet ourselves long enough to sit before God and think about the genuineness of our faith and to test ourselves against God's desire for us. If we want to please God and have genuine faith, we would do well to ask ourselves, "How joyful am I on any given day? Am I maturing in my faith – or am I at status quo or even sliding backward? Do I offer encouragement to those around me? Are most of my relationships harmonious and peaceful (at least most of the time)?" These responses will help us stay strong and genuine in our faith.

Ask yourself those questions and monitor the genuineness of your faith. Ask God to help you improve in the areas that need improvement.

SHOCKING CHOICE

*I am shocked that you are turning away so soon from God, who called you
to himself through the loving mercy of Christ. You are following a different way
that pretends to be the Good News but is not the Good News at all. You are
being fooled by those who deliberately twist the truth concerning Christ.*

GALATIANS 1:6-7

Would you ever take your new cell phone or your other latest
technological gadget and decide that, since it's working too well,
you'd like to swap it out for a broken one? Of course not. But that's basically
what the new believers in Galatia were doing. After Paul and Barnabas had
a successful ministry at several cities in the province of Galatia (Acts 13:
2–14:28), they were later accused of making Christianity too easy for
Gentiles. Some Jewish Christians thought the Gentile believers should have
to follow all of the Jewish laws and regulations. In a sense, they believed
that Gentiles needed to become Jewish first in order to become Christians.
Paul had preached freedom in Christ; the believers in Galatia wanted to
return to the system of trying to be saved by keeping rules. And Paul was
shocked. Their choice made no sense. The Galatians had deserted the Good
News of grace and freedom in Christ with the message that they had to earn
salvation by their own efforts, which is rather *bad* news.

Thankfully, Paul struck down this lie with a statement as strong as any
he made in the New Testament: "Let God's curse fall on anyone ... who
preaches a different kind of Good News" (Gal. 1:8). The stakes involved –
between believing that you can earn your salvation or that you accept what
Jesus did on your behalf – have eternal consequences.

*Are you trying to keep sets of rules in order
to assure your salvation, or are you obedient
to God because you have been saved?*

THE GOOD AND THE PERFECT

My old self has been crucified with Christ. It is no longer I who live,
but Christ lives in me. So I live in this earthly body by trusting
in the Son of God, who loved me and gave himself for me.
GALATIANS 2:20

If we're honest, most of us don't particularly feel like we're shining examples of Christ living in us. The old self doesn't feel crucified and dead; in fact, at times it feels more alive than ever. We feel more like Paul's description of his own personal battles in Romans 7:18: "I want to do what is right, but I can't." If that's the case, how can these statements in Galatians 2:20 be true?

The point is not that we're perfect as believers. We are in process. The old self has been crucified, and Christ lives in us as believers. That was a one-time transaction, and because of it, God looks at us as though we are indeed already perfect.

But that still leaves us with day-to-day living. Why do we struggle so much? Because we still live in our earthly bodies that are prone to sin. But with Christ in us, we are new creations. With Christ in us, our self-centered lives become Christ-centered. Our old lives, our old habits, our old ways of thinking have been nailed to Christ's cross and are dead. Now we have new lives empowered by the resurrected Christ who lives in us by the Holy Spirit. Because of Christ, we are renewed day by day as we trust in Jesus. He is working in us to complete us, perfect us, and make us more like Himself.

Christ lives in you. How might that
make a difference in how you live today?

ALL ONE

There is no longer Jew or Gentile, slave or free, male and female. For you are all one in Christ Jesus. And now that you belong to Christ, you are the true children of Abraham. You are his heirs, and God's promise to Abraham belongs to you.

GALATIANS 3:28-29

Differences divide families, neighborhoods, communities, and nations. Differences in race, nationality, culture, social stratum, language, gender, and skin color push people from each other. The news media continually report stories of civil unrest, hate crimes, bigotry, terrorism, and "ethnic cleansing." The more we become a global village, the more, it seems, we splinter and divide. This passage, however, describes a quite different situation. For those who belong to Christ, there is togetherness, oneness, unity. And instead of conflict, there is peace.

Unity in Christ transcends racial barriers, social status, and gender distinctions. Acceptance in the family of God is based only on Christ and what He has done. All who believe are welcome. All who believe become the true children of Abraham, his heirs, and part of the promise God had made to His servant many years before: "All the families on earth will be blessed through you" (Gen. 12:3).

If you have ever felt the sting of prejudice and the loneliness of rejection, you know that this passage shouts good news. If you have been prone to prejudice against those different from you, the passage shouts correction. All believers are on equal footing at the cross. All who come in faith are welcome and accepted into God's worldwide family.

How do you treat other believers who come from different cultures genders, or social strata? Does anything need to change?

A PRAYER FOR REST IN THEE

Grant me, most sweet and loving Jesus,
to rest in Thee above every creature,
above all glory and honor,
above all power and dignity,
above all riches and arts,
above all joy and exultation,
above all fame and praise,
above all hope and promise,
above all merit and desire,
above all gifts and rewards which Thou can give and pour forth,
above all joy and jubilation which the mind is able to receive and feel;
in a word, above angels and archangels and all the army of heaven,
above all things visible and invisible,
and above everything which Thou, O my God, art not. Amen.

Thomas à Kempis

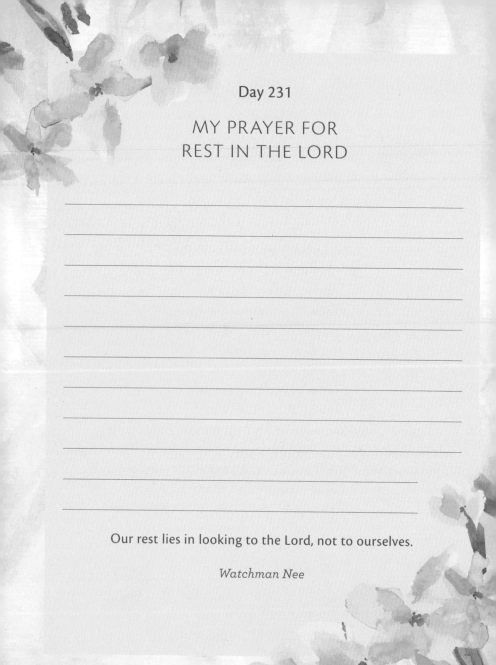

Day 231

MY PRAYER FOR
REST IN THE LORD

Our rest lies in looking to the Lord, not to ourselves.

Watchman Nee

Day 232

CHILDREN AND SLAVES

And because we are his children, God has sent the Spirit of his Son into our hearts,
prompting us to call out, "Abba, Father." Now you are no longer a slave but
God's own child. And since you are his child, God has made you his heir.

GALATIANS 4:6-7

*P*aul's straightforward discussion about slaves sounds scandalous to
our modern ears. Slavery in the New Testament Roman Empire was, in
most instances, quite different from the slavery that exists in parts of our
world today. Slaves in Paul's day were often treated well, and in many cases
they preferred the opportunities slavery afforded to the daily uncertainties
they might have faced as free people. Yet they were still slaves – without any
of the rights that the free people had. If a slave was fortunate enough to be
adopted into his master's family, however, he gained all the same rights as
the natural-born children of the family.

Paul used the concepts of slavery and adoption to illustrate that before
Christ came, people were enslaved to trying to be good enough by obeying
the law. But those who believe in Christ are adopted as God's children – they
are no longer slaves, but heirs. Slaves cannot inherit anything that belongs
to their masters, but children (even adopted children) do.

We are no longer slaves to our sin or to any law or religious ritual. As
believers, we have been adopted as God's children. As adopted children of
God, we are heirs of all His promises. We are His dearly beloved; He is our
Abba Father, our Daddy.

*Remind yourself, as Paul has reminded you, that you are
a child of God, your loving and gracious heavenly Father.*

FRUITFUL

*But the Holy Spirit produces this kind of fruit in our lives: love, joy,
peace, patience, kindness, goodness, faithfulness, gentleness,
and self-control. There is no law against these things!*

GALATIANS 5:22-23

The term *fruit* describes these character qualities as by-products of a life filled with the Holy Spirit. Apples grow on an apple tree because it is an apple tree; likewise, these fruits grow in believers because they are filled with the Holy Spirit.

We can't grow these fruits by wishing, hoping, visualizing, or gritting our teeth with determination. They grow when we are committed to staying in tune with the Spirit and cultivating lives that please Him. No one will perfectly exemplify all of the fruits all of the time – our sin natures preclude that. But when we're trusting God, He will mature the right fruit at the right time. The Holy Spirit gives us love for neighbor or enemy even when we don't feel particularly loving, joy despite difficult circumstances, peace in times of turmoil, patience during daily aggravations, kindness in a rude society, goodness when surrounded by corruption, faithfulness though commitment is scarce, gentleness when the prevailing mood is pushy self-centeredness, and self-control to be able to stand against temptation in a world of wild hedonism.

Do you want overflowing love, ebullient joy, deep peace, strong patience, contagious kindness and goodness, enduring faithfulness, consistent gentleness, and steady self-control? Yield your will to God, and allow Him to work in and through you.

*What evidences of the fruit of the
Spirit do you see in your life?*

WHAT WILL YOU HARVEST?

*You cannot mock the justice of God. You will always harvest
what you plant ... So let's not get tired of doing what is good. At just
the right time we will reap a harvest of blessing if we don't give up.*

GALATIANS 6:7, 9

God's justice cannot be mocked. Through the ages unbelievers have mocked belief in God, the idea of God, and even God Himself. Paul was not referring to that kind of mockery, however; here he was speaking to believers, issuing a warning that if we're not careful, we can deceive ourselves into thinking that our actions have no consequences. Instead, Paul says, "You will always harvest what you plant." Believers are not immune to consequences for their sinful actions. Being saved and being free in Christ does not allow us to do as we please. We cannot act as if God will override our choices to plant sin and evil. While we can count on His promise to cause "everything to work together for the good of those who love God" (Rom. 8:28), we will still be creating plenty of pain for ourselves along the way. We will harvest pain and sorrow if we plant to please our own plans and purposes.

God has a better way. He wants us to use our freedom to sow to please the Spirit and reap blessing in this life and eternal life in the next. Paul went on to explain that we sow to the Spirit by doing good to all people. By doing good to all, especially our brothers and sisters in Christ, we express our love for them and our love for God.

Think of a way you can do what is good for someone else today.

FLOODED WITH LIGHT

*I pray that your hearts will be flooded with light so that you can understand
the confident hope he has given to those he called – his holy people who
are his rich and glorious inheritance. I also pray that you will understand
the incredible greatness of God's power for us who believe him.*

EPHESIANS 1:18-19

Imagine an intrepid explorer with a magnificent longing and love for ancient lost treasure. One day during an excursion deep into the jungle, he discovers a magical treasure chest. He opens the chest and finds it overflowing with the most precious treasure he has ever seen. He quickly closes it, amazed at his good fortune. He opens the chest again and this time discovers a different treasure – a document that tells the explorer that each subsequent opening of the chest will yield new treasures. This document also reveals that this cycle will continue forever and that he will never tire of his newfound treasure.

So it is with our relationship with God. Not only have we come to know the Father, but through wisdom and revelation given by the Spirit, we can continually come to know Him better. As we walk with Him, every day is a new opportunity to know more about "the incredible greatness of God's power for us who believe him." The God who "purchased our freedom with the blood of his Son and forgave our sins," the God who "has showered his kindness on us, along with all wisdom and understanding" (Eph. 1:7-8) is the God who wants to continue to reveal more of Himself to us. Like the magical treasure found by the explorer, God constantly surprises and delights us.

What have you learned about God today?

Day 236

GOD'S MASTERPIECE

*God saved you by his grace when you believed. And you can't take credit for this;
it is a gift from God. Salvation is not a reward for the good things we have done,
so none of us can boast about it. For we are God's masterpiece. He has created us
anew in Christ Jesus, so we can do the good things he planned for us long ago.*

EPHESIANS 2:8-10

Seemingly since the dawn of Christianity, believers have grappled with the way of salvation: What role do we play in God's saving of us? In this chapter Paul wonderfully articulates for believers the relationship between faith and works, and in doing so he puts his foot down on our futile attempts to contribute to our salvation. He first describes our state apart from God: We were dead in our sins, following the desires of our sinful nature. Then God, by His grace and because of His great mercy and love for us, saved us from sin and wrath. In ages to come He will express His kindness to us and reveal the incomparable riches of His grace! What a glorious salvation and eternal hope!

In Ephesians 2:8-9, Paul explains how our salvation is secured. We are not saved by the good things we have done; instead, we are saved by God's grace when we believe. And even our faith is not our own contribution – it is a gift from God! In verse 10, Paul explains that the true *eternal* work belongs to God: We are *His* workmanship, created for good works, yes, but works that He has prepared in advance for us. We do these works as our expression of love and gratitude for the infinite love and tender mercy God has shown us.

*Trust in the love and mercy of God for you.
Look for ways He has prepared for you to show His love to others.*

LIVING FOR GOD

Grant, O Lord, that I may not lavish away the life
which Thou hast given me on useless trifles,
nor waste it in vain searches after things
which Thou hast hidden from me.
Enable me, by the Holy Spirit, so to shun sloth and negligence,
that every day may discharge part
of the task which Thou hast allotted me;
and so further with Thy help that labor which,
without Thy help must be ineffectual,
that I may obtain in all my undertakings,
such success as will most promote Thy glory,
and the salvation of my own soul,
for the sake of Jesus Christ. Amen.

Samuel Johnson

Day 238

MY PRAYER OF
SUBMISSION TO GOD

_____
_____
_____
_____
_____
_____
_____
_____
_____
_____
_____
_____

Whether you eat or drink, or whatever you do,
do it all for the glory of God.

1 Corinthians 10:31

COME BOLDLY

Because of Christ and our faith in him, we can now
come boldly and confidently into God's presence.
EPHESIANS 3:12

Have you ever wanted to talk to the leader of your country – to point out a need that you see is unmet, or to suggest an idea, or to try to understand what he or she is thinking on a particular issue? What if you were summoned to that leader's office? You'd probably feel a bit intimidated by the power he or she represents. But you'd also feel extremely privileged to have been given a bit of that person's valuable time to bring your requests and suggestions.

Now consider meeting with the most powerful person in the universe – not a president or a king, but the One who is the Creator and Sustainer of all things. Do you think you could ever get an appointment with such a person? Do you think He'd care about your desires or needs? Do you think He'd take time out of His busy schedule to meet with you?

Yes. Yes. And yes!

Paul says confidently that you can approach God at any time with freedom and confidence. Because of Christ's work on the cross and in your life, you can enter directly into God's presence through prayer. The writer of the book of Hebrews made a similar statement, "So let us come boldly to the throne of our gracious God. There we will receive his mercy, and we will find grace to help us when we need it most" (Heb. 4:16). What an awesome privilege!

Whatever your need or situation,
talk with God about it. He's approachable.

CHRIST, OUR SOURCE

He makes the whole body fit together perfectly. As each part
does its own special work, it helps the other parts grow,
so that the whole body is healthy and growing and full of love.
EPHESIANS 4:16

Have you ever thought about the importance of your head to your very existence? Probably not – but without your head and the brain it houses, you would not be able to breathe, eat, or live. In a sense, your body is constantly looking to your head as the source of its life.

In the same way, we Christians, who are Christ's body, look to Him "who is the head of his body, the church" (Eph. 4:15) as our source of life, growth, and continuing function. To sustain us, He has given various gifts to all the members in the body. Each member has his or her own special functions in the body, and each member is necessary for the body to work properly. In order for the body to grow spiritually and build itself up in love, each member must do the work God has prepared for him or her to do.

As a believer and member of Christ's body, *you* are important. You have been specially gifted to do your own special work in order to build up the body of Christ. When you do your part and others do theirs, the body of Christ functions as it is meant to on this earth, bringing more people into the Kingdom.

Have you found your role in the body of Christ? Look to Him
for direction and grace to do what He has prepared for you.

IMITATING YOUR DAD

Imitate God, therefore, in everything you do, because you are
his dear children. Live a life filled with love, following the example of Christ.
He loved us and offered himself as a sacrifice for us, a pleasing aroma to God.

EPHESIANS 5:1-2

I f you're a parent, you know that one of the most joyful aspects of parenting is seeing your child imitating you. Perhaps you have a son who has stood by your side at the bathroom mirror as you put on your tie for work, or a daughter who has tried her hand at applying makeup after watching you. Good parents desire to be good role models for their children so that they are worthy to be imitated. Parents want their children to imitate the good things and not the bad ones!

Our Father in heaven has shown incomprehensible kindness and compassion to us and has forgiven all our sins. As dearly loved children, we are to imitate our heavenly Father, by loving others, being kind and compassionate to each other, and forgiving each other. As we "carefully determine what pleases the Lord" (Eph. 5:10), live "like those who are wise" (Eph. 5:15), "understand what the Lord wants [us] to do" (Eph. 5:17), and "give thanks for everything" (Eph. 5:20), we are imitating our heavenly Father. Living this way will leave no room for immorality, impurity, greed, and other deeds of the flesh that Paul mentions in this chapter. Living this way will show others that we have new natures, "created to be like God — truly righteous and holy" (Eph. 4:24).

*Remember the kindness and compassion God has
shown you as you seek to be kind and forgiving of others.*

THE FULL ARMOR OF GOD

A final word: Be strong in the Lord and in his mighty power. Put on all of God's armor so that you will be able to stand firm against all strategies of the devil.

EPHESIANS 6:10-11

While some would have us believe that the Christian life is for weak people, these verses reveal quite the opposite. The Christian life is a battlefield and believers are the warriors, going out daily to do battle on behalf of our faith in a world that scoffs at, scorns, and persecutes us. We must put on all of God's armor so that, like the knights of medieval days, we will be able to stand our ground. The armor is spiritual and the battle is virtually unseen, but they are real. Evil rulers and authorities of the unseen world, mighty powers in the dark work, evil spirits in the heavenly places – these are not battles for the faint of heart.

God doesn't send us into the battle to fend for ourselves. He provides us with full armor. We buckle on the belt of truth so that no lies can cause us to doubt. We wear the body armor of God's righteousness to guard our hearts from temptation. We have on shoes that provide peace that comes from the Good News, so that we will be fully prepared. Our shield of faith stops the fiery arrows the devil shoots at us. The helmet of salvation guards our minds against Satan's lies. We fight back with the sword of God's Word, putting the lies of the enemy to flight.

Clearly, not for the faint of heart. The battle is real, but the armor is there. Are you dressed?

In prayer, dress yourself in each piece of God's armor today.

WORTHY OF THE GOSPEL

*Above all, you must live as citizens of heaven, conducting yourselves
in a manner worthy of the Good News about Christ. Then, whether I come
and see you again or only hear about you, I will know that you are standing
side by side, fighting together for the faith, which is the Good News.*

PHILIPPIANS 1:27

Paul urges the believers in Philippi to conduct themselves "in a manner worthy of the Good News about Christ."

This statement seems odd for it appears to contradict what we know about the Good News – that God sought us, came down to us, and saved us while we were yet sinners, based on nothing we did to earn our salvation. In other words, we are most decidedly *not worthy* of the Good News. And although we know that we have been saved by grace through faith, we also know that we are woefully unable to live perfect lives. We attempt to conduct ourselves as God would like us to, but so often we fail. We know in our hearts that we simply cannot live as citizens of heaven or conduct ourselves in a manner worthy of the Good News.

So where does that leave us? Paul's challenge is for believers to remember that because of the grace of God that has come to us, we have been freed to serve God and our neighbors in love – all the while knowing that such service does not earn us God's Kingdom. We have already been given the Kingdom; we serve because we desire to return love to God in thankfulness and to give love to others as a way of passing along God's love in this world. When we conduct ourselves this way, we are indeed acting in a manner worthy of the Good News.

*As you walk through your busy day, keep in mind
Paul's admonition to walk worthy of the Good News.*

A PRAYER FOR REFUGE

In You, O LORD, do I take refuge;
let me never be put to shame!
In Your righteousness deliver me and rescue me;
incline Your ear to me, and save me!
Be to me a rock of refuge,
to which I may continually come;
You have given the command to save me,
for You are my rock and my fortress.

Psalm 71:1-3

Day 245

MY PRAYER FOR
REFUGE IN GOD

_____

_____

_____

_____

_____

_____

_____

_____

_____

_____

Prayer should be the means by which I, at all times,
receive all that I need, and, for this reason,
be my daily refuge, my daily consolation, my daily joy,
my source of rich and inexhaustible joy in life.

John Chrysostom

WHEN YOU'RE AWAY

Dear friends, you always followed my instructions when I was with you.
And now that I am away, it is even more important. Work hard to show
the results of your salvation, obeying God with deep reverence and fear. For God
is working in you, giving you the desire and the power to do what pleases him.

PHILIPPIANS 2:12-13

It's easy to be a Christian around other Christians, isn't it? We know what's expected of us (usually) and what's taboo. It's not always so easy when we're surrounded by nonbelievers. Have you ever taken a business trip with some colleagues and found yourself invited to places where you didn't feel comfortable or put in situations you didn't want to be part of? Or have you ever traveled alone and found yourself tempted by certain in-room movies or other sinful situations because "no one will ever know"?

The problem is, *two* people will know: you and God. Paul says to us, as he said to the Philippian Christians, that we must live for Christ no matter who is or isn't around. We are accountable for our actions everywhere we go, and so we should obey God with deep reverence and fear (awe) at all times and in all places.

It won't always be easy. It may mean feeling out of it with the group. It may mean making the choice to obey even if the temptation to disobey is strong and persistent. The good news is that "God is working in you, giving you the desire and the power to do what pleases him."

Is your Christian life consistent no matter where you are
or who you're with? If not, what needs to change?

FINISHING WELL

*No, dear brothers and sisters, I have not achieved it, but I focus on this
one thing: Forgetting the past and looking forward to what lies ahead,
I press on to reach the end of the race and receive the heavenly prize
for which God, through Christ Jesus, is calling us.*

PHILIPPIANS 3:13-14

*P*aul pictures a race where the runners expend all their energy to win the prize. With eyes on their goal, nothing matters but finishing the race and finishing well.

Paul's goal was to know Christ, to be like Christ, and to be all that Christ had in mind for him. Paul had reason to forget what was behind – he had held the coats of those who stoned Stephen (Acts 7:57-58) and had pursued Christians to their imprisonment and death (Acts 9:1-2). Christ knocked him down (literally) and turned his life around. The former Christian-persecutor became a Christian who would take the Good News across much of the known world.

So what's in your past? What dark secrets linger there, threatening you with feelings of shame or guilt? Paul says to put the past behind and to look forward to what is ahead. Perhaps you can't literally "forget" the past, but you can ask God to help you move on so that whatever is in your past no longer hampers your present or your future. Because your hope is in Christ, you can look ahead with confidence to what God wants you to become.

Don't let anything divert you from your goal of knowing Christ. With the focus of a dedicated athlete, press on. Lay aside everything harmful and anything that might distract you from finishing well.

*What do you need to do to put the past behind you
and put your focus on finishing well?*

THE SECRET

*I know how to live on almost nothing or with everything. I have learned the
secret of living in every situation, whether it is with a full stomach or empty,
with plenty or little. For I can do everything through Christ, who gives me strength.*
PHILIPPIANS 4:12-13

In this letter written during his imprisonment in Rome, Paul expressed an
unusual attitude toward the security that comes with financial stability:
He's not overly impressed with it. In our materialistic age in which we are
encouraged to make as much money as possible so we can provide for every
need and retire comfortably, such a mindset strikes us at first as foolish,
perhaps even dangerous.

Paul wrote, however, that he had faced both situations of having nothing
and having everything. He had experienced both a full stomach and hunger.
He knew what it was to have both plenty and little. The secret of being able
to live happily in any situation is to rely on Christ for the needed strength.

What about you? Are you currently facing financial difficulty, or are you
comfortable? Is your stomach full or empty? Do you have plenty or only a
little? In whatever situation you find yourself, you need reliance on Christ.
In times of want, you need Him to help you stay faithful, to answer your
prayers for sustenance, to be your comfort. In times of plenty, you need Him
to help you stay faithful, to keep you from becoming overly self-confident or
proud, and to give you peace so that you don't join the rat race of constantly
wanting more.

Whatever situation we find ourselves in, we, like Paul, can trust that we
can do all things through Christ, who gives us strength.

*Whether you're in a time of want or of plenty, are you
relying on Christ to give you the strength you need?*

DON'T DRIFT AWAY

But you must continue to believe this truth and stand firmly in it.
Don't drift away from the assurance you received when you heard the Good News.
COLOSSIANS 1:23

Paul began his letter to the believers in the city of Colosse by encouraging them about their growth in the knowledge of God and their walk with Him. He then directed their vision upward to the glorious majesty of the supremacy of Christ: All things in heaven and earth were created by Jesus and for Jesus; in Him all things hold together; through the blood of Christ God is reconciling all things to Himself.

This was more than just a poetic opening; Paul was purposely bringing the church in Colosse back to the focus of their faith – Jesus Christ Himself – because the believers were being infiltrated by false teaching. In Colosse, this teaching was later called *Gnosticism* (from the Greek word for "knowledge," *gnosis*) for it emphasized that only those with special knowledge (received by some mystic initiation) could be saved. In other words, you had to be in the "in group" to really be saved. Gnosticism distorted Christian teaching by denying Christ as God and Savior and denying that all who call upon Jesus can be saved, hence Paul's focus on Christ at the beginning of this letter.

Paul's caution comes down to us today as well: Don't drift away from the assurance you received. Many will come along who want to cause you to doubt your faith, the truth of God's Word, the assurance of your salvation.

Keep your boat anchored in the Word, and you won't find yourself drifting away.

Are you anchored to the Rock of your salvation?

LIFE IN CHRIST

*Don't let anyone capture you with empty philosophies
and high-sounding nonsense that come from human thinking
and from the spiritual powers of this world, rather than from Christ.*

COLOSSIANS 2:8

Empty philosophies and high-sounding nonsense." Take a look through the religion section of any bookstore and you can understand what Paul meant. The variety of opinions is astounding, but they all have one thing in common: They "come from human thinking and from the spiritual powers of this world, rather than from Christ." That ought to give us pause.

But how do we know that what we believe is the truth? If so many other opinions are out there, how can we know that the Bible is the one and only truth? Just because *it* tells us it is doesn't make it so ... does it?

Search deep within your heart. What has happened to you since you believed? Paul wrote that believers have been "buried with Christ" and "raised to new life" (Col. 2:12). How are you wearing this new life? It ought not be a weight on you of rules and regulations (as Paul explained in the rest of the chapter); rather, your obedience to Christ comes out of your relationship with Him.

Just as you accepted Christ Jesus as your Lord, you follow Him by letting your roots grow down into Him and your life be built on Him. The experience of that relationship gives you assurance that what He says is the truth. No other religion offers peace, joy, fellowship with God, and salvation by faith alone.

What has changed in your life since you became a believer?

WALKING IN GOD'S WAYS

Lord, make us to walk in Thy way:
Where there is love and wisdom,
there is neither fear nor ignorance;
where there is patience and humility,
there is neither anger nor annoyance;
where there is poverty and joy,
there is neither greed nor avarice;
where there is peace and contemplation,
there is neither care nor restlessness;
where there is the fear of God to guard the dwelling,
there no enemy can enter; where there is mercy and prudence,
there is neither excess nor harshness;
this we know through Thy Son, Jesus Christ our Lord.
Amen.

St. Francis of Assisi

I DESIRE TO WALK
IN GOD'S WAYS

_____

_____

_____

_____

_____

_____

_____

_____

_____

_____

_____

Faith never knows where it is being led,
but it loves and knows the One who is leading.

Oswald Chambers

WORKING FOR THE LORD

Work willingly at whatever you do, as though you were working for the Lord
rather than for people. Remember that the Lord will give you an inheritance
as your reward, and that the Master you are serving is Christ.

COLOSSIANS 3:23-24

Have you ever felt like no one appreciates you? Working hard behind the scenes, almost anonymously, you feel overlooked, neglected, taken for granted. Employers make mistakes. Bosses become bossy. Supervisors reward incompetence. Teachers fail. Managers mismanage. That comes with living in a sinful world with fallible, sinful human beings. And yet it hurts when you're the one to get the shaft, the blame, or the fallout of bad decisions.

Regardless of the job or work situation, however, God knows what's going on. He perceives the attitude; He sees the work. He knows whether someone is giving the best effort or just getting by. Thus, God tells us through the apostle, we should work "for the Lord rather than for people." Certainly this would entail working hard, earning our wages, and being honest.

Understanding whom we serve can also free us from the trap of seeking earthly rewards and acclaim. No amount of money can match God's "inheritance," and no accolades can compare with God's "Well done!" that awaits all who trust Christ and serve Him.

Regardless of the reactions of coworkers, classmates, and friends, focus on the Lord and work for Him. The rewards He offers are beyond what you can imagine.

*What difference will it make for you today if you consider that
you are working for the Lord, not merely for any employer?*

MAKING THE MOST OF IT

*Live wisely among those who are not believers, and make the most
of every opportunity. Let your conversation be gracious and attractive
so that you will have the right response for everyone.*

COLOSSIANS 4:5-6

*P*aul may have been in prison, but his message was never chained; he
asked the believers in Colosse to pray that he would continue to
proclaim the message of Christ as he should. He went on to exhort the
Colossian believers to "live wisely among those who are not believers, and
make the most of every opportunity" (Col. 4:5).

"How?" they might have asked.

Paul answered. "Let your conversation be gracious and attractive so that
you will have the right response for everyone" (Col. 4:6).

Coming at the end of his request for prayer, Paul's instruction provides a
clue as to how he – and we – can cooperate with God as He opens doors for
our message. When our conversation is gracious, we extend grace to others
in a gentle, understanding way. When it is attractive, it is tasteful, kind,
and respectful to the listener. Conversation that is gracious and attractive
enables us to walk through doors that God has opened.

Living wisely among unbelievers will not come easily. You may not always
feel like you have the "right response for everyone." God doesn't ask for
perfection; all He asks of you is sensitivity to the Holy Spirit, wariness toward
sin and temptation, willingness to monitor your speech, and readiness to
walk through the doors that may open before you.

*In what ways can you make your speech
more gracious and attractive so that
you can make the most of every opportunity?*

RINGING OUT

So you received the message with joy from the Holy Spirit in spite of the severe suffering it brought you. In this way, you imitated both us and the Lord ... And now the word of the Lord is ringing out from you to people everywhere.

1 THESSALONIANS 1:6, 8

The Thessalonian believers probably couldn't help but smile at Paul's prayer for them. It was heartfelt, genuine, and full of thanks for their continued joy despite their troubles. Paul was grateful for his spiritual children. They had come to Christ under great persecution in the very pagan city of Thessalonica – a city firmly entrenched in idol worship. These people had welcomed Paul and had received with joy the gospel message he preached.

But instead of just being secure in their salvation, however, the believers there ended up having a strong desire to tell everyone everywhere of their new faith in God. But not without cost. Their conversion to Christianity brought "severe suffering" in the form of some kind of persecution. That didn't stop these believers, however. So strong was their faith and so great was their joy that they evangelized even as they endured.

The Christian faith ought to fill believers with such joy that they cannot help but spread God's Good News wherever they go. Like a fragrant perfume, their faith should refresh everyone they meet. What about you? Has your faith brought you joy? Are you a refreshment to others just because of who you are in Christ?

How will you let the Good News "ring out" from your life today?

THE WORD AT WORK

Therefore, we never stop thanking God that when you received
his message from us, you didn't think of our words as mere
human ideas. You accepted what we said as the very word of God –
which, of course, it is. And this word continues to work in you who believe.

1 THESSALONIANS 2:13

No loving father would let his kids cross a busy street by themselves. They might make it to the other side without getting hit, but the odds aren't good. A dad who neglects his children's safety isn't taking his parental responsibility seriously. In the same way, mature Christians shouldn't let new believers step into the world without holding their hands spiritually and offering input and guidance.

Paul wasn't about to let the Thessalonians who had just come to Christ go their own way without some help. They weren't spiritually strong enough. Thessalonica's lurid temptations and ungodly philosophies could have easily broadsided them, causing them to stumble in their faith or even to fall away. The strong opposition they were experiencing for their beliefs could have run them over.

So, like a good parent, Paul did a bit of guiding and advising. He urged them to move forward and let the Holy Spirit continue to work in them. Paul told them to hold tightly to God's Word, for it had changed the Thessalonians in the past and would continue to change them.

God's Word is at work in you as well. Every time you pick up the Bible and read it, it goes to work in your heart and life. Are you listening?

In what ways are you letting God's Word work in your life?

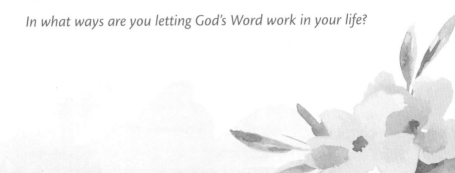

A PRAYER FOR LOVE

*May God our Father and our Lord Jesus bring us to you very soon.
And may the Lord make your love for one another and for all people
grow and overflow, just as our love for you overflows.*
1 THESSALONIANS 3:11-12

When Paul wrote to the Thessalonians, his love and concern for them were apparent in every word. When he prayed for them, he asked the Lord to make their love for one another overflow. Paul prayed that the Thessalonian church might become a loving, supporting community of faith. The strong, silent, loner Christian didn't fit into Paul's understanding of how God works among His people.

Believers need each other. God uses other believers to strengthen us and make us holy. Jesus said, "I am giving you a new commandment: Love each other. Just as I have loved you, you should love each other. Your love for one another will prove to the world that you are my disciples" (John 13:34-35). The writer to the Hebrews told us, "Let us not neglect our meeting together, as some people do, but encourage one another" (Heb. 10:25).

As you pray for strength to be faithful to God, you should expect His answer to come through those believers who worship every Sunday with you. God may speak to you through the pastor, a friend at church, or even an acquaintance who makes a statement out of the blue (seemingly) that strikes you right to the core. Likewise, you should earnestly pray that God might use you to strengthen other believers. After all, we're a family – and will be forever!

*What's your attitude toward other believers?
Do you have a core group who supports and
prays for you – and for whom you do the same?*

A PRAYER OF SUBMISSION

Use me then, my Savior, for whatever purpose,
and in whatever way Thou may require.
Here is my poor heart, an empty vessel; fill it with Thy grace.
Here is my sinful and troubled soul;
quicken and refresh it with Thy love.
Take my heart for Thine abode;
my mouth to spread the glory of Thy name;
my love and all my powers,
for the advancement of Thy believing people;
and never suffer the steadfastness
and confidence of my faith to abate,
that so at all times I may be enabled from the heart to say,
"Jesus needs me, and I Him; and so, we suit each other."
Amen.

Dwight L. Moody

Day 259

MY PRAYER OF SUBMISSION

_____

_____

_____

_____

_____

_____

_____

_____

_____

_____

_____

Therefore submit to God.
Resist the devil and he will flee from you.

James 4:7

HOLINESS AND HONOR

God's will is for you to be holy, so stay away from all sexual sin.
Then each of you will control his own body and live in holiness and honor –
not in lustful passion like the pagans who do not know God and his ways.
1 THESSALONIANS 4:3-5

There might be times when, all alone, we are tempted to do wrong. We might be home alone or traveling alone. It's then that the television set can become a great temptation. With no one around and the door locked – remote in hand – a person can let the imagination run wild through the promiscuous images all too available on the adult channels.

Television didn't exist in Paul's day, but sexual immorality has been around since the dawn of time, and the believers in Thessalonica were no strangers to it. Paul wanted the Thessalonians – men and women alike – to steer clear of sexual sin and other bad behavior. He urged them to control their bodies and live in ways that honored God – not being like the pagans who, in their ignorance of the Lord, embraced their lustful passions and acted in immoral ways.

Some believers in Thessalonica either didn't understand this message because they were brand new to the faith or had conveniently forgotten it. So Paul used the media of his day – a letter – to remind them to live pure and holy lives. If they were to crave anything, it should be holiness and honor.

The words resonate today. Sexual immorality, lustful passion, immorality, and adultery are still around and not too difficult to find. And God's words are the same to us: He wants us to be holy and to stay away from sexual sin.

How are you doing in this area?
Are you staying away from sexual sin?
If not, what do you need to do to be back in God's will?

FOCUS ON CHRIST

Always be joyful. Never stop praying. Be thankful in all circumstances,
for this is God's will for you who belong to Christ Jesus.
1 THESSALONIANS 5:16-18

These verses contain three commands that seem impossible to obey. The difficulty lies in the words "always," "never," and "in all circumstances." We wonder how we can perpetually be joyful, pray, and be thankful, especially when encountering painful trials, inscrutable problems, and extreme conflicts. Yet this is what God wants us to do – it is His will.

The last phrase of this verse – "belong to Christ Jesus" – holds the answer. When we consider Christ's work on the cross in the past, His intercession for us right now, and what He has promised to do for us in the future, we can be joyful and thankful, continually telling God our needs and seeking His direction.

Joy flows from knowing that God loves us. Thankfulness comes from knowing that God is working in our lives, in each and every circumstance. Praying continually is a natural response for those in close relationship with their Creator and Savior.

Note that God does not command us to be thankful *for* all circumstances. Instead, we are to praise Him *in* each one. Regardless of what happens to us, God is with us working out His best for us (see Romans 8:28).

Focus on Christ, and live with joy.

Are you always joyful? Always praying?
Always thankful in all circumstances?
This is God's will, so consider what you need to do
to make these a part of your daily life.

Segment header

GOD IS JUST

In his justice he will pay back those who persecute you.
And God will provide rest for you who are being persecuted
and also for us when the Lord Jesus appears from heaven.

2 THESSALONIANS 1:6-7

These words were written to first-century followers of Christ, who were living as a small minority in a culture violently opposed to their faith. Persecuted and harassed, many were rejected by family and friends and denied employment. Others suffered great physical harm. They looked for rescue. They yearned for justice. And then they heard this encouraging message from Paul – God is just. Regardless of their present difficulties, these believers would be rewarded for their faithfulness.

Pressed on every side, we cry out for relief from trials and persecution and troubles. At times, a seemingly endless hoard of problems and pressures surround us like a hostile army, threatening to attack and destroy. We can see no exit, no hope, only disaster and defeat. With thick clouds blocking the sun, we wonder if we'll ever see light again. Now listen to this clear word from Paul – God is just. In His justice, He will pay back those who persecute us. The all-powerful Creator loves us. The all-knowing Sustainer understands us. The supreme Ruler cares about us. He promises to give us rest.

In the meantime, we seek to live worthy of our call, and we pray for the power to accomplish all the good things our faith prompts us to do (1 Thess. 1:11). We want to honor our Lord Jesus by the way we live (1 Thess. 1:12). It isn't easy, but it's worth it – for eternity!

Whatever unjust situations you or your loved ones face today, know that God Himself is just and will bring perfect justice.

ARE YOU READY?

Now, dear brothers and sisters, let us clarify some things about the coming of our Lord Jesus Christ and how we will be gathered to meet him.

2 THESSALONIANS 2:1

The book of Revelation makes it clear that Jesus will return to take His people to be with Him in heaven forever. At that time, God will live among His people and "will wipe every tear from their eyes, and there will be no more death or sorrow or crying or pain" (Rev. 21:4). The promise is secure, but we don't exactly know when or how this will happen. In fact, Paul had explained in his first letter to the Thessalonian church that Jesus' return "will come unexpectedly, like a thief in the night" (1 Thess. 5:2).

However, then as now, many people have various opinions about how and when Jesus' return will happen. While there is scriptural evidence for various opinions, the bottom line is that we simply do not know exactly the method or time of Jesus' return – but that's a good thing. If we knew the method, we might be tempted to read into all earthly occurrences to determine the timing. If we knew the time, we'd be tempted to live as we choose and come to Christ at the last minute. God has made it very clear that Jesus' return will occur unexpectedly.

Our job is not to determine the when or the how, but to simply live as best as we can, share our faith with as many as we can, and be ready!

What do you think about when you meditate on the return of Jesus? If He came today, would you be ready?

A PRAYER FOR PROTECTION

Pray, too, that we will be rescued from wicked and evil people,
for not everyone is a believer. But the Lord is faithful;
he will strengthen you and guard you from the evil one.

2 THESSALONIANS 3:2-3

In many parts of the world, Christians aren't persecuted for their faith. Oh, they may be ridiculed or even shunned by others for their beliefs, but for the most part, they can worship freely and share openly about God without being jailed or worse.

However, that isn't the case in other parts of the world, and it wasn't the case in Thessalonica during Paul's time. Believers there experienced much trouble and suffering from those hostile to the gospel. That's why Paul encouraged the Thessalonian believers to "stand firm and keep a strong grip on the teaching we passed on to you" (2 Thess. 2:15). And that's why Paul asked the believers to pray for him and his fellow travelers as they continued to spread the Good News. The threats were very real. Paul requested prayers that they would be "rescued from wicked and evil people."

Faith in God doesn't mean an easy life; in fact, it may bring distress and trials. Pray for those who face severe persecution for their faith. Pray that they will be rescued from wicked and evil people. Pray for yourself and your loved ones that the Lord will "lead your hearts into a full understanding and expression of the love of God and the patient endurance that comes from Christ" (2 Thess. 3:5). Pray that the Lord of peace will "give you his peace at all times and in every situation" (2 Thess. 3:16).

Take time to pray for the believers who face
severe persecution for their faith. Pray that God
will care for them and give them His peace.

TO BE LIKE JESUS

O Lord, give us more charity, more self-denial,
more likeness to Thee. Teach us to sacrifice our comforts
to others, and our likings for the sake of doing good.
Make us kindly in thought, gentle in word, generous in deed.
Teach us that it is better to give than to receive;
better to forget ourselves than to put ourselves forward;
better to minister than to be ministered unto.
And unto Thee, the God of love, be all the glory and praise,
both now and for evermore.
Amen.

Henry Alford

MY PRAYER FOR
CHRISTLIKE CHARACTER

_____

_____

_____

_____

_____

_____

_____

_____

_____

I have now concentrated all my prayers into one,
and that one prayer is this, that I may die to self,
and live wholly to Him.

Charles Spurgeon

FILLED WITH LOVE

*The purpose of my instruction is that all believers would be filled with love
that comes from a pure heart, a clear conscience, and genuine faith.*

1 TIMOTHY 1:5

As the beginning of this letter attests, Paul not only spread the
Good News, but also spent much time battling false teachers who
infiltrated churches after he left. Paul wrote letters and often sent trusted
representatives to various problem places to help the believers know truth
from error.

Timothy was one of those representatives. Paul had met Timothy in
Lystra and had invited him to join in the missionary travels (Acts 16:1-3).
Apparently on a visit to Ephesus, Paul and Timothy found widespread
problems with false teaching in the church. When Paul moved on, he left
Timothy to "stop those whose teaching is contrary to the truth" (1 Tim. 1:3).
Apparently the false teachers had the believers all caught up in discussions
about esoteric things that were not helping them mature in their Christian
lives but instead were simply wasting time and energy. Instead, the focus
should be "that all believers would be filled with love." What kind of love?
The kind that comes from a *pure heart* that is devoted to God and free from
corruption, a *clear conscience* that is free from guilt and impure motives,
and a *genuine faith* that is focused on Christ alone.

After all, Jesus said, "Your love for one another will prove to the world
that you are my disciples" (John 13:35). Such love should characterize our
lives and our relationships. Such love shows who we are and to whom we
belong. Such love draws others to Christ.

*How can you be sure that such love
characterizes your life and your relationships?
What's the status of your heart,
your conscience, and your faith?*

AN AMBIANCE OF PRAYER

I urge you, first of all, to pray for all people. Ask God to help them; intercede on their behalf, and give thanks for them. Pray this way for kings and all who are in authority so that we can live peaceful and quiet lives marked by godliness and dignity.

1 TIMOTHY 2:1-2

How can you "pray for all people"? If you made a list of all your family and friends, you'd have a lengthy prayer list. Add to that list your acquaintances, and then add the leaders at work, at church, and in your country and you might feel like you could never get all those people prayed for – at least not in any helpful way.

Paul wrote that in our prayers for all people we need to do only three things – ask God to help them, ask Him to intercede on their behalf, and thank God for them. Whether it is your dearest friend, your neighborhood acquaintance, or your country's leader, you can pray in this way. Ask God's hand to move in their lives.

You may not feel like you can do much. Your friend may be far away or may be facing a difficult time in life that you can't fix. You don't know what's really going on in the life of that acquaintance. You probably won't have a chance to talk personally to the president or king. But you *can* pray.

The point is not that you must pray through dozens of names every day. Instead, be open to the Holy Spirit's leading. When a particular person comes to mind, say a quick prayer asking God to help and to intercede. He'll take it from there.

Who has God brought to mind today? Say a prayer for that person. Ask God to help and intercede. Thank God for that person.

PRIORITIES

*For if a man cannot manage his own household,
how can he take care of God's church?*

1 TIMOTHY 3:5

When it comes to priorities, Paul wasn't shy about making clear what was important. Many people might seem to have all of the qualifications for leadership – they look good, speak well, and are knowledgeable. However, Paul took Timothy a step further regarding the types of people he should consider for leadership in the church in Ephesus (and in the churches in general). One of the important qualities was that the man's own family be such a priority that his children are well cared for and well-disciplined and that his home is well managed. All too often, the people who look good up front have spent so much time getting there that they've neglected their families. This does not honor God.

Whether or not you are involved in or aspire to church leadership, the statement here begs the questions, How am I doing with my own family? Am I managing my home well? How are our finances? Am I spending enough time with my spouse and children? Am I disciplining my children fairly and consistently? Am I teaching them to be respectful? What kind of example am I to them?

When we set priorities in our lives, when we set goals for where we'd like to be in the future, we must always remember the value God places on our families. We ought not be leading in other places if we neglect to lead our families.

Where does my family fall in my list of priorities?

LOVE DEMONSTRATED

Don't let anyone think less of you because you are young.
Be an example to all believers in what you say, in the way you live,
in your love, your faith, and your purity.

1 TIMOTHY 4:12

Love takes the central position in Paul's list of five important characteristics. He uses all five to challenge Timothy to be an example. The first two highlight public actions: what you say and how you live. The last two focus on the inner life: faith and purity. Love holds the two aspects (public and private) together.

As noted in first Timothy 1:5, our love should be "from a pure heart, a clear conscience, and genuine faith." Love like that will affect what we say and how we live; it will affect our faith and our purity. Like many of the other passages concerning love, this one creates a high standard. And to "be an example" to all other believers in this way – that's a huge challenge as well; in fact, it can be overwhelming. Timothy had a huge job in Ephesus dealing with the false teachers and may have felt himself to be too young, not up to the task. Paul says, "Nonsense! Just be a good example. Live right. You'll gain the respect you deserve."

Do you want to be a good example to others – fellow believers, unbelievers, your children, your grandchildren? Think of Christians you know who are examples to you. They're not perfect, but you sense the love that shines through them. To be a good example, you merely need to love. The rest will fall in line.

What kind of example are you to others?
What of Christ do they see in you?

PAYBACK

Never speak harshly to an older man, but appeal to him respectfully as you would to your own father ... Treat older women as you would your mother.

1 TIMOTHY 5:1-2

inancial institutions extend credit for us to purchase items; of course, they expect to be paid back within certain set terms and guidelines. To refuse payback is to risk having the item repossessed.

Consider most parents' investments in the lives of their children. Our parents' contributions to our natural, material, emotional, physical, and spiritual vitality would tally up to more than everything we owe on our mortgages and debts. Yet what parents have ever run a tab and expected their children to repay the cost of diapers, formula, clothing, shoes, medical care, and food from the time they were born until they leave home? Most parents care for their children – feed, clothe, and pay for numerous kinds of fun and education – simply out of love.

Yet what happens on the other end? When we are old enough to be on our own, what do those same loving parents get from us? Do they ever hear from us? Do we show our appreciation for all they did, or are they merely a nuisance? Have we ever taken the time to listen to the wisdom they might be able to impart?

Paul would advise us, as he advised Timothy, to treat our elders with respect. Even if your parents had many faults, they still deserve your respect and honor. After all they have done for you, what can you do for them?

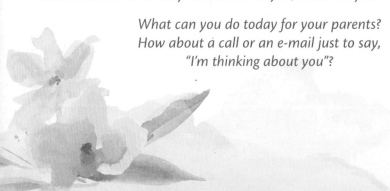

What can you do today for your parents?
How about a call or an e-mail just to say,
"I'm thinking about you"?

A PRAYER TO THE OMNISCIENT FATHER

You have searched me, LORD,
and You know me.
You know when I sit and when I rise;
You perceive my thoughts from afar.
You discern my going out and my lying down;
You are familiar with all my ways.
Before a word is on my tongue
You, LORD, know it completely.
Where can I go from Your Spirit?
Where can I flee from Your presence?
If I go up to the heavens, You are there;
if I make my bed in the depths, You are there.
If I rise on the wings of the dawn,
if I settle on the far side of the sea,
even there Your hand will guide me,
Your right hand will hold me.
Search me, God, and know my heart;
test me and know my anxious thoughts.
See if there is any offensive way in me,
and lead me in the way everlasting.

Psalm 139:1-4, 7-10, 23-24

Day 273

MY PRAYER TO THE OMNISCIENT FATHER

_____

_____

_____

_____

_____

_____

_____

_____

_____

_____

To know that God knows everything about me
and yet loves me is indeed my ultimate consolation.

R. C. Sproul

MISPLACED LOVE

For the love of money is the root of all kinds of evil. And some people, craving money, have wandered from the true faith and pierced themselves with many sorrows.

1 TIMOTHY 6:10

Paul warned young Timothy that wrong behaviors and painful results can often be traced back to an unhealthy pursuit of money. Usually, money goes in three directions: toward our desires, toward our responsibilities, and toward our generosity.

The first area covers our nonessential wants: entertainment, toys, vacations, etc. The second covers the costs of living: mortgage or rent, utilities, vehicle expenses, food, clothing, and other necessities. The third area has to do with charitable giving: worshipping by giving back to the Lord part of what He has first given to us, contributing to local charity organizations or missionaries, or donating to help a family in need. Is that the order in which you spend your paycheck? First your desires, then your responsibilities, and finally, if there's any left over, you might give to help someone else? Actually, your money allocations should be exactly the opposite.

Take some off the top the minute you get your paycheck. Meet your commitment to those you've chosen to help. Next, take care of your responsibilities (a savings plan in this area would be a wise investment). Finally, have a little fun.

Paul doesn't say that money is the root of all kinds of evil; it's the *love of* money that can get us into trouble. When you recognize that all you have is from God by giving right off the top to Him, you will keep your money in the right perspective.

What's your attitude toward your money?
What should your attitude be?

WELL-PLACED TRUST

*That is why I am suffering here in prison. But I am not ashamed of it,
for I know the one in whom I trust, and I am sure that he is able to guard
what I have entrusted to him until the day of his return.*

2 TIMOTHY 1:12

This was probably Paul's last letter. He had been imprisoned for a second time (the imprisonment at the end of the book of Acts was a first imprisonment) and was awaiting execution. Writing from prison, Paul declared his confidence in Christ. He was not ashamed of his situation or his Lord, and despite his suffering, he continued to boldly proclaim his faith. Although Paul knew that he probably would be executed soon, he stood strong. Paul was convinced of the truth of the gospel and of the strength and faithfulness of his Lord and Savior. He knew the One in whose hands he had placed his present and his future.

Living for Christ is not always smooth; in fact, the way can be rough. During those difficult times, doubts creep in. Fearing for our lives and considering our dire circumstances, we may lose sight of the Savior. But that's when we need Him most.

Although not facing martyrdom in a Roman dungeon, you still may feel imprisoned and under assault, with no hope of rescue or release. You may be in a difficult job, a difficult marriage, or a difficult financial situation. Maybe you're facing a debilitating illness or dealing with a prodigal child. In short, you're suffering. That's when you need to refocus your attention on the truth, remembering the One in whom you trust.

Christ will rule over all earthly powers. He will guard your faith and salvation. He loves you. He will bring you home.

*Can you say with Paul that you know the One in whom
you trust and that you're sure He is able to guard what
you've entrusted to Him until the day of His return?*

KEPT PURE

If you keep yourself pure, you will be a special utensil for honorable use.
Your life will be clean, and you will be ready for the Master
to use you for every good work.

2 TIMOTHY 2:21

"I f you keep yourself pure." Sounds like an impossibility. After all, we are tainted by sin, we live in a sinful world, we are surrounded by evil and temptation. How can we possibly be pure enough for God to use?

God knows it isn't easy. After all, He's been here. "Since he himself has gone through suffering and testing, he is able to help us when we are being tested" (Heb. 2:18). We are not called to isolate ourselves from the world, for we would be unable to witness to those who need the Good News. But we *are* called to be pure, and we do that by refusing to yield to temptation and, when we sin, by immediately going to God for forgiveness and cleansing. We keep ourselves pure by staying away from corrupting influences, drawing close to those who help us mature in our faith, and keeping short accounts with God.

When we keep ourselves pure, we will be able to be used by God for special works that He wants us to do. What a privilege to be called by God for special works on His behalf. What a privilege to live a life that is pure and clean before Him. What a privilege that we are able to live such lives because of what He has done for us.

Do you want purity, forgiveness, and purpose in life?
Come to God. Forgiveness and cleansing are only a prayer away.

THE OWNER'S MANUAL

All Scripture is inspired by God and is useful to teach us
what is true and to make us realize what is wrong in our lives.
It corrects us when we are wrong and teaches us to do what is right.
God uses it to prepare and equip his people to do every good work.

2 TIMOTHY 3:16-17

The owner's manual for a new car is packed with helpful information and advice – on everything from how to turn on the windshield wipers to how to change a tire. The manufacturer wants to be sure that you have everything you need to operate and maintain this expensive and complex piece of machinery.

Infinitely more valuable and complex than automobiles are human beings, special creations of their loving Creator. In a confusing and dangerous world, we need care and guidance. God has provided just that in His "owner's manual," the Bible. Written by chosen, godly people as they were inspired by the Holy Spirit, this book, God's Word, contains everything we need to live right. It teaches what is true, points out what is wrong in our lives, corrects us, and then teaches us how to do right. God uses His Word to equip us "to do every good work."

"The word of God is alive and powerful. It is sharper than the sharpest two-edged sword, cutting between soul and spirit, between joint and marrow. It exposes our innermost thoughts and desires" (Heb. 4:12). In every story, every parable, every prophecy, every teaching, God confronts us with Himself, telling us how to live to please Him.

The Bible is God's instruction manual, handbook,
spiritual first-aid kit, and love letter.
Read it, study it, learn it, and apply it.

FOUGHT, FINISHED, FAITHFUL

I have fought the good fight, I have finished the race, and I have remained faithful.
2 TIMOTHY 4:7

The end was near, and Paul knew it. He had been set free from a Roman prison at an earlier time, but he sensed that this wasn't going to be the case this time. In fact, Paul compared his life to that of an offering poured out to the glory of God. "As for me, my life has already been poured out as an offering to God. The time of my death is near" (2 Tim. 4:6).

Paul had fought the good fight. He had traveled much of the world spreading the Good News. He had written letters, prayed for the churches, fought the false teachers, argued for the faith, faced persecution and suffering, and finally, he would be executed. The race was finished. The finish line was in sight. The reward was waiting because he had remained faithful through it all.

What can you say of your spiritual life? What if today were the end for you? Are you planning to be more faithful in the future when you have more time and less stress? Are you willing to fight the good fight when people aren't so hostile? Are you hoping the finish line is still several miles away?

Remember that you don't know the day or the hour when God will call you home. Today is the day to get right with God so that when the time comes, you will have fought, finished, and been found faithful to the end.

If you were to die today, would others say
that you've fought, finished, and been faithful?

A PRAYER OF DEDICATION

O Lord, Thou knowest what is best;
let this or that be done as Thou wilt.
Give what Thou wilt, how much Thou wilt,
and at what time Thou wilt.
Do with me as Thou knowest, and as best pleases Thee,
and is most for Thy honor.
Put me where Thou wilt, and do with me
in all things according to Thy wilt.
I am in Thy hand, turn me round which way Thou wilt.
Lo, I am Thy servant, ready to obey Thee in all things;
for I don't desire to live for myself, but for Thee:
I wish it may be perfectly and worthily. Amen.

Thomas à Kempis

Day 280

I DEDICATE MY LIFE
TO THE LORD

_____

_____

_____

_____

_____

_____

_____

_____

_____

_____

Let your heart therefore be wholly true to
the LORD our God, walking in His statutes and
keeping His commandments.

1 Kings 8:61

WALK YOUR TALK

Such people claim they know God, but they deny him by the way they live.
TITUS 1:16

Paul wrote to Titus, his son in the faith, to guide Titus in his leadership responsibilities on the island of Crete. Titus was a Greek believer who had been trained and nurtured by Paul. Like Timothy, Titus was one of Paul's closest friends and traveling companions who traveled on behalf of Paul to various locations. At this time, Paul had left Titus on the island of Crete to appoint elders in the new churches. Paul wrote to Titus to give him guidance in choosing the people who would fill those important positions in the churches. Paul also warned Titus about the infiltration of false teachers and encouraged Titus to be a good example to the believers.

Titus had his hands full – for the Cretans were known for being "liars, cruel animals, and lazy gluttons" (Titus 1:12). For Titus to identify new believers who had the ability to mature in the faith and blossom as leaders was a tough task indeed. Titus would need discernment to find the people who matched the qualifications Paul laid out in this chapter. Unlike the people mentioned in 1:16, the people Titus chose would claim to know God and *prove* their faith by the way they lived.

What about you? Do you claim to know God but deny Him with your life? Or would you meet Paul's standards as one who proves your faith by the way you live?

Do you live what you say you believe?
What would the people closest to you say?

GOD'S GRACE

For the grace of God has been revealed, bringing salvation to all people.
TITUS 2:11

Grace. Through the centuries, learned theologians and regular folks have tried to understand it and explain it: "unmerited favor"; "getting what we don't deserve"; "God's Riches At Christ's Expense." None of these noble efforts fully does justice to the term. As fallen creatures, the best we can hope for is an occasional glimpse of the truth. Even though we only see "imperfectly as in a cloudy mirror" (1 Cor. 13:12), what we witness in those moments of revelation is truly amazing.

In this letter, Paul wrote about the different people who would make up the churches – older men and women, younger men and women, husbands, wives, children, slaves – and then went right into verse 11 that points out that the grace of God has been revealed and brought salvation to *all* people – male, female, young, old, married, unmarried, rich, poor. All are saved by grace alone. Paul wrote to the church in Ephesus, "God saved you by his grace when you believed. And you can't take credit for this; it is a gift from God. Salvation is not a reward for the good things we have done, so none of us can boast about it" (Eph. 2:8-9).

The truth is, God gave us all the blessings of salvation even though He owed us nothing but judgment for our sin. We don't deserve it; we just receive it. That's grace.

What does the grace of God mean to you?
How will you live in His grace today?

OUR MOTIVATION FOR DOING GOOD

He saved us, not because of the righteous things we had done,
but because of his mercy. He washed away our sins, giving us a new birth
and new life through the Holy Spirit. He generously poured out the Spirit
upon us through Jesus Christ our Savior. Because of his grace he declared
us righteous and gave us confidence that we will inherit eternal life.

TITUS 3:5-7

In these three verses is the gospel in a nutshell. We have been saved – not because of any goodness or good works on our part, but strictly because of God's mercy and grace upon us. When He saved us, He washed away our sins. We were born again and given new life through the Holy Spirit. That Spirit has been generously poured out on us so that we are able to live for Christ. We have been declared righteous in His sight because of what Jesus Christ has done for us. And we can have full confidence that we will one day inherit eternal life.

This is what we believe; this is what the Christian faith is all about. No other religion on earth offers salvation as a free gift for simply accepting someone's sacrifice on our behalf. No other religion requires nothing of us but faith and obedience out of love for God and gratitude to Him for the new life we've been given. No other religion offers help along the way by the indwelling of a Holy Spirit. No other religion gives us the promise of confidence that we will indeed reach our reward in heaven.

The next time someone asks you what you believe, be ready with the basics from these verses. And let that person know that this offer can't be found anywhere but in the one true God.

Meditate on God's amazing grace and mercy shown to you
in Christ. Memorize the key points about your faith so
you'll be ready to share when the opportunity arises.

"I'M PRAYING FOR YOU"

I always thank my God when I pray for you, Philemon, because I keep hearing about your faith in the Lord Jesus and your love for all of God's people.

PHILEMON 1:4-5

We are often drawn to prayer by tragedies and difficult circumstances in our lives. We tell God all about our problems and ask for His help – and rightly so. Paul was certainly in difficult circumstances when he wrote this letter to Philemon. He was under house arrest in Rome, awaiting a trial before Caesar. He certainly had much to pray for. But his attention in prayer was also focused on others. In his letter to Philemon, Paul didn't forget to tell Philemon that he was praying for him – that he was thanking God for him.

Are there brothers or sisters in Christ who have encouraged you? Have you told them how much you appreciate them and that you are praying for them? Are you praying daily for those people in your life who mean so much to you? Are you thanking God daily for your spouse, your children, your parents, your siblings, your coworkers, your boss, your friends, and your neighbors? Are you bringing them before God's throne when they have concerns and needs?

Lay out a weekly plan of praying for the people in your life so you can take the time to really pray for them. Then resolve to tell them how much they mean to you. And you can honestly say, "I'm praying for you."

Start your weekly prayer list today. Spread all those people out across your week and take a few minutes each day to pray over that day's list. You'll be amazed at the blessings you receive!

THE ACCURATE REFLECTION OF GOD'S GLORY

*The Son radiates God's own glory and expresses the very character of God,
and he sustains everything by the mighty power of his command.
When he had cleansed us from our sins, he sat down in the place
of honor at the right hand of the majestic God in heaven.*

HEBREWS 1:3

What an incredibly rich, all-encompassing description of who Jesus Christ really is! Seldom are so many of His magnificent traits all brought together into one verse. Yet even this one verse is but a sample of the richness and depth of the book of Hebrews.

Written by an unknown author, the book of Hebrews resonates with language and description that make every verse worthy of silent meditation. The subject of this letter, clearly written to fellow Jews (Hebrews), explains once and for all that Jesus really is the Messiah promised in their Scriptures (our Old Testament). Replete with Jewish history and filled with familiar characters from the Old Testament, this book patiently walks the Jews through their own familiar promises and shows how those promises point directly to Jesus.

The subject throughout the treatise is consistent. Jesus Christ, the eternal Son of the divine Father, is superior to every other religious figure and form. (In chapter 1, for example, He is compared with angels – the most powerful and transcendent beings most of us can imagine – and they come up short when compared to the Son of God.) What Jesus has accomplished and is still achieving in the eternal realm enables us to be perfect and holy. Therefore the Hebrews, and we today, are challenged repeatedly by the author to take this message to heart, listening "very carefully to the truth we have heard" (Heb. 2:1), for that truth changes our lives and our eternity.

Choose a couple of verses from this chapter and meditate on them for a few moments. Thank God for sending His Son.

A PRAYER FOR A SINCERE HEART

Father in Heaven! You have loved us first,
help us never to forget that You are love so that
this sure conviction might triumph in our hearts
over the seduction of the world,
over the inquietude of the soul,
over the anxiety for the future,
over the fright of the past,
over the distress of the moment.
But grant also that this conviction might discipline
our soul so that our heart might remain faithful and sincere
in the love which we bear to all those whom You
have commanded us to love as we love ourselves.
Amen.

Søren Kierkegaard

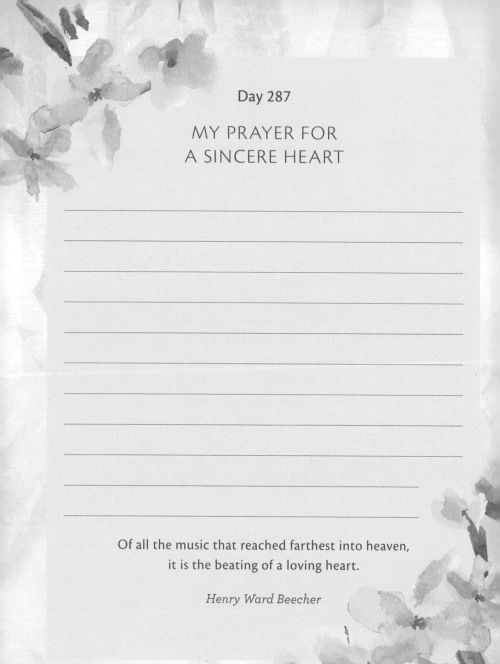

Day 287

MY PRAYER FOR
A SINCERE HEART

_____

_____

_____

_____

_____

_____

_____

_____

_____

_____

_____

Of all the music that reached farthest into heaven,
it is the beating of a loving heart.

Henry Ward Beecher

SOMEONE WHO REALLY UNDERSTANDS

Since he himself has gone through suffering and testing,
he is able to help us when we are being tested.

HEBREWS 2:18

"What do *you* know about it?" Persons in great pain and misery sometimes throw this question in the face of those who are trying to console them. The rejection is especially acute if the one offering solace has never been through similar misery herself. "How can you tell me 'Everything is going to be all right' or 'It's really not as bad as it seems'? You don't know anything about this!"

On the other hand, someone who has actually experienced the situation the sufferer is presently enduring innately senses what needs to be done or said – or left unsaid. That is exactly what kind of person, what kind of comforter, Jesus is. He was made "in every respect like us" (Heb. 2:17). He Himself suffered, just as we do; He Himself was tempted, just as we are. This is why He is able to help us so effectively – He has been through and understands whatever painful, dreadful situation we may face. He is able to minister as "our merciful and faithful High Priest" (Heb. 2:17) precisely because He went through suffering and temptation and therefore *understands* both those afflictions and us. So, says the writer, He is able to help us when we are being tempted, and He offers a perfect sacrifice that obliterates sin when we fall.

Thank Jesus for being willing to become human
so that He could truly understand pain, fear, suffering,
temptation, hurt – all those emotions that are a part of life.
Take whatever you're facing to Him today,
knowing that He understands.

LISTEN UP

Remember what it says: "Today when you hear his voice,
don't harden your hearts as Israel did when they rebelled".
HEBREWS 3:15

What a privilege that God would speak to us and make Himself heard in our hearts! Those outside the community of believers consider such a phenomenon absurd, unbelievable, an imagined fantasy. Most followers of Jesus cheerfully testify that it has happened to them – God has spoken in one way or another and given direction, guidance, or comfort.

Some skeptics immediately evoke the inherent problem of whether it really is the voice of God we're hearing or just our own wishful thinking – or the aftermath of that spicy meal we had late last night. For sincere believers, however, the real problem is that even when we *know* God has spoken to us, we fallen humans have a tendency to harden our hearts and not listen to His voice when it addresses us. It's not that we don't know whether God has spoken to us; it's that we don't want to conform to what He says when He *does* speak.

The writer of Hebrews warns every subsequent generation reading these words not to follow the example of the Israelites who, on the verge of entering the Promised Land, missed out because they did not listen to God. Not once, but three times the writer repeats, "Today when you hear his voice, don't harden your hearts" (Heb. 3:7-8, 15; 4:7). Evidently it's an urgent matter. We'd better pay attention.

Ask the Lord to help you have a listening ear
and a soft heart when He speaks to you.

RADICAL HEART SURGERY

For the word of God is alive and powerful. It is sharper than the
sharpest two-edged sword, cutting between soul and spirit, between
joint and marrow. It exposes our innermost thoughts and desires.

HEBREWS 4:12

Most of us avoid the surgeon's knife if we can. When faced with a choice between taking some pills or undergoing surgery, we choose the less radical solution if at all possible. The thought of a sharp knife cutting into our internal organs makes us queasy.

Similarly, we often avoid the most effective cure for our spiritual sicknesses, perhaps without realizing it. Our biggest problem, the author of Hebrews explains, is hardness of heart, so that even when God speaks to us, we don't listen. The author tells us that the cure for that hard-heartedness is the very Word of God itself.

The Word, he wrote, is like a scalpel. It strips away the calloused outer layers of flesh, passes through those defenses that we build up to protect ourselves from God's interference, and goes straight down into our hearts. The razor-sharp Word penetrates with astonishing accuracy right to the very core of our being, exposing "our innermost thoughts and desires." Yet this sharp knife is not an executioner's sword – God has no interest in slaying us. Instead, like a surgeon's knife, God's Word is an instrument of healing. The process of exposing and eradicating the root of our spiritual illness may indeed be painful for a while, but the result is health and wholeness.

Nobody likes the pain of surgery, but wouldn't you rather be well?
Are you letting God's Word penetrate your heart and life?

HE UNDERSTANDS

And he is able to deal gently with ignorant and wayward people
because he himself is subject to the same weaknesses.

HEBREWS 5:2

Jesus is not Superman. Though we recognize and appreciate His supernatural powers, we do not often recognize and appreciate His *vulnerability*. Apart from Herod's foiled attack on the infant Jesus, we don't remember many real threats to His life until the day He voluntarily laid it down for us.

But those who lived closer to the historical Jesus, like the writer of the book of Hebrews, were impressed very much by His human susceptibility. He knew what it was to be hungry, tired, and cross with your friends. He knew what it was to anticipate with fear a gruesome destiny. The Gospel writers, reflecting the memories of eyewitness disciples, made special mention of those human weaknesses that showed Jesus to be a normal human being – His need for rest and refreshment, his curt remarks to thick-headed followers, His cries of agony, His falling to the ground, exhausted, under the weight of the cross He carried.

Reflecting on Jesus' sufferings, the writer of Hebrews sees them as the very means by which God perfected Him to be the High Priest we all need. Jesus represents us before God and can deal gently with us because He intimately understands our all-too-human foibles. It's comforting to know that the one person who stands between us and the perfect justice of God knows exactly what it feels like to be human.

Reflect on the fact that Jesus became
a human for your sake. Thank Him that in
His intercession for you, He truly understands.

STARTING OVER?

So let us stop going over the basic teachings about Christ again and again.
Let us go on instead and become mature in our understanding.
Surely we don't need to start again with the fundamental importance
of repenting from evil deeds and placing our faith in God.
HEBREWS 6:1

Start all over again? Indeed not! When Jesus said, "Follow me," to His disciples, He did not mean to do so in cycles, with breaks, time-outs, and spiritual sabbaticals in between periods of zeal and commitment. Nor did He expect them to need to go back to square one every few months like penalized pieces of a board game and start the process all over again.

Yet surprisingly many people do begin their Christian walk over and over again with the most basic baby steps of faith. To mature in the faith might mean commitment, taking real steps of faith into unknown territories, needing to trust God through lengthy times of waiting. So they stay at the starting point when they can blame their sins on ignorance and their lack of commitment on misunderstanding. It's much safer that way – or so it seems. But there's nothing safe about thinking that the Christian life is a perpetual series of start-overs.

The writer of Hebrews was appalled at the arrested development of the people to whom he was writing. By this time they should have been teaching others, yet they were still like babies in the nursery needing to go over rudimentary teachings that they should, by now, have understood and accepted. The writer challenges them to move forward and deeper, not to constantly go back to square one and start over.

Where are you in your Christian walk?
Are you willing to go deeper into a more mature
faith? What steps do you need to take?

A PRAYER TO A FORGIVING GOD

Who is a God like You,
who pardons sin and forgives the transgression
of the remnant of His inheritance?
You do not stay angry forever
but delight to show mercy.
You will again have compassion on us;
You will tread our sins underfoot
and hurl all our iniquities into the depths of the sea.

Micah 7:18-19

Day 294

MY PRAYER TO OUR
FORGIVING AND MERCIFUL GOD

_____

_____

_____

_____

_____

_____

_____

_____

_____

_____

God pardons like a mother, who kisses
the offense into everlasting forgiveness.

Henry Ward Beecher

ALIVE FOREVER

Therefore he is able, once and forever, to save those who come to God through him. He lives forever to intercede with God on their behalf.

HEBREWS 7:25

The references to the ancient King Melchizedek in this chapter may seem a bit disconcerting, but the author was drawing upon a story well known by his Jewish readers from the book of Genesis. Because Melchizedek was both a king and a priest, and because no record exists of the beginning or end of his life, the author used him to describe the role Jesus has as both King and High Priest.

The point is that Jesus' high-priestly role is similar to but greater than that of any priest Israel ever had in its long history. While Israel's priests sacrificed animals to atone for the people's sins (and had to continue to do so), Jesus offered *Himself* as the once-and-for-all sacrifice for sin. Not only that, He "lives forever" so "his priesthood lasts forever" (Heb. 7:24). Because Jesus has already conquered death, He never will die again. Therefore, the priestly work He does – standing before God in our defense, pleading on our behalf on the basis of His blood – will never cease.

Nothing can add to what Jesus did to save us; the matter was settled completely at the cross. No more sacrifices are needed because "Jesus did this once for all when he offered himself as the sacrifice for the people's sins" (Heb. 7:27). Nothing can take away from the intercession He now makes for us before God; after all, He *died* to make our relationship with God possible.

Does your awareness that Jesus is alive and interceding constantly on your behalf lead you to be lax and lethargic ... or brimming with energy to serve Him?

Day 296

WRITTEN ON YOUR HEART

*"But this is the new covenant I will make with the people of Israel on that day,
says the Lord: I will put my laws in their minds, and I will write them
on their hearts. I will be their God and they will be my people".*

HEBREWS 8:10

What Jesus inaugurated with His blood is the authentic covenant that God had intended all along for His people. Since the time of Moses, the Israelites had experienced a foreshadowing of what was to come. The layout and furniture in the Tabernacle and Temple, the system of blood sacrifices to atone for sin, the role of the priests – all of this was the old covenant ("Old Testament") God had with His people. But "when the right time came, God sent his Son" (Gal. 4:4). Through the prophet Jeremiah, whom the writer quoted here in chapter 8, God promised a *new* covenant.

The essential difference between the two covenants is that under the old arrangement, the laws were "out there," written on stone tablets – laws that served only to point out sin and the need for forgiveness. Paul wrote, "Why, then, was the law given? It was given alongside the promise to show people their sins. But the law was designed to last only until the coming of the child who was promised" (Gal. 3:19).

In this new covenant, God writes His laws in our hearts and minds, so we all understand them. That can happen because Jesus' death conquered sin and opened the pathway between God and us. Under the new covenant established through Jesus, God's Word, written upon our hearts, is His communication to *us*.

Are you listening?

*What you read in God's Word becomes part of your
very being and stays with you when you close this
book and go out the door. How will His Word
in your heart affect your life "out there" today?*

THE PERFECT SACRIFICE

*Just think how much more the blood of Christ will purify our consciences
from sinful deeds so that we can worship the living God. For by the power of
the eternal Spirit, Christ offered himself to God as a perfect sacrifice for our sins.*

HEBREWS 9:14

These are among the most sobering verses of the entire Scriptures. We stand in hushed awe looking on as Christ, empowered by the Holy Spirit, offers Himself "to God as a perfect sacrifice for our sins."

The apostle Peter wrote that "God paid a ransom to save you from the empty life you inherited from your ancestors. And the ransom he paid was not mere gold or silver. It was the precious blood of Christ, the sinless, spotless Lamb of God" (1 Pet. 1:18-19). We've been ransomed (bought back from sin) by the blood of Christ. The writer of Hebrews explains further that Christ's blood is much more efficacious than the blood of animal sacrifices because animal blood could only cover sin, it couldn't cleanse the consciences of those who committed the sins: "It is not possible for the blood of bulls and goats to take away sins" (Heb. 10:4). Jesus Christ's blood, however, actually *purifies* our hearts, washes away the sin that resides there, and enables us to worship with clear consciences. We are not just forgiven, we are cleansed, made whole, renewed, and consecrated to God because of the blood of Jesus.

Each time we come back to this eternal truth, we are soberly reminded that we have been purified from deeds that led to death. Therefore, we are free to worship without hindrance, regret, or disgrace. Jesus' sacrifice was not just adequate, it was perfect.

*Your sin has been atoned for. You have been bought
back from slavery to sin by the blood of Christ.
You can now have a personal relationship with God.
Meditate on these awesome truths.*

ONCE FOR ALL

*Let us go right into the presence of God with sincere hearts fully trusting him.
For our guilty consciences have been sprinkled with Christ's blood to
make us clean, and our bodies have been washed with pure water.*

HEBREWS 10:22

Since Christ has cleansed us and made us acceptable to God by His shed blood, where do we go from there? Why, deeper into God's presence, of course! That's why He cleaned us up in the first place – so we could approach God. "So then, since we have a great High Priest who has entered heaven, Jesus the Son of God, let us hold firmly to what we believe ... Let us come boldly to the throne of our gracious God. There we will receive his mercy, and we will find grace to help us when we need it most" (Heb. 4:14, 16).

Sometimes, however, we act like the purification we receive from Jesus is primarily to make us feel better so we can speed back into our world. Knowing we need forgiveness, we go to Jesus. But once acquired, we treat that pardon like a warning instead of like a ticket from the policeman who pulls us over. Relieved, we gratefully stick the warning in our pocket, rev up our car, and recklessly zoom off again.

Instead, the author of Hebrews urges, since God has sacrificed His only Son so that we can come closer to Him, we should linger and do so. He makes us clean specifically so that we can enjoy fellowship with Him, our hearts lifted high in gladness, at ease in His pure presence. Once cleansed, let's stay awhile.

*How do you view the forgiveness you receive from God because
of Christ? Does it send you back out to sin some more,
or does it cause you to sit in awe in God's presence?*

JUST PASSING THROUGH

All these people died still believing what God had promised them.
They did not receive what was promised, but they saw it all from a distance and
welcomed it. They agreed that they were foreigners and nomads here on earth.
HEBREWS 11:13

This world is not my home, I'm just a-passin' through," go the words of the familiar old spiritual. That might seem to be merely a placebo for those who are unsuccessful in this world. For those who can't make it in this competitive marketplace, the next best thing is to dismiss the present reality and set their hopes on heaven. But that's not what the writer is saying here. Many of the people listed in this "Hall of Faith" were rich, competent, and powerful. All of them were familiar to the writer's audience, and their stories can be read in the Old Testament. None of them was perfect; their sins and foibles are readily told in Scripture.

Yet in spite of all the material wealth and power these people had, and in spite of all their personal imperfections, they deliberately lived as foreigners and nomads on this earth, keeping a light grip on this life and looking intently toward the promises of God. They had faith, described here as "the confidence that what we hope for will actually happen; it gives us assurance about things we cannot see" (Heb. 11:1). These and many other "heroes of faith" are held up for our admiration and emulation precisely because they eschewed loyalty to the visible world and considered themselves citizens of God's heavenly Kingdom instead. They lived by faith, not by sight.

How would your actions be different if you were
intensely conscious that you are no more than a
foreigner passing through this world on your way to a
home country that God Himself is preparing for you?

A PRAYER FOR ASSURANCE

O Lord, reassure me with Your quickening Spirit;
without You I can do nothing.
Mortify in me all ambition, vanity, vainglory,
worldliness, pride, selfishness, and resistance from God,
and fill me with love, peace and all the fruits of the Spirit.
O Lord, I know not what I am, but to You I flee for refuge.
I would surrender myself to You,
trusting Your precious promises
and against hope believing in hope.
Amen.

William Wilberforce

Day 301

MY PRAYER FOR ASSURANCE

_____

_____

_____

_____

_____

_____

_____

_____

_____

_____

_____

Prayer crowns God with the honor and glory due to His name,
and God crowns prayer with assurance and comfort.
The most praying souls are the most assured souls.

Thomas Brooks

EYES ON THE PRIZE

We do this by keeping our eyes on Jesus, the champion who initiates and perfects our faith. Because of the joy awaiting him, he endured the cross, disregarding its shame. Now he is seated in the place of honor beside God's throne.

HEBREWS 12:2

In today's world of lax promiscuity and a credit-driven economy, almost no one remembers what delayed gratification is. Previous generations understood that many of the things one wants most in life cannot be had easily or instantly. Mature adults know that attaining anything worthwhile takes time, toil, perseverance, and sometimes even suffering.

The writer of Hebrews describes our spiritual pilgrimage as an endurance race, a race so wearying that many times we feel like giving up and quitting. The only way to make it, to keep running all the way to the end, is to keep our eyes fixed on Jesus, who runs before us setting the pace. Not only does He demonstrate that it is possible to complete this race and win it, He encourages us along because He knows how we feel. In order to be crowned victor, Jesus not only had to endure the normal difficulties of the race, but He also had to endure suffering, abuse from competitors, and shame on His way to crossing the finish line. That's when He was honored.

The Christian life is not easy (nothing worthwhile is); we do not attain instant perfection (as much as we might like it). Instead, we are in a long-distance race that we run only against ourselves, always with our eyes on Jesus, always moving toward the finish line. As we meditate on what He did for us, we are strengthened to keep going.

In your Christian life, are you running strong,
or are you beginning to feel weary?
Ask Jesus to give you the strength you need.

OUR SPIRITUAL LEADERS

Obey your spiritual leaders, and do what they say. Their work is to watch over your souls, and they are accountable to God. Give them reason to do this with joy and not with sorrow. That would certainly not be for your benefit.

HEBREWS 13:17

How often is the story told (in the latest novel or movie) of an overbearing ogre in the role of leader who is disobeyed by the hero or heroine in the story? The moral? Being disobedient and a nonconformist against those in authority is your duty, for it makes all things better. So what's a real-life leader to do?

Leadership involves making tough choices, looking out for the organization *and* the needs of the people, looking into the future while keeping a careful eye on the present. Leadership is difficult and good leaders are rare indeed. Church leaders often find themselves in the difficult positions of trying to do the right thing when they know they'll upset at least someone in the process. They know they are responsible to God for the souls in their care – and those souls are often willing to cause trouble despite the care they receive!

The writer of Hebrews counsels us to obey those whom God has placed over us, for our own good. The task of the spiritual leader is very difficult. Our spiritual leaders seek to please God, and they get great joy out of seeing us prosper spiritually. We make it easy on them and on ourselves when we refuse to be upset and disobedient but instead work together with them to serve the Lord.

Pray for the leaders in your church. Consider all the responsibilities they have in running your church. Consider what you can do to help and encourage them.

Day 304

AN OPPORTUNITY FOR JOY

*Dear brothers and sisters, when troubles come your way,
consider it an opportunity for great joy. For you know that when
your faith is tested, your endurance has a chance to grow.*

JAMES 1:2-3

These words sound like a contradiction in terms! Troubles are for complaining, crying, and praying; joy just doesn't come into the equation. But that doesn't mean it *shouldn't* be there. After all, everything about the Christian faith turns what we consider to be "normal" upside down. Joy in troubles? Why not?

The writer of this letter was James, the half-brother of Jesus. Writing to "Jewish believers scattered abroad" (James 1:1), James wanted these believers to be able to face their troubles and to grow through them. For many of these early believers, their faith created a whole new series of troubles. Instead of complaining, crying, or giving up, James challenged the believers to have joy because their faith would have a chance to grow and deepen during the difficult times.

Think about it. When everything's going great in your life, are you in the Word and on your knees, or do you get lax about those things? Most often, it's the troubles that bring us back to God. When our faith is tested, we have a chance to grow. God loves us enough to put us through our paces. He wants us to be "fully developed ... perfect and complete, needing nothing" (James 1:4).

*In what ways can you consider your troubles
and difficulties as opportunities for joy?*

FAITH AND WORKS

*So you see, faith by itself isn't enough.
Unless it produces good deeds, it is dead and useless.*

JAMES 2:17

Wait a minute, you might think to yourself, *I thought all I needed was faith to be saved.* You might remember the apostle Paul's words in Galatians 2:16, "We know that a person is made right with God by faith in Jesus Christ, not by obeying the law," and in Romans 3:28, "We are made right with God through faith and not by obeying the law." So how can it be that "faith by itself isn't enough"? Isn't this a contradiction?

One thing you can be sure of – God's Word does not contradict itself. His Word is truth and can be trusted completely. So how do we understand what Paul and James are saying? The answer: We read and study more deeply.

In Galatians and Romans Paul was writing to people dealing with Judaizers – Jews who were teaching that Christians had to *do* certain acts, such as circumcision and obeying Jewish laws, to be saved. Hence, Paul focused on salvation by faith alone.

James was writing to people who thought intellectual agreement alone was enough – and then they kept on living in ways that displeased God (like showing favoritism). Hence, James focused on how their faith should make a difference in how they treated people and even the words that came out of their mouths.

The bottom line – we can't *earn* salvation; we can only accept it. However, once accepted, our relationship with Jesus should have an effect on every aspect of our lives.

*We are not saved by good works
but for good works. Has your faith made a
discernible difference in how you live?*

WATCH YOUR MOUTH

*People can tame all kinds of animals, birds, reptiles, and fish, but no one
can tame the tongue. It is restless and evil, full of deadly poison.*
JAMES 3:7-8

Have you ever experienced this phenomenon – your mouth running off ahead of you, spewing deadly poison before you even realize what has happened? Then you know firsthand why it is that "no one can tame the tongue." It is indeed "restless and evil, full of deadly poison." This is not a new phenomenon. Proverbs 13:3 says, "Those who control their tongue will have a long life; opening your mouth can ruin everything." Indeed, opening our mouths often gets us into trouble.

Jesus explained why: "It is what comes from inside that defiles you. For from within, out of a person's heart, come evil thoughts ... wickedness, deceit ... slander, pride, and foolishness" (Mark 7:20-22).

So what can we do?

We can't tame our tongues, but as believers, we have the Holy Spirit within who will help us. Paul wrote to the Romans, "I plead with you to give your bodies to God because of all he has done for you. Let them be a living and holy sacrifice – the kind he will find acceptable ... Don't copy the behavior and customs of this world, but let God transform you into a new person by changing the way you think" (Rom. 12:1-2). In fact, one of the fruits of the Spirit is self-control (Gal. 5:23).

You don't have to do it alone. You've got help from the Holy Spirit Himself. Ask Him.

*Do you need some mouth control? Ask the Holy Spirit
to grow the fruit of self-control in your life and
to continue to transform you from the inside out.*

A PRAYER FOR GOD'S PRESENCE

Into Thy hands, O Lord, I commend myself,
my spirit, soul, and body:
Thou didst make, and didst redeem them;
and together with me, all my friends and all that belongs to me.
Thou hast vouchsafed them to me, Lord, in Thy goodness.
Guard my lying down and my rising up,
from henceforth and for ever.
Let me remember Thee on my bed, and search out my spirit;
let me wake up and be present with Thee;
let me lay me down in peace, and take my rest:
for it is Thou, Lord, only that makes me dwell in safety.
Amen.

Lancelot Andrewes

Day 308

MY PRAYER FOR
GOD'S PRESENCE

_____

_____

_____

_____

_____

_____

_____

_____

_____

_____

_____

_____

_____

Those who know Your name trust in You,
for You, Lord, have never forsaken
those who seek You.

Psalm 9:10

WATCH HIM RUN

So humble yourselves before God. Resist the devil, and he will flee from you.
JAMES 4:7

Picture Satan running for cover! It almost sounds impossible. After all, he's evil and powerful, wreaking havoc all over the world. He's not a little guy in red tights with a pointy pitchfork and long tail. No, he's much bigger and much more frightening.

And we do well to have a certain amount of healthy fear. We ought not mess with his power by delving into witchcraft or séances or spell casting. That's just playing with fire, and we are wise to steer clear.

Yet, as formidable as Satan might be, he is not all-powerful. James writes that all we have to do is resist and he will flee. We put on our armor (as described in Ephesians 6:10-20) – shaking in our shoes, our sword clattering against our shield, our helmet hiding our fear – and Satan sees us coming and runs the other way! He knows that once we have the armor on and decide we're going to fight, he's already lost the battle.

You see, it's not us that make him afraid; it's the fact that behind us stands the God of the universe. Satan knows that taking Him on is always a losing proposition.

But to have that strength, we must humble ourselves before God. Pride will only cause us to slip and fall. Humility lets us stand our ground in the battle. We aren't strong enough to make Satan run; it's our dependence on God that causes Satan to flee.

Do you think you can't resist sin?
Think again. Put on your armor and know that God
fights with you. Then watch Satan run.

PRAYING AND PRAISING

Are any of you suffering hardships? You should pray.
Are any of you happy? You should sing praises.
JAMES 5:13

I t doesn't get much more straightforward than that – if you're suffering, pray; if you're happy, praise! If more of us would simply take that advice, life would be so much simpler.

Too often when we face hardships, our first response is not to pray. Perhaps we just don't think we should bother God with our request; after all, our hardship is probably not as bad as someone else's hardship.

Perhaps we think we can handle the difficulty on our own, and so we don't bring it to God.

Perhaps we figure that since our own wrong choices got us into this particular hardship, God isn't going to help us out.

And what about when we're happy? Too often when we feel good, our first response is not to praise. Instead, we become forgetful of having our quiet time. We aren't driven to prayer because – well – everything is going fine.

James says that it doesn't matter why we're suffering hardship, who caused it, or how we got into it. When we're suffering, we should pray. And when the hardships are over and we're happy again, we ought not forget the provision and comfort that got us through. When we're happy, we should sing praises.

Prayer and praise – each day, each moment calls for one or the other.

Are you praying or praising today?

CHOSEN FOR SPECIAL FAVOR

God the Father knew you and chose you long ago, and his Spirit has made you holy. As a result, you have obeyed him and have been cleansed by the blood of Jesus Christ. May God give you more and more grace and peace.

1 PETER 1:2

What if every day you could feel like a winner – like you had been specially chosen to win any number of prizes in the latest contest? Most of us go through our day-to-day routines with no particular sense of being "winners" who have been selected for special prizes. Yet Peter's opening words in this letter announce, "You have been selected ... by almighty God Himself!"

Peter tells us that God the Father chose us long ago; the Spirit made us holy by setting us apart from worldliness and enabling us to obey; Jesus Christ cleansed us with His blood. This is one of the few places in Scripture where all three members of the Trinity are named together, each distinguished from the others by the particularity of His work in our behalf. Peter says the three persons of the Godhead work for us, doing what we cannot do ourselves and showering us with favor.

Later Peter expands on those blessings. He evokes an incredible treasure already on deposit in the "Bank of Heaven" – salvation from the perils of this world and life everlasting in the presence of Jesus. Our challenge is that to inherit all these "prizes," we must keep on believing in that which we do not yet see.

How must God feel about you if all three members of the Trinity are hard at work in your behalf? Since you've been chosen by God for special favor, how will you celebrate today?

A LIVING TEMPLE

And you are living stones that God is building into his spiritual temple.
What's more, you are his holy priests. Through the mediation of Jesus Christ,
you offer spiritual sacrifices that please God.

1 PETER 2:5

Peter encapsulates in a single verse the passive and active aspects of the Christian life. We are living stones that God is using to build a spiritual edifice for His glory and praise; at the same time, we ourselves have an active role to play in that spiritual temple as we offer "sacrifices" (service) that please Him. He does the design and construction of that spiritual temple, putting us living elements together like many-colored fragments of stained glass to form a beautiful mosaic. We then go about our daily lives, offering everything we do as priestly service to God.

To omit either the passive or the active emphasis is error. Some overemphasize the grace of God to the point of unfruitful passivity. Others work like scurrying ants to achieve spiritual benefit through their own efforts. Both ways of conducting the Christian life are lopsided. Peter's image balances two aspects of truth: Because we are saved by grace, our lives should be fruitful for Him.

To which side do you tend to lean? Do you relish contemplating the glorious beauty of the finished work of Christ, but sometimes neglect to put on your "priestly robes" and serve Him? Or do you hustle around working up a sweat doing "Kingdom work" without stopping from time to time to appreciate the architect and His vision of the temple He is constructing?

Consider everything you do today as your
"spiritual sacrifice" to God, in thanksgiving for being chosen
as one of His living stones with which He is building His temple.

HOW TO RESPOND TO DIFFICULT PEOPLE

Don't repay evil for evil. Don't retaliate with insults when people insult you. Instead, pay them back with a blessing. That is what God has called you to do, and he will bless you for it

1 PETER 3:9

What could be more counterintuitive than this piece of advice? Respond to those who attack you verbally by blessing them and saying nice, kind things in return? Every molecule of our being is charged with readiness to retaliate and meet aggression with aggression. We don't even have to stop and think or plan what to say when we get angry – it just spills out.

As with every other difficult command he gives out, Peter pointed to the example of Jesus and basically said, "There's your model. Copy Him."

But what is perhaps more motivating is that Peter went to some length to explain how God promises to bless people who do this counterintuitive business of returning kindness for insult, sweetness for rancor, blessing for animosity. God watches over those who do right, especially when wrong is being done to them. He listens sympathetically to our complaints addressed to Him (instead of to the person intending to harm us). He rewards us when we keep our tongue reined in.

In 1 Peter 3:10 Peter quoted a portion of Psalm 34 that says, "If you want to enjoy life and see many happy days, keep your tongue from speaking evil." The next time you're attacked verbally, might it be easier not to respond in kind if you know that God will reward you for your self-control and obedience?

Are there individuals from whom you can expect bitter words today?
If so, perhaps you should prepare your heart ahead of time.
Ask God what you can say in return that will
"pay them back with a blessing" and so honor Him.

A PRAYER FOR GOD'S LOVINGKINDNESS

Almighty God, by whose mercy my life has been
yet prolonged to another year, grant that Thy mercy
may not be in vain. Let not my years be multiplied
to increase my guilt; but as age advances,
let me become more pure in my thoughts,
more regular in my desires, and more obedient to Thy laws.
Let not the cares of the world distract me,
nor the evils of age overwhelm me.
But continue and increase Thy lovingkindness towards me;
and when Thou shalt call me hence,
receive me to everlasting happiness,
for the sake of Jesus Christ our Lord. Amen.

Samuel Johnson

MY PRAYER FOR GOD'S LOVINGKINDNESS

_____

_____

_____

_____

_____

_____

_____

_____

_____

_____

Our mind cannot find a comparison too large
for expressing the superabundant mercy
of the Lord toward His people.

David Dickson

KEEP ON KEEPING ON

So if you are suffering in a manner that pleases God, keep on doing what is right,
and trust your lives to the God who created you, for he will never fail you.

1 PETER 4:19

In every chapter of his letter, Peter discussed the suffering that Christians experience because of their faith in Christ. The believers to whom Peter wrote were no strangers to suffering and persecution; Peter himself would one day be martyred for his faith. Here Peter urged sufferers to do two things: Keep on doing what is right, and trust God not to fail them.

Sound advice ... but easier said than done. Let's face it, when we are suffering, the natural reaction is to put some distance between ourselves and whatever is causing the disturbance.

By no means does it feel natural that when we suffer, even according to God's will, we should keep right on doing whatever brought on the persecution. Nor is it all that easy to trust God, who willed us to be in that situation in the first place!

But two considerations compel us. First, as Peter says elsewhere, there's no value in suffering for doing *wrong*, so if we're going to suffer anyway, let it be for doing *right* (1 Pet. 3:13-17).

Second, the God to whom you entrust yourself is "the God who created you." He has the right to do whatever He purposes to do with what He made. So, since you are His creation, trust Him to do right with what is His own. You can do that because you know God will never fail you.

Ask God to help you trust Him, to keep on doing what is right,
and to have faith that He will never fail you.

HOLD ON!

In his kindness God called you to share in his eternal glory by means
of Christ Jesus. So after you have suffered a little while, he will restore,
support, and strengthen you, and he will place you on a firm foundation.

1 PETER 5:10

Almost every adventure movie contains a scene where someone is dangling helplessly over an abyss, desperately hoping another person will come to the rescue. The only thing the imperiled person can do is *hold on!* This is Peter's message from beginning to end of his letter. Hold on! Deliverance is coming!

Peter never once denied the pain and suffering in believers' lives; rather, he openly acknowledged that these are part and parcel of the life of all who follow Jesus, just as they were inherent in *His* life. But Peter promised that this will only be a stage, a temporary phase of our walk with Christ, and that far better things are in store for us.

The theme of Peter's entire book is "out of weakness and testing come strength and glory." Here near the end Peter piled verbs on top of one another promising that after we have suffered a little while, God Himself will restore us, support us, strengthen us, and place us on a firm foundation. Peter's words echo, perhaps, what the Master said to him one dark night: "Simon, Simon, Satan has asked to sift each of you like wheat. But I have pleaded in prayer for you, Simon, that your faith should not fail. So when you have repented and turned to me again, strengthen your brothers" (Luke 22:31-32).

You can trust Peter's counsel. He obviously knew what he was talking about.

Ask the Lord to strengthen you for the day ahead
so that you can persevere and hold on.

EVERYTHING YOU NEED

By his divine power, God has given us everything we need for living a godly life.
We have received all of this by coming to know him, the one who called us
to himself by means of his marvelous glory and excellence.

2 PETER 1:3

Peter knew Jesus better, perhaps, than almost any other human being ever knew Him. Peter walked with Him, listened, learned, saw miracles, and observed Jesus for almost three years in a day-to-day close relationship. In fact, on certain occasions when Jesus left everyone else behind, He called Peter, James, and John to come along with Him; they were specially chosen to see some things that no one else witnessed. Peter alluded to some of these in this letter.

But though he knew Jesus as a man, Peter calls Him "God," "Savior," and "Lord" in the first two verses, and in this third verse refers to His "divine power." This is one of the few places in Scripture where Jesus' divinity is so blatantly and clearly asserted, and by one who knew Him well. But what is striking about that divine power here is that Peter assures us that *we* have access to it.

Christianity is not a mere matter of imitating Christ's example (a major theme of Peter's first letter); it's also a matter of knowing Him better and better. We are not on our own to live up to the high standards God has put before us. The better we know Him, the more of that divine power we have. Peter tells us, Christ has given us everything we need to live a godly life.

Do you realize the divine power that is available to you?
What does it mean for you today that God has given
you everything you need to live a godly life?

WORSE OFF THAN BEFORE

*And when people escape from the wickedness of the world
by knowing our Lord and Savior Jesus Christ and then get tangled up
and enslaved by sin again, they are worse off than before.*

2 PETER 2:20

*A*h, what a relief to escape a dark, fetid environment and come out into the brightness and light of the open sky. Feel fresh breezes of clean, pure air upon your face. Breathe in deeply and gratefully. Then, decide to turn around and duck back down into that dank dungeon. Doesn't make sense, does it?

Of course not; yet Peter stopped us short by reminding us that this is precisely what some people were doing. Having known the liberating joy of following Jesus up out of the foul stench of their captivity to sin, they later willingly return to that sin under a pretext of freedom. Encouraged by false teachers who were themselves enslaved to sin, they returned to the way of life from which Jesus had already freed them. They thought freedom meant doing whatever they wanted and then just asking Jesus to forgive them. They forgot that sin has horrible entanglements and consequences.

Judgment is real; sin is deadly. Hopefully Peter's description causes you to shiver. He warns that once you've found the escape from wickedness, once you've breathed the fresh air of freedom in Jesus, don't return again to slavery to sin. If these words make you stop and examine yourself carefully, that's good! It means the Spirit of God is still at work in you.

*Have you allowed yourself recently to toy with some sin
that had enslaved you in the past? Are you thinking,
"Christ has set me free, so now this won't be a problem
for me like it used to be"? If this sounds like how
you've been thinking, read this chapter again.*

WHEN SCOFFERS COME

*Most importantly, I want to remind you that in the last days
scoffers will come, mocking the truth and following their own desires.*

2 PETER 3:3

*B*eing laughed at is a bitter experience. From early childhood, through grade school, high school, and even in adult life, we worry over whether our clothing might elicit negative notice, we are mortified if an opinion provokes a guffaw, we hope that our lack of abilities on the playground or on the job won't make us objects of derision. The memory of peers laughing at us is painful, sometimes leaving a wound that doesn't heal for years. No wonder we all dread the possibility that it will happen again.

The devil knows this and uses our fear of being laughed at against us. Since Christians believe in the unseen, we can be sure that the enemy of our souls will attack that very life of faith. One of his stronger weapons is the threat of scornful laughter. Listen to some prominent speakers or some celebrities and you will quickly find that scoffers have indeed come "mocking the truth and following their own desires." This ought not surprise us, for Peter had already given warning.

Be prepared for the scoffers who will laugh at what you believe. Their ignorance need not cause *you* embarrassment. You know the truth. They are the ones who will one day look very foolish indeed.

*Pray not to be caught off guard but to be ready
for the scoffers who might come your way.
Ask God to fix your eyes on His coming so that
you live a holy, godly life in anticipation of it.*

A PRAYER FOR AID IN TIME OF NEED

We beseech Thee, Lord and Master, to be our help and succor.
Save those among us who are in tribulation;
have mercy on the lowly; lift up the fallen;
show Thyself unto the needy; heal the ungodly;
convert the wanderers of Thy people;
feed the hungry; release our prisoners;
raise up the weak; comfort the faint-hearted.
Let all the people know that Thou art God alone,
and Jesus Christ is Thy Son,
and we are Thy people and the sheep of Thy pastures.
Amen.

St. Clement of Rome

Day 322

MY PRAYER FOR AID
IN TIME OF NEED

_____

_____

_____

_____

_____

_____

_____

_____

_____

_____

_____

Have you ever noticed how much of Christ's life
was spent in doing kind things?

Henry Drummond

STEP INTO THE LIGHT

So we are lying if we say we have fellowship with God but go on living in spiritual darkness; we are not practicing the truth. But if we are living in the light, as God is in the light, then we have fellowship with each other, and the blood of Jesus, his Son, cleanses us from all sin.

1 JOHN 1:6-7

The sun is amazing. Moments before dawn, as the earth spins on its axis and revolves around the sun, our planet positions us to begin to see the sun. But well before it is visible wherever we are, we see its approach brighten dark skies. As the sun's reflections on the moon dissipate, and seconds before the full sun appears to our eyes, we can drive without headlights and see clearly enough to take a stroll. That's how powerful the sun is! But it's nothing more than a candle compared to the light of God!

When God reveals Himself to us through the person of Jesus Christ and draws us to Himself by the Holy Spirit, He brightens our darkened lives. We begin to understand Him and His ways. We sense the warmth of His presence in our fellowship. As we position ourselves to receive God's full presence in us, our minds illuminate to the truth reflected to us by His Word. His Word shines light on our past and our present, and guides us into our future. If we submit to God's Word and turn from the darkness of our sins, the Lord purifies us and ignites His purposes in our lives.

John encourages us to remain in the light of our heavenly Father. We cannot do that apart from remaining in His Word and applying God's precepts to our steps in this life.

Are you living in the light, as God is in the light?
What do you do when God's Word shines on you?

GOD FIRST

*Do not love this world nor the things it offers you, for when you
love the world, you do not have the love of the Father in you.*

1 JOHN 2:15

The same John who wrote this verse saying, "Do not love this world," also penned those precious words, "For God loved the world so much that he gave his one and only Son, so that everyone who believes in him will not perish but have eternal life" (John 3:16). Is this a contradiction? Is the world loved or not? We get no help from the vocabulary because John used the same Greek words for *love* and for *world* in both passages. Apparently, God gets to love the world, but we don't.

Exactly!

God created the world and knows how to love it. He particularly loves those for whom He gave His Son – us. We, on the other hand, must not love the world; instead, God wants us to love *Him*. And actually, we will treat the world with greater respect as we love God than we will if we make the world our god and try to love it. As Paul explained in Romans 1:25, we have been deceived if we exchange worship of the Creator for worship of the creation.

This doesn't mean you have to hate everything about your life. God wants you to live life to the fullest (John 10:10). Instead, you must always love God most and hold loosely the things of this world. In the end, only your love of God will last forever.

*Do you love the world and what it offers you,
or can you readily let it go in order to love God first?*

LOVE AS YOU'VE BEEN LOVED

We know what real love is because Jesus gave up his life for us.
So we also ought to give up our lives for our brothers and sisters.

1 JOHN 3:16

Our orders are to live as Jesus lived and to love as He loved. John also recorded these words that Jesus told His disciples, "So now I am giving you a new commandment: Love each other. Just as I have loved you, you should love each other. Your love for one another will prove to the world that you are my disciples" (John 13:34-35). Jesus went the full distance to show us the nature of love. He gave up His life for us: "There is no greater love than to lay down one's life for one's friends" (John 15:13).

How, we might ask, do we give up our lives? One aspect of laying down our lives includes the possibility of anonymity. If we literally "give up our lives," we will not be around to be thanked. If we figuratively "give up our lives," we probably shouldn't expect thanks – and we can't be thanked or applauded or interviewed as a hero if we remain anonymous. What we do is for others, not for appreciation or recognition.

You can probably think of five people who could benefit from an anonymous note of encouragement. Someone near you probably has a specific financial or material need that you could meet without drawing attention to yourself. Don't overlook the joy of spending a day looking for opportunities to practice kindness purely at random!

Which of those five people will you "give up your life" for today?

FIRST LOVE

We love each other because he loved us first.
1 JOHN 4:19

Throughout the centuries, Christians have developed a number of ways to point to God's existence. For instance, we argue from the design in the universe that there must be a Master Designer, or we say that the universal sense of right and wrong is a clue to a moral absolute and Creator.

One approach the Bible employs we could call "the argument from love." John, who describes himself as the apostle Jesus loved (see John 13:23; 20:2; 21:7, 20), penned the phrase, "God is love" (1 John 4:16). Unfortunately, the world has muddied up the word *love*. Many see love as something that can come and go, or the word is thrown around and means nothing: "I *love* chocolate!"

The kind of love Jesus shows us can only come from Him. The apostle Paul described it as patient and kind, not jealous or boastful or proud or rude, not demanding its own way, not irritable, keeping no record of being wronged, rejoicing when the truth wins out. "Love never gives up, never loses faith, is always hopeful, and endures through every circumstance" (see 1 Cor. 13:4-7). Clearly, that kind of love comes by way of God alone.

Our capacity to love offers another evidence for God's existence. If we are naturally selfish, then loving comes supernaturally! Whenever we note the presence of love, we are noting God's presence. Whatever genuine love we see, feel, or hear about came from Him. We love because He first loved us.

In the past few days, in what ways have you seen evidence of God through love? What can you do to show others by your actions that God is love?

GOD HAS A TESTIMONY

And this is what God has testified: He has given us eternal life, and this life is in his Son. Whoever has the Son has life; whoever does not have God's Son does not have life.

1 JOHN 5:11-12

*F*ormer *Chicago Tribune* investigative reporter Lee Strobel used to be a hardened atheist. As a journalist, his natural bent was to check facts and seek logical conclusions to come up with an accurate news story. But he is married to a believer, and her faith influenced him. Instigated, Strobel began to investigate and to write about his pursuit of the work of God. Subsequently, through interviews with theologians, thorough critique of theories denying God's existence, and the testimonies of others besides his wife, Strobel became a believer. He has published his findings in several books so that others might believe. Now Strobel is a Bible teacher and has influenced many with the case he makes for the truth of Christianity.

The evidence that God has given eternal life through His Son lies in His Word and in the lives of His followers. We have the Son and so have life; those who do not have the Son do not have life. Like Strobel, many who have sought to prove Christianity to be false and have seriously studied and investigated have become believers. Why? Often because they saw the evidence in the lives of those who have life.

You are influencing every person you meet for or against the Christian faith. Who knows what that person you meet today might be investigating about the claims of Jesus?

What is your life saying today about Jesus?

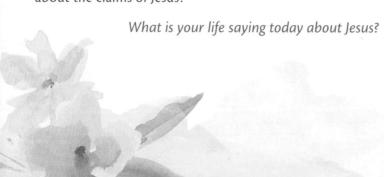

A PRAYER IN PRAISE OF THE CREATOR

Thank You for making me so wonderfully complex!
Your workmanship is marvelous – how well I know it.
You watched me as I was being formed in utter seclusion,
as I was woven together in the dark of the womb.
You saw me before I was born.
Every day of my life was recorded in Your book.
Every moment was laid out
before a single day had passed.
How precious are Your thoughts about me, O God.
They cannot be numbered!
I can't even count them;
they outnumber the grains of sand!
And when I wake up,
You are still with me!

Psalm 139:14-18

Day 329

MY PRAYER IN PRAISE
OF THE CREATOR

_____

_____

_____

_____

_____

_____

_____

_____

_____

_____

_____

We are God's productions, His compositions.

David Jeremiah

FINDING THE TRUTH

If anyone comes to your meeting and does not teach the truth about Christ,
don't invite that person into your home or give any kind of encouragement.
Anyone who encourages such people becomes a partner in their evil work.

2 JOHN 1:10-11

These are harsh words in a world where so many want to be viewed as tolerant, open-minded, and able to see things from many points of view. While there is value in being able to see a situation from many perspectives and being sensitive to people's situations, Satan has been crafty in taking this way across the line. Indeed, we are being slowly but surely seduced into believing that all kinds of lies, evil, wickedness, and sin are actually okay if there are "consenting adults" or "mitigating circumstances" or "an end that justifies the means." To believe otherwise is to be "narrow-minded."

God's Word rescues us from confusion and gives us the truth. Anyone who does not teach the truth does not deserve our hearing, our money, our hospitality, or our encouragement. That's how important God regards the truth, and that's how important it must be to us.

That means, then, that we need to *know* the truth, and we do that by studying God's Word and listening to those people who *do* teach the truth about Jesus. Let others call you narrow-minded; after all, Jesus said, "You can enter God's Kingdom only through the narrow gate. The highway to hell is broad, and its gate is wide for the many who choose that way. But the gateway to life is very narrow and the road is difficult, and only a few ever find it" (Matt. 7:13-14).

*Ask God to continue to teach you truth from His Word and to
give you discernment when listening to the teaching of others.*

SEAL OF APPROVAL

*Dear friend, don't let this bad example influence you. Follow only
what is good. Remember that those who do good prove that they are
God's children, and those who do evil prove that they do not know God.*

3 JOHN 1:11

The international community is familiar with seals of approval that re-assure customers that products meet high standards. For example, the European "Trusted Shops" seal indicates that its bearer delivers goods and services on the Internet in a manner that meets strict requirements for consumers. In the United States, we have the Food and Drug Administration (FDA), Dairy Association (USDA), and Pharmacopoeia (USP) seals that reassure people purchasing these products that they are not tainted in any way but are safe to use or consume. In Africa, Asia, and other regions, similar warranties exist for public safety.

John joyfully places his spiritual seal of approval on two friends in the church, Gaius and Demetrius. Gaius is a leader whom fellow church members attest has benefited the believers and the work of the gospel, despite the fact that a man named Diotrephes was attempting to stir up trouble. Demetrius may have carried this letter from John to Gaius. Ultimately, John explained, anyone who does what is good has God's approval, regardless of what some people may accuse.

However, the world's standards often are not aligned with the Christian worldview. While it may feel good to gain a stamp of approval from the people around us, this is not what we should seek. We would do well *not* to meet with the approval of people whose ideas and practices are not in submission to our highest authority, God. The stamp of approval we should seek is the one that only God can give.

To whom are you looking for approval?
How can your life today gain God's "seal of approval"?

RESERVATIONS REQUIRED

So I want to remind you, though you already know these things,
that Jesus first rescued the nation of Israel from Egypt,
but later he destroyed those who did not remain faithful.

JUDE 1:5

Many of us use online calendars or carry daily planners to keep ourselves organized. We especially make note of important reservations we have made for a meeting, flight, event, dinner out, and other happenings.

Jude's letter provides a personalized reminder to Christians regarding the most important appointment of our lives: our eternal destiny announced on Judgment Day. Jude repeated his brother James's earlier warnings about false teachers and went on to post additional reminders for all his readers to note.

Note: Jude reminds us that, despite all that God has miraculously performed to deliver us out of bondage, there are those who still will attempt to hinder us in our faith. Yet God has made a reservation for those who pervert the gospel: "doomed forever to blackest darkness" (Jude 1:13).

Note: Watch out for people who are divisive; this is not of God's Holy Spirit.

Note: Stand firm in Jesus Christ, who gave His life for us and loves us. Pray. Show mercy toward one another. Keep the faith!

Finally, Jude reminds us that God has a place reserved for us in eternity. This appointment is confirmed by God – not by our ability to save ourselves – and He will take us into His magnificent presence with great joy because of Christ.

The appointment with God for eternity isn't in your planner,
for you don't know when it will occur. But how about
a daily appointment with God? Can you set aside time
to talk with Him and read His Word each day?

FOREVER AND EVER

*He is the faithful witness to these things, the first to rise from the dead,
and the ruler of all the kings of the world. All glory to him who loves us
and has freed us from our sins by shedding his blood for us.
He has made us a Kingdom of priests for God his Father.
All glory and power to him forever and ever! Amen.*

REVELATION 1:5-6

"Who's in charge around here anyway?" we sometimes mutter under our breath. Bad service at a restaurant or lack of help at a store can cause us to instantly seek the manager – the person in charge.

Perhaps some might mutter that way about planet Earth. "Who's in charge around here?" we ask as suffering and evil run rampant. If indeed there is a Manager in charge, we wonder how powerful He really is, if He cares, or if He's even on the premises.

Although the book of Revelation can seem overwhelming and mysterious with its indecipherable imagery and visions, in essence it is about who is in charge and explains unequivocally that the Manager has everything under control. Here's all you need to know to get started. The book of Revelation was a vision God gave to the apostle John. The vision is, in many ways, very similar to the visions the ancient prophets Isaiah, Ezekiel, and Daniel saw. God's plan and purposes for planet Earth and its inhabitants have never changed. In the end, in the final battle between good and evil (the battle that has been raging since before time began), God wins! Revelation is like a grand coronation ceremony of God's Son, Jesus Christ. It pictures Jesus as the King of kings, as the ultimate authority in heaven and on earth.

Who's in charge? God is. And when you're with Him, you're on the winning side.

*Reflect on what it will be like to meet this
glorious King of kings. Then, with the apostle John,
proclaim, "All glory and power to him forever and ever!"*

OVERCOMING

"Look how far you have fallen! Turn back to me and do the works
you did at first. If you don't repent, I will come and remove
your lampstand from its place among the churches".

REVELATION 2:5

The words sound harsh – if you don't repent, you will be removed. But ultimately, that's been the message of the Good News since it was first uttered (and the message of the Old Testament prophets before that). "Repent of your sins and turn to God," John the Baptist had preached (Matt. 3:2). To do so brings heaven and eternal life. By extension then, to refuse to repent is to turn away from God, which brings judgment and eternal death. The message of judgment is as real as the message of forgiveness.

In chapters 2 and 3, the apostle John wrote to seven churches that were located along a major Roman road. A letter carrier could take John's message from Patmos, across the sea, to Ephesus on the coast. He could then make a circuit to the rest of the cities mentioned. John wrote Jesus' words of commendation and rebuke to the various churches – and these messages can be applied today. To the church in Ephesus, Jesus spoke of how they had fallen into sin and called them to repentance. Otherwise judgment would come. To the church of Smyrna, He gave encouragement and hope. He warned the churches in Pergamum and Thyatira not to tolerate false teachers. "Repent of your sin," Jesus repeated (Rev. 2:16).

Words of forgiveness and encouragement; words of warning and judgment. In the end, only two options will remain: repent or face judgment.

What warnings given to these churches might apply to you today?
What do you need to do about it?

BLESS THE LORD

I bless Thee, O Lord,
though I am powerless, Thou strengthens my weakness.
Thou stretch forth from above Thy helping hand
and bring me back unto Thyself.
What shall I render to Thee, O all-good Master,
for all the good things Thou has done
and continue to do for me, the sinner?
I will cease not to bless Thee all the days of my life,
my Creator, my benefactor, and my guardian.
Amen.

St. Basil the Great

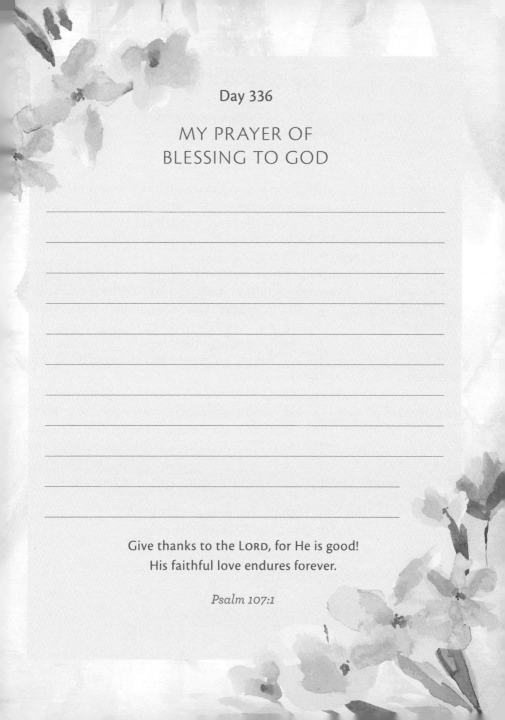

Day 336

MY PRAYER OF
BLESSING TO GOD

_____

_____

_____

_____

_____

_____

_____

_____

_____

_____

_____

Give thanks to the LORD, for He is good!
His faithful love endures forever.

Psalm 107:1

HE'S KNOCKING

"Look! I stand at the door and knock. If you hear my voice and open the door, I will come in, and we will share a meal together as friends".

REVELATION 3:20

In this powerful picture, Jesus stands at the door of the church and knocks. He wants to enter, to be welcomed in, to fellowship with the believers there. Note that although the Lord desires to enter, He allows individuals to open the door. Jesus doesn't force His will on them, pounding at the door, prying it open. Instead, He stands and knocks.

The church at Laodicea had become "lukewarm" (Rev. 3:16); that is, they had allowed their passion for Christ to cool and had become enamored with themselves and their wealth instead. Eventually, Jesus was no longer with them. Thus, He stood on the outside, knocking, hoping to get their attention so that He might enter and change their lives.

Where is Jesus for you? Outside or inside? Is He a stranger, or do you "share meals" together? What concerns occupy your thoughts and desires? Relationships? Career? Possessions and power? Perhaps even survival? Do they threaten to push Jesus aside and move Him to the fringe of your life?

Whatever your situation, know that the Lord is standing near. Through the din and demands, hear His gentle knock. Push through the clutter and open the door.

Then welcome Christ and give Him His rightful place at your table.

Has Jesus been pushed outside of your life?
Listen ... you can hear Him knocking.

HOLY, HOLY, HOLY

*Each of these living beings had six wings, and their wings were covered
all over with eyes, inside and out. Day after day and night after night
they keep on saying, "Holy, holy, holy is the Lord God, the Almighty –
the one who always was, who is, and who is still to come".*

REVELATION 4:8

The words ring out over the horizon of time itself: "Holy, holy, holy!" The first person to record hearing that heavenly refrain was the prophet Isaiah. He wrote that the Lord "was sitting on a lofty throne ... Attending him were mighty seraphim, each having six wings ... They were calling out to each other 'Holy, holy, holy is the Lord of Heaven's Armies!'" (Isa. 6:1-3).

Hundreds of years later, while exiled on the island of Patmos, John was allowed to hear this eternal chorus: "Holy, holy, holy is the Lord God, the Almighty." The song comes down to us from heaven, giving us a glimpse into the eternal glory and holiness that is God's.

Perhaps we don't think enough about this concept of holiness. What does it mean? Holiness is perfect moral character. God will never do anything that is not perfect. We can trust Him completely, for everything He does is in line with His perfect holiness.

When life beats us up and we wonder if things will ever change, when the ebb and flow of life's routine weighs us down and we wonder if things will ever get better, we ought to sit for a moment and ask for a glimpse of heaven. The song is being sung there continuously. "Holy! Holy! Holy!" The prayer of praise rings on, and one day we will join the chorus!

*Today, take a moment to join the heavenly
chorus in praising God, for He is holy, holy, holy.*

WORTHY IS THE LAMB

And they sang in a mighty chorus: "Worthy is the Lamb
who was slaughtered – to receive power and riches and wisdom
and strength and honor and glory and blessing".

REVELATION 5:12

The Lamb who was slaughtered is worthy to receive all things! The angels sing with joy of Jesus Christ as the Lamb, for just as the blood of a lamb painted on doorposts protected the Israelites from the angel of death in Egypt, so Jesus' blood saves us from death. And just as the animal sacrifices offered throughout the centuries on altars in the Tabernacle and Temple gave forgiveness from sin, Jesus' blood gives forgiveness for all sin for all time to those who believe. Indeed, John the Baptist had proclaimed upon seeing Jesus, "Look! The Lamb of God who takes away the sin of the world!" (John 1:29).

But why blood? Why did Jesus have to be "slaughtered"? In the Old Testament, the sacrifice of an animal and the blood shed made forgiveness of sin possible. Blood represents life. The death of an animal (of which the shed blood was proof) fulfilled sin's penalty and allowed God to then grant forgiveness to the sinner making the sacrifice. The sacrifices helped the people understand that sin has dire consequences and should never be taken lightly.

All those sacrifices pointed forward to a day when the sinless Lamb of God would come and be the final sacrifice for all sin. Now anyone who comes to Him in repentance and faith will be saved. That's why Jesus is worthy, and that's why the angels sing!

Meditate on the sacrifice Jesus made to save you.
Thank Him for being the Lamb of God who
takes away the sin of the world.

READY AND WAITING

As I watched, the Lamb broke the first of the seven seals on the scroll.
REVELATION 6:1

Here in chapter 6 begins the "meat" of the book of Revelation. Chapters 6-16 describe "seal," "trumpet," and "bowl" judgments. The seals referred to in this chapter are on the scroll described in chapter 5 – the scroll that has "writing on the inside and the outside" and is "sealed with seven seals" (Rev. 5:1). Christ alone was found worthy to break the seals, open the scroll, and set into motion the events that will culminate in His future reign.

As Christ breaks each seal, a new form of devastation occurs on the earth. Christ does not *send* disaster; the mechanism for evil already exists in the hearts of people. Humankind's capacity to hurt, kill, and destroy has been well documented throughout history. Famines and plagues have taken place for centuries. In these final days, as the end draws near, evil will be unleashed in all its fury. Christ allows it to take place – in His timing and within His parameters. Nothing happens outside of the plan. Evil is shown for what it is. Those who side with evil will seek to hide; those who love the Lord will be saved.

While many have given various opinions about how these visions will actually play out, we can know one thing for sure: God is in control. He left much of this vision purposely unclear so we would study it and stay alert. The point is not to figure it all out; the point is to be ready and waiting when He returns.

If Jesus Christ comes today, are you ready and waiting?

HEAVENLY PRAISE

After this I saw a vast crowd, too great to count, from every nation and
tribe and people and language, standing in front of the throne and before
the Lamb. They were clothed in white robes and held palm branches
in their hands. And they were shouting with a mighty shout,
"Salvation comes from our God who sits on the throne and from the Lamb!".

REVELATION 7:9-10

The sixth seal had been opened and its fury unleashed. So great was the unbelievers' fear of God that they desired death (Rev. 6:15-16). Then suddenly four angels stood at the four corners of the earth and held back the winds of judgment (Rev. 7:1). Then God placed a special seal on His own. This seal was a sign of spiritual and eternal protection. Those sealed would be set apart from God's judgment of an impenitent world. They would not face God's wrath, for they have been saved by the blood of the Lamb.

Some groups of Christians believe that believers will be taken to heaven in what is called the Rapture and that they will not have to go through this time of great tribulation. They believe that the seal described here will be placed on people who become believers during that time. Others believe that all believers alive at the time of the end will go through this tribulation. Whatever the case, the point is that God seals and protects His own.

The number 144,000 may be a symbolic number, representing completeness. No one will be lost or forgotten. In fact, all will be part of that "vast crowd, too great to count" that will stand before the Lamb celebrating His final triumph. Waving palm branches, the traditional symbol of victory, people from all over the world will extol God for the salvation He has provided through His Son. What a great day that will be!

*Praise God today for all He has done for you
and for believers all over the world!*

A PRAYER FOR UNDERSTANDING

Eternal God, who is the light of the minds that know Thee,
the joy of the hearts that love Thee,
and the strength of the wills that serve Thee;
grant us so to know Thee
that we may truly love Thee,
and so to love Thee that we may fully serve Thee,
whom to serve is perfect freedom, in Jesus Christ our Lord.
Amen.

St. Augustine

Day 343

MY PRAYER FOR
UNDERSTANDING

_____

_____

_____

_____

_____

_____

_____

_____

_____

_____

_____

Faith consists, not in ignorance, but in knowledge,
and that, not only of God, but also of the divine will.

John Calvin

WHEN THE LIGHTS GO OUT

*Then the fourth angel blew his trumpet, and one-third of the sun was struck,
and one-third of the moon, and one-third of the stars, and they became dark.
And one-third of the day was dark, and also one-third of the night.*

REVELATION 8:12

*A*bout 50 million North Americans found themselves in the dark the afternoon of August 14, 2003. As a result of a downed 345,000-volt power line in the state of Ohio, electricity was lost for almost the entire northeastern part of the United States. The complete darkness halted work, travel, and communication. And when night fell, the darkness was darker and quieter than anything many had experienced. Imagine, then, what it will be like when the fourth trumpet is blown and one-third of the sun, the moon, and the stars become dark!

Again, this had been foretold by Old Testament prophets. Isaiah wrote, "The heavens will be black above them; the stars will give no light. The sun will be dark when it rises, and the moon will provide no light" (Isa. 13:10). Joel prophesied, "The day of the LORD is upon us. It is a day of darkness and gloom, a day of thick clouds and deep blackness" (Joel 2:1-2). Amos said, "That day [of the Lord] will bring darkness, not light" (Amos 5:18). Such darkness sets the stage for the next three trumpet judgments that will unleash demonic activity on the earth.

We may look at our world now and feel that the darkness is already creeping in. To believers, Jesus said, "You are the light of the world – like a city on a hilltop that cannot be hidden" (Matt. 5:14). The darkness surrounds us, but we have the Light of the world in us.

*Is the light of your life shining in the dark places
where people need to receive Christ?*

HARD HEARTS

But the people who did not die in these plagues still refused to repent
of their evil deeds and turn to God. They continued to worship demons
and idols made of gold, silver, bronze, stone, and wood – idols that can
neither see nor hear nor walk! And they did not repent of their murders
or their witchcraft or their sexual immorality or their thefts.

REVELATION 9:20-21

Unfortunately, some people never learn. Many times the person released from prison returns to a life of crime, only to end up back behind bars. While many do attempt to turn their lives around, many more just cannot or will not change. Their sin becomes normal to them, and they don't want to repent. So it is with the people described here in Revelation 9.

As the last trumpets are blown, demonic forces invade the earth. Ironically, these demonic forces can only attack and destroy those "who did not have the seal of God on their foreheads" (Rev. 9:4). That is, the demons can only torment their own worshippers! And they do! Yet the plagues, the devastation, and the presence of evil in all its fullness do not drive these people to God. Despite being attacked by the demons, these people refuse to repent and, in fact, they continue to "worship demons and idols." Their hearts are hard.

This outpouring of judgment will be meant to bring people to see their need for repentance, turn from evil, and be saved. This is why there must be a final judgment and eternal punishment. God is doing everything to bring people to Himself, and some will refuse. Those people must get what they desire – eternal separation from God. On Judgment Day, they will reap what they have sown.

Have you ever met a hard-hearted person?
Why do you think that person refused to believe?

SECRETS MEANT TO BE KEPT

When the seven thunders spoke, I was about to write.
But I heard a voice from heaven saying, "Keep secret
what the seven thunders said, and do not write it down".
REVELATION 10:4

People want to know the future. Many attempt to find out by way of horoscopes or palm readers. Sadly, their attempts are foolish at best.

Believers also want to know the future – and we ought to find it quite amazing that God anticipated that need and met it by way of this revelation. In fact, God talked about the future throughout history through many of His prophets. Because they spoke for God and their prophecies came true, we can trust that the book of Revelation will also come true.

Yet there are some things that we aren't meant to know – as is clear in this verse. A similar message was given to the prophet Daniel: "What I have said is kept secret and sealed until the time of the end" (Dan. 12:9). Jesus told His disciples, "No one knows the day or hour when these things will happen, not even the angels in heaven or the Son himself. Only the Father knows" (Mark 13:32).

While we could speculate about what we aren't told, it is far more valuable to seriously consider what we *have been* told. God has told us that difficult times will come, but in the end He wins – and by extension, all of us who have chosen His side will win also.

God's Word tells us how to live holy lives and to be ready for His return. And that's all we really need to know.

What are you doing with what you already know
about God and how He wants you to live?

GRATITUDE FOR GOD'S REIGN

And they said, "We give thanks to you, Lord God, the Almighty,
the one who is and who always was, for now you have assumed
your great power and have begun to reign".
REVELATION 11:17

*A*t the time of the end, as evil and destruction prevail, many will turn away from God, seeing the growth of evil as evidence against His existence. Even today, many refuse to believe in a God of love because they think that such a God could not allow evil to exist. Even believers sometimes wonder why people have to suffer and why evil goes unpunished.

The Scriptures encourage us to take the long-range view of history. The twenty-four elders, who sit in God's throne room, paint this long-range view for us in their prayer of praise to the Almighty. They thank "the one who is and who always was" for controlling all of history. They praise Him for administering His perfect justice at the appropriate time. God's justice will ultimately prevail, and God's servants will ultimately be vindicated.

In fact, we ought to be glad that God *doesn't* administer His divine judgment every time we sin; otherwise, none of us could survive. Instead, He gave His Son to die on our behalf so we could have life to the fullest. He takes evil and turns it around for good. He takes the pain we've experienced and helps us reach out to others.

The time of reckoning *will* come when God will right all wrongs. Be patient. Heaven is on its way!

Give thanks to the Lord God, the Almighty,
the One who is and who always was.
Praise Him that heaven is on the way!

SATAN'S DAYS ARE NUMBERED

And they have defeated him by the blood of the Lamb and by their testimony.
And they did not love their lives so much that they were afraid to die.

REVELATION 12:11

Satan's power appears to be everywhere; his influence pervades cultures across the globe – through the Internet, the printed word, movies, television, and almost any other possible outlet. Yet here in these verses we discover several things about Satan.

Satan had been cast out of heaven (Rev. 12:7-8). Satan was at one time a beautiful angel who, in his pride, wanted to be equal with God. A battle ensued and Satan and his followers among the angels lost the battle and were cast out of heaven. Satan still leads this army of demons as they wreak havoc on the earth.

Satan is a deceiver (Rev. 12:9). He lies and manipulates people to make them believe whatever he wants.

Satan goes before God accusing us day and night (Rev. 12:10). Make no mistake. Satan loves no one – not even those who love him. He just wants to separate as many people as possible from God. And those in the opposite camp – Christians – He hates most of all.

Satan is already defeated (Rev. 12:11). The blood spilled by Jesus on the cross defeated him completely, and Jesus' resurrection took away Satan's powerful final weapon – death.

Satan's days are numbered (Rev. 12:12).

As you look at your world, remember that God will one day set all things right. In the meantime, don't fear Satan or his power. The blood of Jesus and your personal story of salvation have defeated him.

*Satan is very real, but very vulnerable. His time
is short, so he is hard at work. Ask God to use you
to turn people away from him and back to God.*

TEACH ME YOUR WORD, O LORD

You are my portion, LORD;
I have promised to obey Your words.
I have sought Your face with all my heart;
be gracious to me according to Your promise.
I have considered my ways
and have turned my steps to Your statutes.
I will hasten and not delay to obey Your commands.
Though the wicked bind me with ropes,
I will not forget Your law.
At midnight I rise to give You thanks
for Your righteous laws.
I am a friend to all who fear You,
to all who follow Your precepts.
The earth is filled with Your love, LORD;
teach me Your decrees.

Psalm 119:57-64

Day 350

MY PRAYER FOR
GROWTH IN THE WORD

_____

_____

_____

_____

_____

_____

_____

_____

_____

_____

_____

The Bible is the one Book to which any thoughtful man
may go with an honest question of life or destiny
and find the answer of God
by honest searching.

John Ruskin

THE GREAT DIVIDE

And all the people who belong to this world worshiped the beast.
They are the ones whose names were not written in the Book of Life
before the world was made – the Book that belongs to the Lamb who
was slaughtered. Anyone with ears to hear should listen and understand.

REVELATION 13:8-9

Other than Antarctica, every continent in the world has a continental divide. One of the continental divides in North America runs like a spine all the way to the tip of South America. Also known as the Great Divide, this land line separates by its massive mountains the waters that drain into the Pacific from those that flow into the Atlantic Ocean and the Arctic Sea. Throughout the world, such natural divides create a separation within a country or sometimes they form the boundaries between countries.

There is a great divide of another sort in the book of Revelation: All who believe in Jesus Christ and whose names are written in the Book of Life will be divided from those who reject God's Word and Jesus Christ. In fact, the Book of Life alone determines the eternal destiny of every person who has ever lived. At the final judgment, John wrote that "the books were opened, including the Book of Life ... And anyone whose name was not found recorded in the Book of Life was thrown into the lake of fire" (Rev. 20:12, 15).

One great divide, two destinies. If you have believed in the Lord Jesus Christ as your Savior and accepted His sacrifice on your behalf, your name is recorded in the Book of Life, never to be erased (Rev. 3:5). That book is the register of heaven's citizens. If your name is there, rejoice! Your eternal destiny is secure.

Is your name in the Book of Life?
Are you certain of your eternal destiny?

BASKING IN PARADISE

And I heard a voice from heaven saying, "Write this down:
Blessed are those who die in the Lord from now on. Yes, says the Spirit,
they are blessed indeed, for they will rest from their hard work;
for their good deeds follow them!".
REVELATION 14:13

On any vacation break, we attempt to escape the chores of work, school, and other everyday tasks. Some take a trip or just enjoy resting at home for a few days. In Europe, families often are rewarded with an entire month of relaxation. These breaks are given by employers so that workers can rest and recharge.

We may be used to short vacations, but can we even conceive of basking in paradise for eternity? Unfathomable rest awaits all of us who place our faith in Jesus Christ. Not only rest, but also rewards. Can we imagine how God will reward the souls of His weary children?

Revelation 13 describes the onslaught of evil as Satan makes his final desperate attempt to deceive as many as he can. Those who refuse the mark of the beast will suffer terribly. Satan has control of the world's economy, and being a believer means persecution and death. Into this darkness shines a ray of light.

Revelation 14 draws back the curtain and gives us a glimpse of heaven's glories, showing what awaits those who endure to the end. Suffering is not meaningless; faith has eternal value; rewards for service and perseverance are beyond imagining.

Take heart. God knows the difficulties you face today. He knows you're trying to be faithful. He sees your good deeds, even if no one else does. Thank God for His promises of rest and reward. Both will one day be yours.

Are you resting in the promises of God?

COMPREHENDING ANGELS

Then I saw in heaven another marvelous event of great significance. Seven angels were holding the seven last plagues, which would bring God's wrath to completion.
REVELATION 15:1

What comes to mind when you think of an angel? Perhaps it's the children clothed in wings and foil halos at the church Christmas program. Or chubby figures strumming harps. Or benevolent messengers between God and humans.

If you were to really see an angel, however, you would probably be scared out of your socks. Whenever angels appeared in Scripture, they usually had to pick the person up off the ground and tell him or her not to be afraid. Clearly, these beings are glorious and powerful. And while they do serve as God's messengers helping believers all over the earth, they are more than that. They are warriors, often at battle in the spiritual realm. In fact, an angel told Daniel why a prayer took so long to be answered: "Since the first day you began to pray ... your request has been heard ... I have come in answer to your prayer. But for twenty-one days the spirit prince of the kingdom of Persia blocked my way. Then Michael, one of the archangels, came to help me ... " (Dan. 10:12-13).

Here in Revelation, the angels stand ready to pour out seven bowls full of God's wrath upon the earth. These mighty angels do God's bidding, setting in motion the plagues that will "bring God's wrath to completion."

For those who believe, this will be a "marvelous event" indeed!

The next time you see an angel figurine or picture, consider the true power of God's angels. Thank God that these faithful messengers do His bidding.

KEEPING WATCH

*"Look, I will come as unexpectedly as a thief! Blessed are all
who are watching for me, who keep their clothing ready so they
will not have to walk around naked and ashamed".*

REVELATION 16:15

We know that Jesus is coming back, but we don't know *when* He's coming back. Jesus said, "No one knows the day or hour when these things will happen ... So you, too, must keep watch! For you don't know what day your Lord is coming ... You also must be ready all the time, for the Son of Man will come when least expected" (Matt. 24:36, 42, 44).

Paul wrote to the believers in Thessalonica, "You know quite well that the day of the Lord's return will come unexpectedly, like a thief in the night" (1 Thess. 5:2). Peter wrote, "The day of the Lord will come as unexpectedly as a thief" (2 Pet. 3:10).

If we knew a thief was going to visit our house on a particular night, we'd be doubly sure to lock our doors and check all the windows. Human nature as it is, if we knew that Jesus was going to return on a particular day, we might be tempted to live as we pleased and then say a prayer for repentance and forgiveness the morning before His return.

But we aren't given that option. We're to be constantly ready, anticipating that Jesus could come at any moment and constantly working to share the Good News with as many as we can. Working, witnessing, waiting, and watching – these should characterize our lives as we anticipate our Lord's return.

*Are you working, witnessing, waiting, and watching for Jesus?
Which is the most difficult for you?*

GOD'S FAITHFUL MESSAGE

One of the seven angels who had poured out the seven bowls
came over and spoke to me. "Come with me," he said, "and I will
show you the judgment that is going to come ... "

REVELATION 17:1

God's voice echoed to Adam and Eve in the garden. God dispatched spiritual messengers to Abraham and Sarah, telling them their descendants would outnumber heaven's stars. God instructed Moses to deliver His commands to Pharaoh and the Hebrew slaves. God mercifully called judges who became rescuing leaders of the Israelites who cried out for deliverance. Through one prophet after another, God spoke both divine promises and judgments to disobedient and divided Israelite tribes.

Angels proclaimed to shepherds the news of Jesus' birth to save the people from their sins. Jesus called disciples to continue preaching the message of God's Good News. God gave His own Son in order to call us to Himself. The Almighty's voice knocked Paul to his knees on the Damascus road and converted him from a murderer to a missionary preacher and author of most of the New Testament. Now in Revelation, God's angels shout His final messages to John, and John relays God's message to us. Are we listening?

God has been a compassionate communicator to humankind from creation to Revelation. His words, recorded by those He inspired, are a faithful record for all. God has equipped us to translate His truths for any language, ethnicity, and age group in order to communicate His love to all people. God has not and will not fail to speak to us. We need only to listen.

In what ways can you listen faithfully to God's voice?

A PRAYER TO OUR AWESOME GOD

Great art Thou, O Lord, and greatly to be praised;
great is Thy power, and infinite is Thy wisdom.
Grant me, O Lord, to know and understand
whether first to invoke Thee or to praise Thee;
whether first to know Thee or call upon Thee.
I will seek Thee, O Lord, and call upon Thee.
I call upon Thee, O Lord,
in my faith which Thou hast given me,
which Thou hast inspired in me
through the humanity of Thy Son,
and through the ministry of Thy preacher.
Amen.

St. Augustine

Day 357

MY PRAYER TO OUR
AWESOME GOD

_____

_____

_____

_____

_____

_____

_____

_____

_____

_____

_____

We are never nearer Christ than when we
find ourselves lost in a holy amazement
at His unspeakable love.

John Owen

MESSIAH OR MONEY?

The merchants who became wealthy by selling her these things will stand
at a distance, terrified by her great torment. They will weep and cry out.

REVELATION 18:15

Money has its place. Everyone needs money to live. We should strive
to make enough money to care for our families and to be able to
help our churches and other ministries build God's Kingdom. When wealth
becomes our primary goal, however, we are guilty of greed and will find
ourselves dissatisfied and even tempted into sin.

Paul wrote to Timothy that "the love of money is the root of all kinds of
evil. And some people, craving money, have wandered from the true faith
and pierced themselves with many sorrows" (1 Tim. 6:10).

The person who desires money above all else does so at great personal
expense. That's what chapter 18 is about; John sees a vision of final
judgment on a world economy based completely on wealth and luxury. The
word *Babylon* describes this immoral and corrupt system that gives great
promises but offers nothing of lasting value. When it collapses, those who
depend on it have nothing.

Money cannot satisfy our souls. Wealth may seem to make life easier,
but it will leave us empty. When our lives are over, we will leave this world
the way we entered it: naked and owning nothing. We should set aside our
desire for wealth and instead look forward to the riches of God's Kingdom.
Our concern should be about our souls and the souls of those we love.

Are you overly concerned with money?
Ask God to give you the proper perspective
on what's really important.

ANTICIPATING THE WEDDING FEAST

"Praise the LORD! For the Lord our God, the Almighty, reigns. Let us be glad and rejoice, and let us give honor to him. For the time has come for the wedding feast of the Lamb, and his bride has prepared herself".

REVELATION 19:6-7

John was granted a vision of that day in the future when God's people – the bride – will celebrate their union with Jesus, the Lamb. In John's vision, a voice from God's throne leads God's people in praise: "Praise the LORD! For the Lord our God, the Almighty, reigns." This grand celebration commemorates the ultimate reason Jesus came to the earth. He came to buy His people back from their slavery to sin so that they could become joyful members of His eternal Kingdom. Like a loving husband, He comes to the feast leading His bride.

What will the wedding feast be like? Seated at this feast will be all those who have trusted Christ for salvation – from every nation of the world since the beginning of time. Jesus said, "I tell you this, that many Gentiles will come from all over the world – from east and west – and sit down with Abraham, Isaac, and Jacob at the feast in the Kingdom of Heaven" (Matt. 8:11). Imagine! You might have a seat right beside Moses, or David, or Daniel, or your great-great-grandparent who began a legacy of faith in your family.

Keep this vision of your joyful union with Christ and with all other believers before you as you serve Jesus on this earth. You've sent in your R.S.V.P. and your seat will be waiting. Praise the Lord!

Besides Jesus, of course, who do you look forward to meeting when you get to the great wedding feast?

REBELS WITHOUT A CAUSE

Blessed and holy are those who share in the first resurrection.
For them the second death holds no power, but they will be priests
of God and of Christ and will reign with him a thousand years.

REVELATION 20:6

In this chapter, John's vision unveils the destiny of Christian martyrs and saints: Those who have uplifted the name of Jesus throughout the ages – in spite of suffering, trials, hardships, oppression, and more – will be enthroned with the Lord to reign with Him.

This chapter has probably engendered more debate than any other portion of Scripture. What exactly is happening here? Opinions about this chapter fill numerous books, but the bottom line is this: God is in control of history. Satan will be chained up for a time so that he can't deceive the nations. Jesus will reign during this glorious time. However, people's hearts are hard. When Satan is released again, he will gather an army for that final battle – "a mighty army, as numberless as sand along the seashore" (Rev. 20:8).

In other words, if people's hearts are hard, even living under the reign of Jesus Christ Himself does not deter them from evil. When evil again presents itself, they run toward it. Satan will not repent; people who choose rebellion also will not repent, no matter how many chances they are given. The source of rebellion is not God or Satan, but the human heart. When God's judgment comes, it will be completely just.

What strikes you most when you think about the final battle between good and evil and the final judgment? How do these future realities make a difference in your life today?

GOD'S FAMILY REUNION

I heard a loud shout from the throne saying, "Look, God's home is now among his
people! He will live with them ... He will wipe every tear from their eyes, and there
will be no more death or sorrow or crying or pain. All these things are gone forever".

REVELATION 21:3-4

There's nothing quite like a family reunion. Whether it's summertime
or special holidays that bring us together, family reunions give us the
chance to celebrate a common heritage and enjoy one another.

But oh, the reunion of God's family in glory; what a time that will be!
John cannot tell us the date; only the Father knows and will reveal it in the
end. As best as he can, John describes the new Jerusalem as he saw it in his
vision. With many symbols we can relate to, he illustrates where God will
live. He explains how Christians will live forever in God's presence in a place
where sadness is gone, where God makes everything new, where streets are
paved with gold, where God Himself is the light. The gates have the names
of the twelve tribes of Israel and the foundation stones have the names of
the twelve apostles of Jesus – symbolizing that all the faithful believers in
the time before Christ and all who followed Him after will be present in
the city. We will all be part of one grand family. There will be no divisions
because of language, physical appearance, or culture. Every tribe, language,
and nation will contribute to an innumerable, harmonious throng.

God promises to make all things new. It is beyond our imagination,
beyond our ability to even comprehend. Heaven is a mystery, but we've
been given a glimpse. What a wonderful place it will be! What a wonderful
family! What a wonderful God!

What family members or neighbors
need your prayers for their salvation so that
they can join God's family forever?

STAY THE COURSE

Look, I am coming soon, bringing my reward with me to repay
all people according to their deeds. I am the Alpha and the Omega,
the First and the Last, the Beginning and the End".

REVELATION 22:12

How do people find their way through life? In ancient days, people steered by the stars. Mariners steered their crafts on courses mapped by the skies, eventually adding technological advances, such as special navigational clocks to stay their courses. From stargazing to handmade maps and handheld compasses to today's powerful computerized geographic information data systems aboard ships and in cars, we have been determined to find the way to stay on course and not get sidetracked or lost.

People may know where they are physically, but many are lost spiritually. They have no direction. They try different methods to find meaning in life, only to end up empty and frustrated.

Jesus says that He is the Beginning and the End. He is the final destination. If we want to arrive in the new Jerusalem, we need to go the right way – and Jesus Himself is the way, the truth, and the life (John 14:6). God's Word is the only navigation system that will get us there. We must be guided by the Father, Son, and Holy Spirit. Walking in the light of God's truth, He will direct our paths. God has made the way through the blood of Christ. We have only to stay the course our God in heaven provides: to abide in Him and obey His word until the end.

Are you staying on a righteous course,
or do you feel like you've been sidetracked?
What will you do to get back on track with God?

A PRAYER FOR RENEWAL

O gracious and holy Father,
grant us wisdom to perceive Thee,
diligence to seek Thee,
patience to wait for Thee,
eyes to behold Thee,
a heart to meditate upon Thee,
and a life to proclaim Thee,
through the power of the Spirit of Jesus Christ our Lord.
Amen.

St. Benedict

Day 364

MY PRAYER FOR RENEWAL

_____

_____

_____

_____

_____

_____

_____

_____

_____

_____

Do not conform to the pattern of this world,
but be transformed by the renewing of your mind.
Then you will be able to test and approve what
God's will is – His good, pleasing and perfect will.

Romans 12:2

Day 365

MY PRAYER OF THANKS FOR GOD'S FAITHFULNESS THIS YEAR

_____

_____

_____

_____

_____

_____

_____

_____

_____

_____

_____

_____

_____

_____